DETHRONING THE DECEITFUL PORK CHOP

FOOD AND
FOODWAYS

SERIES EDITOR:
JENNIFER JENSEN WALLACH

Dethroning the Deceitful Pork Chop

RETHINKING AFRICAN AMERICAN
FOODWAYS FROM SLAVERY TO OBAMA

EDITED BY JENNIFER JENSEN WALLACH

The University of Arkansas
Fayetteville
2015

ISBN: 978-1-55728-679-6
e-ISBN: 978-1-61075-568-9

19 18 17 16 15   5 4 3 2 1

Designed by Liz Lester

♾ The paper used in this publication meets the minimum requirements
of the American National Standard for Permanence of Paper for Printed
Library Materials Z39.48-1984.

Library of Congress Control Number: 2015938420

Cover image: Dolores Harris, daughter of Farm Security Administration client
George Harris, with canned food prepared by her mother. Dameron, Maryland.
Courtesy of the Library of Congress, LC-USZ62-130380.

In memory of
Julie Watkins, editor and friend

CONTENTS

Part II: Representations

Part III: Politics

FOREWORD

I remember it almost like it was yesterday. I was sitting in the living room of my best friend, opening my mail. After a stack of junk mail and bills, I finally reached the padded parcel, having saved the best for last. Inside were my copies of Jessica Harris's *Iron Pots and Wooden Spoons: Africa's Gifts to New World Cooking* (1989) and *The Welcome Table: African American Heritage Cooking* (1995). Though it was still early in the Internet era and thus before Amazon.com, I had nonetheless managed to find a book dealer who had both books and was willing to part with them at an affordable graduate student price. After reading through them multiple times, flagging pages and taking notes, the books took their rightful place on my bedside table beside another African American food studies classic: Vertamae Grosvenor's *Vibration Cooking: Or, the Travel Notes of a Geechee Girl* (1970).

Having been introduced to the term "foodways" while conducting research for historian Hasia Diner (*Hungering for America: Italian, Irish, and Jewish Foodways in the Age of Migration*, 2001), my initial research about African Americans, or Blacks, and foodways revealed several references to Harris and Grosvenor. This was clearly the launching point, the inevitable place to start! Years later, I would have the privilege to meet both authors, but even before then I would have numerous conversations that helped to shape my thinking about African American foodways. One of these discussions took place at the first Southern Foodways Symposium (1998) with food writers Donna Battle Pierce and Toni Tipton Martin. The three of us, along with others, had spirited conversations about the soon-to-be released, first-of-its-kind study by literary scholar Doris Witt. Among other exciting aspects, her forthcoming book, *Black Hunger: Soul Food and America,* offered a systematic, in-depth look at the inner workings of African American food culture. Witt brought numerous methodologies and analytics to bear on the interrogation of the term "soul food." We were in for a treat!

Years later, while attending the Grits, Greens and Everything in Between symposium (2000), I would share the podium with Witt and others, and I would also meet independent foodways scholar Howard Paige, a specialist on African American foodways in the Great Lakes Region. The conference, sponsored by the Culinary Historians of Chicago and Roosevelt University, was considered the first national meeting on soul food and provided most of the authors for the collection of essays edited by Anne Bower, *African American Foodways: Exploration of History and Culture.*

Since the late 1990s, several monographs and articles have been published that further our understanding of the histories and cultures of African American food relations. Though countless articles have been written on food and slavery from several disciplines, the subfield of African American food studies was, more or less, born from such studies as Rafia Zafar's "The Signifying Dish: Autobiography and History in Two Black Women's Cookbooks" (see *Feminist Studies* 25, no. 2), Witt's *Black Hunger*, and my *Building Houses out of Chicken Legs: Black Women, Food, and Power.* Frederick Opie's *Hog and Hominy: Soul Food from Africa to America* added to this development. From Opie's subsequent blog, *Food as Lens* (http://www.food asalens.com/), to Tipton Martin's *The Jemima Code*, "a pop-up exhibit and book curated to explore the culinary treasures African American cooks left behind in [their] cookbooks" (http://thejemimacode.com/about/), and from Kimberly Nettles-Barcelon's *Gastronomica* essay, "'Saving' Soul Food," to Adrian Miller's James Beard award winner, *Soul Food: The Surprising Story of an American Cuisine*, the fields of food studies, African American studies, gender and women's studies, folklore, geography, and anthropology have been richly rewarded and expanded in the forming of this subfield. And this is just the beginning. At this moment, dissertations are being produced, food activism is taking place on behalf of people of color (in particular), articles are being thought through, and conversations are being held to better understand African American food histories, to better unpack the importance of religion, gender, sexuality, region, and nation on contemporary food habits, to figure out how to combat food insecurities in sustainable ways, and to detail the myriad of ways that African Americans have deployed resistance using food and food practices.

Building on what can arguably be considered a watershed moment in African American food studies, *Dethroning the Deceitful Pork Chop:*

Rethinking African American Foodways from Slavery to Obama continues this construction by beginning with the goal of resisting a singular
interpretation of Black food culture. As editor Jennifer Jensen Wallach
writes in her introduction, *Dethroning the Deceitful Pork Chop* offers
new sets of questions, different analytical approaches, and a variety
of methodologies to advance the argument "that food practices have
been and continue to be sites of resistance for African Americans."
This volume expands our thinking and moves our minds in directions
that have been, in some cases, tangential. Wallach explains:

> Although particular foods, including, of course, watermel-
> ons and chickens, are undeniably worthy of contemplation, our
> research reveals that the symbolic or sentimental significance of
> which foods were cooked or consumed has often been consid-
> ered less important than having the right to eat with dignity or
> just plain having enough to eat.

The essays in this volume explore the right to eat sustainably and
with dignity, in ways that will excite you and move you to explore
even more obscure archives and repositories, read texts in new ways,
search visuals for different meanings (hidden and in plain view), look
at kitchen and restaurant landscapes with fresh eyes, watch cooking
shows with more cynicism, and visit farmer's markets with more purpose but also with a healthy skepticism.

Personally, I cannot wait to use this collection of essays in my
classroom and in my own research. I am excited to see what our early
labor in the field has produced, but also I am animated by the ways in
which I can circle back to use what I helped to create in order to hear
more, do more, write more, say more, and fight for more. Reading this
anthology took me back to the mid-1990s when I opened that padded
package; this volume will be as dog-eared as the others, taking its
rightful place in the food studies canon but also being immensely useful in helping to birth even more knowledge about African American
food histories and cultures!

PSYCHE WILLIAMS-FORSON
University of Maryland, College Park

SERIES EDITOR'S PREFACE

The University of Arkansas Press series Food and Foodways explores historical and contemporary issues in global food studies. We are committed to telling lesser-known food stories and to representing a diverse set of voices. Our strength is work in the humanities and social sciences that uses food as a lens to examine broader social, cultural, environmental, ethical, and economic issues. However, we recognize that food—perhaps the most central of all human concerns—is not only a barometer by which to gauge social, cultural, and environmental conditions, but also a source of pleasure. In addition to scholarly books, we publish creative nonfiction that explores the sensory dimensions of consumption and celebrates food as evidence of human creativity and innovation.

This essay collection, *Dethroning the Deceitful Pork Chop: Rethinking African American Foodways from Slavery to Obama,* represents the current state of the growing subfield of African American food studies. The fifteen essays collected here utilize a wide variety of methodological perspectives and explore African American food expressions from the time of European contact up through the present. This volume offers fresh insights into a field that is only now beginning to reach maturity, helping to fulfill the Food and Foodways series mandate to publish research on rich but underexplored topics. The contributors demonstrate that throughout time Black people have used food practices as a means of resisting white oppression overtly—through techniques like poison, theft, deception, and magic—or more subtly as a way of asserting humanity and ingenuity, revealing both cultural continuity and improvisational finesse. Collectively, the authors complicate generalizations that conflate African American food culture with southern-derived soul food and challenge the tenacious hold that stereotypical Black cooks like Aunt Jemima and depersonalized Mammy have on the American imagination. They survey the abundant but still understudied archives of Black food history and establish an ongoing research agenda that should animate scholars of American food culture for years to come.

JENNIFER JENSEN WALLACH

ACKNOWLEDGMENTS

This collection was born after a conversation with the then-director of the University of Arkansas Press, Larry Malley, at the Southern Historical Association meeting in Mobile, Alabama, in 2012. I casually asked Larry for some advice about which publishing project I should tackle next, and I left the conference with a mandate to find and collect the most recent scholarship in the field of African American food studies. Larry's enthusiasm and his instinct for a good book project were impossible to resist. I am grateful for his always-sound advice, unwavering support, and fabulous home-cooked meals. I hope he feels that his faith in me and this project has been rewarded. I am grateful also to Julie Watkins, the first editor I worked with on this project. Julie, who tragically passed away before this book went into production, was an unfailing champion and friend. Her imprint can be seen throughout these pages and, indeed, throughout the Food and Foodways series, which she cofounded.

An author could not ask for better people to work with than the staff of the University of Arkansas Press. Mike Bieker, the current director of the University of Arkansas Press, has been incredibly supportive not only of this volume but also of food studies in general. I appreciate his enthusiasm, warmth, and accessibility. I am grateful for editor David Scott Cunningham's savvy, skill, and wit. I appreciate Melissa King's creativity and collaborative spirit. I am also grateful to Deena Owens for helping me get the little details right.

Finally, I would like to thank the contributors to *Dethroning the Deceitful Pork Chop: Rethinking African American Foodways from Slavery to Obama* for their hard work and patience with what must have seemed like endless requests and reminders. Psyche Williams-Forson and Rebecca Sharpless generously offered advice, read through early drafts of the essays, and graciously added their voices to the volume. I am proud of the book we have all produced together, and I am honored to have had the chance to work with such a dedicated, creative group of scholars.

INTRODUCTION

There was a deep dent in the refrigerator, where the bullet had hit and ricocheted, and the coffee pot on the counter was shattered. They had found the bullet on the opposite counter beside a watermelon I had bought that day. Even then I wondered what the white policemen had said to each other when they saw the watermelon.

MYRLIE EVERS, *For Us, the Living* (1967)

I first read Myrlie Evers's description of the aftermath of the 1963 assassination of her husband, Mississippi civil rights activist Medgar Evers, while in graduate school in the mid-1990s. Those were heady days of continuous intellectual awakenings. They were also overwhelming ones as I immersed myself in African American history and began to come to a piecemeal understanding of the tenacity of white supremacy and of the horrors lurking behind the dominant narrative of American progress that I was slowly learning to disassemble. Myrlie Evers's watermelon was one of many revelations that I associate with that period of discovery. I was struck by its seemingly incongruous presence in the narrative recollection of the most horrific event of her life. Overwhelmed as she was by grief and chaos, why did she notice the watermelon on the counter? What pulled her out of the stupor of a doctor-administered sedative and drew her attention to that seemingly innocuous icon of summertime? How could she summon up the psychic energy to care about what the white policemen thought? Years later, while writing her memoir, why was she still contemplating the fruit?[1]

I did not know it at the time, but my initial, clumsy attempts to answer these questions eventually grew into a full-fledged research agenda and a desire to examine the relationship between food practices and African American subjectivities. More than a decade passed before I would begin to assemble the tools necessary to begin to unpack the relationship between ideas about food and ideas about race that had transformed that inanimate object into a source of anxiety and pain. I could find little in my doctoral coursework to validate my growing sense that food habits were worthy of contemplation. Because my intellectual awakening coincided with an explosion of foodie culture —manifested in expanding culinary programming on television, the deification of high-end chefs, and the proliferation of olive oils and sea salts on grocery store shelves—I found ample support for the idea that African American food culture was interesting and entertaining. However, I found relatively little sympathy for the idea that this inter-est could be transformed into the purportedly rarified substance of *scholarship.*

I thought off and on about that watermelon for years, both about what it symbolized for Evers and about the implications of that object to my understanding of the social world Evers inhabited. While I was slowly mulling this over and writing about other aspects of African American culture, other academics were at work building the inter-disciplinary field of food studies and developing methodological approaches that would empower me and many others to design foodways-oriented research agendas. This intrepid group legitimated the study of food culture by producing a high-quality body of schol-arship filled with fresh insights.[2] These pioneers risked the condem-nation of dismissive colleagues who thought of food as mere fuel for other aspects of human behavior rather than as a subject worthy of investigation on its own terms. These naysayers often labeled food studies research as "scholarship-lite."[3] In this climate, the decision to study food culture had to be accompanied by a fearless disregard for conventional professional wisdom.

Psyche Williams-Forson's landmark *Building Houses out of Chicken Legs: Black Women, Food, and Power* (2006) was one of the boldest and most visionary books to emerge during this period.[4] Not even a decade old, it has already had a profound impact on the fields of African American studies and food studies. For me, and for so many others, Williams-Forson's study was a revelation. Williams-Forson amplifies food studies scholar Doris Witt's seminal claim that "the connection between and frequent conflation of African American women and food has functioned as a central structuring dynamic of twentieth-century U.S. psychic, cultural, sociopolitical, and economic life."[5] Williams-Forson explores "the roles that chicken has played in the lives of black women from the past to the present" and offers a template for how a food item can be decoded to reveal multiple meanings; beginning during the era of slavery and ending in the twenty-first century, she examines chicken and uncovers "a story of feminist consciousness, community building, cultural work, and personal identity."[6] Williams-Forson studies the bird both as a material item, which could nourish black bodies or harm over-indulgers, and as a symbolic one. Although images of African Americans as chicken thieves abound in the iconography of American racism, Williams-Forson uncovers a more complicated symbolic register, coupling aversion and shame with more positive ideas about the fowl, spawned by associations with family dinners, culinary entrepreneurship, and artisanal skill. The end result is a study that demonstrates that it is impossible to come to an understanding of black, female subjectivity—either in the past or the present—without contemplating the chicken.

Following Williams-Forson's lead, we can begin to understand the layers of meaning embedded in Myrlie Evers's watermelon, which had both a somber material reality and a fraught symbolic one. Evers had, after all, purchased the fruit to enjoy alongside her murdered husband. Furthermore, her reaction to the white policemen's presence made it clear that she was painfully aware of the existence of a century's worth of racialized images of black people voraciously consuming the fruit. The white gaze of the policemen who encountered that watermelon and the violent death of Medgar Evers at the hands of white racists occupied different points on the same continuum of what it felt like to live in the grip of white repression in 1960s Mississippi. A deep, empathetic understanding of that particular historical moment demands an engagement with the emotional violence unleashed by the potent symbol of the watermelon as well as with the actual violence perpetrated against the Evers family.

The year after *Building Houses out of Chicken Legs* appeared, a collection of essays, *African American Foodways: Explorations of History and Culture* (2007), edited by literary scholar Anne Bower was published. Bower brought together new food-related research from scholars working in several disciplines.[7] In this collection, an article by Williams-Forson about racist imagery involving chickens is printed alongside anthropologist Robert L. Hall's exploration of the foods of the Atlantic slave trade, sociologist William C. Whit's ruminations on the concept of soul food, Anne Yentsch's archaeological work recovering food habits of the enslaved, Doris Witt's reflections on conducting research at the intersection of culinary and literary studies, Rafia Zafar's analysis of turn of the twentieth-century African American food writing, and Anne Bower's close reading of several cookbooks produced by the National Council of Negro Women. Collectively, these essays testify to the potential of African American food studies to recover lost details about the material, spiritual, and social realities of the black experience in the United States. Implicitly, the seven contributors to the volume established a broad future research agenda. By creating a compelling, but necessarily partial, portrait of African American foodways, they challenged other scholars to pick up where that collection left off.

The fifteen essays collected in *Dethroning the Deceitful Pork Chop: Rethinking African American Foodways from Slavery to Obama* are the result of the concerted efforts of a diverse group of scholars to build on the foundation of *African American Foodways*. Together, we hope to augment that preliminary collection with new sets of questions and some different analytical approaches. Contributors to the volume utilize a variety of methodologies, ranging from library science to literary close readings to spatial analysis to archival research to media studies and beyond. The essays are unified by our shared testimony that food practices have been and continue to be sites of resistance and vehicles for identity construction for African Americans. In the pages that follow, readers will witness African Americans using food as poison and as magic, as a means of expressing a uniquely black aesthetic and as a way of rebelling against the limitations of culinary stereotypes, as a survival mechanism for an isolated black community and as a vehicle for asserting full belonging to the US nation-state.

As the title of this collection suggests, we collectively resist a singular interpretation of black food culture that begins with chitterlings and ends with hoecakes.[8] In contemporary popular culture, the soul food tradition is often depicted as an essentially black way of cooking and eating. These stereotypes persist despite the fact that numerous African American intellectuals have publically questioned the desirability of maintaining a classic southern diet and have challenged cultural oversimplifications for decades. Writing in the pages of the *Crisis* in 1918, the venerable W.E.B. Du Bois promoted wartime food austerity measures, chiding, "As a race we eat too much meat, especially pork." "The deceitful Pork Chop," he proclaimed, "must be dethroned in the South."[9] Similarly, *Dethroning the Deceitful Pork Chop: Rethinking African American Foodways from Slavery to Obama* attempts to decouple the unyielding association of African Americans with pork and to raise new culinary questions. Although many of these essays respectfully acknowledge the pronounced African American imprint on southern cooking, we do not countenance the idea of a fixed, authentically African American way of eating. We examine the foods that developed within the southern plantation system alongside more cosmopolitan food expressions. Both are part of the African American foodways that we seek to document and to explore. Together we grapple with the tenacious hold that stereotypical black cooks like Mammy and Aunt Jemima have had on the American imagination. We chart how various culinary identities have been constructed, modified, and discarded. Finally, we strive to avoid the food fetishism that can be linked to static ideas about authenticity. Readers should not expect to find paeans to mythically perfect sweet potato pie or collard greens in these pages. Although particular foods, including, of course, watermelons and chickens, are undeniably worthy of contemplation, our research reveals that the symbolic or sentimental significance of which foods were cooked or consumed has often been considered less important than having the right to eat with dignity or just plain having enough to eat.

The book is divided into three parts; articles are clustered around these general topics: archives, representations, and politics. It is appropriate that our volume begins with a foreword from Williams-Forson, whose influence is evident throughout the pages that follow. It is bookended with an afterword by Rebecca Sharpless, whose masterful *Cooking in Other Women's Kitchens: Domestic Workers in the South, 1865–1960* (2010) provides a sensitive and detailed account of the lives of an exploited but surprisingly resilient group of culinary laborers. As the editor of this volume, I am grateful that we were able to proceed with our undertaking undergirded by the advice and endorsement of these scholars whose work has been foundational in establishing the emerging subfield of African American food studies.

The contributors to the first part of the book, "Archives," all contend in one way or another with the issue of source material, grappling with how and where we can look for the information needed to construct nuanced black food histories. In the first essay in this segment, Kelly Wisecup examines writings by eighteenth-century European naturalists who recorded their observations about Caribbean-grown cassava. She demonstrates that these authors unwittingly captured the culinary knowledge of enslaved people who learned how to utilize the plant for nourishment as well as for poison, for sustenance as well as for resistance. In his essay, "Native American Contributions to African American Foodways: Slavery, Colonialism, and Cuisine," Robert A. Gilmer challenges the frequent implication that enslaved Africans and Native Americans exchanged gastronomic knowledge under peaceful and voluntary conditions, arguing that "the majority of these exchanges occurred under far less idyllic circumstances: either through European intermediaries, through African American contact with Native American slave owners, or finally between Native American and African American slaves, toiling side by side, and forced into contact through the rise of the plantation system." While Wisecup and Gilmer examine texts and historical episodes for heretofore hidden glimpses into black food culture, the next contributor, Marcia Chatelain, analyzes food writing composed by black women in the nineteenth and twentieth centuries, asking what their recipes and reminiscences can reveal about black female identity construction. Next Katharina Vester does a close reading of *A Date with a Dish,* a classic 1948 cookbook written by *Ebony* food editor Freda De Knight. Vester argues that "the text was meant not only to circulate cooking instructions but also to serve as an archive of African American culinary traditions." Vester documents De Knight's expansive vision of African American food habits, which incorporated southern recipes alongside other regional and international cuisines. Finally, Gretchen L. Hoffman, a scholar of library science, concludes this section with an innovative essay that argues that the current method of cataloging materials related to African American foodways limits the ability of users to locate these items on library shelves. She reminds us that library classification schemes are themselves "socially constructed, artificial representations of knowledge" and that cultural assumptions about issues like race, gender, and region can affect how knowledge is categorized and, by extension, how easily it is accessed.

The second part of the book, "Representations," expands on Vester's thoughtful meditation on the idea of a single, authentic African American cuisine with essays that examine black culinary productions and black cooks in relationship to stereotyped ideas about how African Americans eat and prepare food. The essays in part 2 document black culinary achievement that includes, complicates, and goes beyond the soul food aesthetic. Christine Marks's essay, "Creole Cuisine as Culinary Border Culture: Reading Recipes as Testimonies of Hybrid Identities and Cultures," asserts that Creole cooking demonstrates the "interconnectedness of the histories of African Americans, Native Americans, and white settlers in Louisiana." She claims that although the African influence on this hybrid cuisine had long been under-acknowledged, recipes and finished dishes can be decoded to reveal an indomitable black influence. Anthony J. Stanonis's inventive essay offers a reexamination of the familiar concept of "soul food." He discovers that prior to the 1960s, the phrase "soul food" often referred to spiritual issues, leading Stanonis to conclude that in the black tradition food and spirituality—both mainstream Christian observance and the hidden world of conjure—were often linked. Stanonis convincingly reminds us that "the pot used to cook collard greens might also be used to boil a black cat." In the next chapter, Kimberly D. Nettles-Barcelón reflects on the stereotype of the "sassy" black cook, as manifested in the fictional character of Minnie from the movie *The Help* and in chef Carla Hall's carefully created public persona. In "Mighty Matriarchs Kill It with a Skillet: Critically Reading Popular Representations of Black Womanhood and Food," Jessica Kenyatta Walker combats narrow representations of black eating practices through her examination of the "scripts of soul food" utilized on the short-lived cooking-competition television show *My Mama Throws Down*. Finally, Lindsey R. Swindall concludes this section with her analysis of how issues of race, gender, and social class have influenced First Lady Michelle Obama's decision to advocate publically for healthful eating habits as well as the public response to her initiatives.

Swindall's examination of the first lady's food reform activism provides a useful segue to the final third of the book, "Politics." In the first chapter, Christopher Farrish redirects our attention back to the era of slavery, particularly to the space of the plantation yard, where he isolates both mechanisms of control and fissures that enslaved people could exploit in order to resist total domination. My essay, "Dethroning the Deceitful Pork Chop: Food Reform at the Tuskegee Institute," examines Booker T. Washington's food reform efforts at Tuskegee University, arguing that he designed policies that were aimed at preparing his students for assimilation, should first-class citizenship be offered to them, or for self-sufficiency if faced with continued exclusion. Next Audrey Russek investigates the complicated racial politics of dining while black in the mid-twentieth century, examining the strange phenomenon of restaurants that would serve people of African descent from (or perceived to be from) foreign countries while denying service to black Americans. Angela Jill Cooley's essay describes black food insecurity in Mississippi in the first half of the twentieth century, demonstrating that activist Fannie Lou Hamer conceptualized food as a civil rights concern. In the final chapter, "After Forty Acres: Food Security, Urban Agriculture, and Black Food Citizenship," Vivian N. Halloran situates the work of contemporary African American farmers and food activists into a long historical struggle for black food autonomy.

Cumulatively, these essays reflect the current state of the field of African American food studies, offering myriad ways to reflect on the relationship between food habits and the legacy of the peculiar way that race has been constructed in the United States. The contributors to this volume work together to resist the idea of a singular, essential black culinary identity, uncovering tradition and adaptability, culinary celebration and pragmatism, and, most of all, resiliency.

PART I ▪ Archives

CHAPTER 1

Foodways and Resistance

Cassava, Poison, and Natural Histories in the Early Americas

KELLY WISECUP

While sugar is the food with which Africans in the early Americas are most closely associated, and certainly the food whose value as a com‑ modity and consumable outweighed all others, sugar was produced to be consumed elsewhere and not by the people who produced it. Colonial economies depended on other foods, both those indigenous to the Americas and those imported from as far away as the Pacific, to feed the huge population of enslaved Africans who planted, culti‑ vated, harvested, and processed sugarcane.[1] Moreover, Africans' diets were determined to a large degree by planters' financial concerns and, by the late eighteenth century, their attempts to maintain their labor force without metropolitan oversight. As planter David Collins wrote in his *Practical Rules for the Management and Medical Treatment of Negro Slaves, in the Sugar Colonies. By a Professional Planter*, "It may be laid down as a principle, susceptible of the clearest demonstration, that every benefit conferred on the slaves, whether in food, or cloth‑ ing, or rest, must ultimately terminate in the interest of the owner."[2] Planters' concerns about maintaining control of the slave trade in the face of abolitionist arguments—what Collins called the "interest of the owner"—motivated them to provide slaves with what they deemed to be a regular supply of sustaining food. As Collins noted, food was crucial to maintaining an efficient labor force: "the energy and vigor of an arm depends, next to natural temperament, upon an ample supply of food; therefore, the Planter, who would wish to have his work done with pleasure to himself, and with ease to his slaves, must not abridge them, as is too frequently the case."[3] Far from deriving from concerns about the inhumane conditions of slavery, planters' interest in Africans' diets may be traced to their desires to control their slaves and to maintain their profits and access to the slave trade by "ameliorating" the conditions of slavery.

Considering early African American foodways in the context of plantation slavery thus raises a number of epistemological and methodological quandaries. First, the archive containing records of enslaved Africans' foodways is found in colonial texts whose purpose was not simply to report on the Americas but to justify slavery, to defend planters' behavior, and to present so-called foreign or exotic peoples and practices to European readers. In particular, as Vivian Nun Halloran points out, there is rarely a "written archive of culinary knowledge" for enslaved Africans before the nineteenth century.[4] When African foodways are described in this archive, it is often through a lens shaped by Euro-colonial views and rhetorical practices, elements that supported planters' attempts to preserve the slave trade by controlling representations of Africans. Second, planters' interest in controlling Africans' diets raises the question of how much agency slaves had over their foodways and, more specifically, whether Africans' pre-existing, Old World agricultural knowledge and practices of consumption influenced what they ate. For example, the recent debates about whether African knowledge of rice was transferred to the Americas, especially in South Carolina, and about the degree to which this knowledge influenced planters have revived questions about the degree to which African practices survived the Middle Passage or were remade in the Caribbean.[5] As David Eltis, Philip Morgan, and David Richardson argue in a co-authored article, slaves certainly arrived in Americas with knowledge that was applicable to the forms of agriculture present in the Carolinas and the Caribbean, but "what was basically at issue is who had the power to transform the plantation economy and reorient it to new crops."[6] Planters, they point out, "held the reins of power, experimented keenly, and in essence called the shots," while the larger Atlantic economy and the supremacy of sugar determined what other crops were cultivated.[7]

The essay takes these debates as a starting point for its investigation of African and Afro-Caribbean foodways in the British West Indies, as represented in natural histories, a genre employed by European travelers and men of science who collected botanical specimens and recorded their observations in great detail in order to provide their metropolitan audiences with information about the Americas' flora and fauna. As I explain, natural historians sought to apply principles of "good ordering" to the people, plants, and animals they observed, both by placing them into categories according to their species or use and by extending these categories to rule humans' behavior.[8] Yet, as I argue, this very impulse to rhetorical and material order also makes natural histories into valuable resources that provide insights into Africans' foodways: specifically, how enslaved peoples employed their knowledge of food as a form of resistance. Africans' knowledge of uniquely New World foods, particularly cassava, a root that could be processed into flour and that became a major component of slaves' diets, destabilized the categories with which natural historians sought to order phenomena on plantations, including Africans themselves. These moments of textual disruption show how Africans employed their knowledge of Caribbean foods for both survival and resistance, while also indicating how enslaved Africans influenced the content and the form of colonial texts. My focus on literary or rhetorical evidence of Africans' foodways in the Caribbean might be productively combined with historical studies of slaves' provenance and agricultural knowledge to uncover the range of uses to which Africans throughout the Americas put their foodways and to broaden scholars' understandings of the archives in which accounts of such foodways appear.

Natural Histories and Plantation Slavery

Natural histories were a "scientific discipline, intellectual obsession, and literary form" employed by men of science in Europe and in the Americas and by collectors seeking to gain approval in metropolitan scientific circles.[9] They responded to the "explosion of information" produced by travel to and settlement in the Americas, for they offered a form with which writers created a "catalog of nature," and they allowed travelers and natural philosophers alike "to find techniques for presenting timely accounts of recent discoveries, while also assimilating and organizing a vast, rapidly growing body of reports."[10]

They also fed the desire for New World exotica back in Europe, that is, the desire to collect, observe, and possess objects from the Americas, with the goal of displaying one's wealth and sophistication.[11]

Often filling several large volumes, natural histories usually began with a preface or introduction describing the writer's goals and sometimes the conditions under which he collected information and made observations. The history itself was divided into chapters or books, each devoted to the close description of objects in a particular category, usually including air and climate, diseases, animals, vegetables, animals living in water, insects, and so on. These chapters reflected the categories in which natural historians classified flora and fauna, and they likewise elucidated the qualities of individual specimens. A specimen's place in a category exposed its similarity to and difference from other specimens, in this way illuminating the unique features of that object. Natural historians applied their prior knowledge and education to create these categories, so that while they did devise new names when they encountered plants or animals unknown in Europe, Old World perspectives shaped the ways that they encountered, described, and presented New World phenomena on paper.

As Christopher P. Iannini has pointed out, natural histories and West Indian plantation slavery were inextricably connected in the eighteenth century. Planters sometimes collected specimens for natural historians; others wrote their own natural histories. Moreover, the Caribbean's lush flora and fauna, extreme weather, and geography attracted the curiosity of many European men of science. Finally, as Iannini writes, natural histories were at the center of debates about slavery: they "emerged as a crucial medium not only for the circulation of natural knowledge among physicians, planters, botanists, gardeners, merchants, and investors but also . . . for assessing the moral significance of colonial slavery as a new and seemingly necessary dimension of modern social and economic life."[12] In particular, natural histories grappled with the ways that plantation slavery confused the category of the "object." Despite their use of categories to identify and classify objects according to their "place" in natural systems, natural historians found that some objects eluded their categories and that the category of the "thing" itself was far from coherent in the West Indies. Iannini points out that "things" in the Caribbean included not just entities like sugarcane and cockroaches but also chattel slaves, "at once property and person, commodity and laborer, object of study and bearer of knowledge."[13] Indeed, natural historians had to confront the fact that in the West Indies "the boundary between specimen and naturalist, thing and agent, is neither clear nor stable"; for example, the slaves whose commerce and labor drove the West Indian economy were also potential sources of knowledge.[14] Even as writers attempted to apply natural historical forms to people as well as to things in the Caribbean, they found that Africans disrupted this order and their categorization as things.

In this chapter, I extend Iannini's focus on natural historians' concerns about slave agency by examining the particular dietary practices and culinary knowledge that Africans in Barbados and Jamaica employed both for survival and for resistance. Africans' practices of consumption existed in tension with both planters' and natural historians' attempts to order slaves and their practices. I examine these moments of contradiction and disruption in the context of Africans' foodways both to explore how Africans' material practices shaped natural histories' content and form and to investigate how natural histories represent Africans' multiple uses for food, including uses antithetical to planters' and natural historians' purposes.

Food and Order

Natural histories imposed order on the Caribbean's natural phenomena by classifying flora, fauna, and, ultimately, people, and this order doubled as a foundation for plantation management. In one of the first English natural histories of the Caribbean, printed in 1657, gentleman and Royalist exile Richard Ligon described observations made during his three years' stay in Barbados, where he worked as an overseer or plantation manager.[15] Ligon arranged the objects he encountered in categories that ordered things by type and by their relation to one another, from food, drink, commodities imported, and commodities exported to buildings and materials with which to build. For example, he commented in his section on food, "The next thing that comes in order, is Drink."[16] And he noted after a discussion of the difficulty of importing butter to Barbados, "I am too apt to fly out in extravagant digressions for, the thing I went to speak of, was bread only, and the several kinds of it."[17] Even when Ligon's desire for delicacies he would have enjoyed in London distracted him from his "order," he always returned to the organization of the natural history.

Ligon extended this rhetorical ordering to justify the treatment of animals and humans and to establish the relations among and differences between humans. He commented that when planters used "good ordering" to care for their hogs, by creating a "Park rather than a Sty" for them, the animals grew "so large and fat, as they wanted very little of their largeness when they were wild. They are the sweetest flesh of that kind, that ever I tasted."[18] Planters' ability to order the conditions in which hogs lived allowed the animals to achieve ideal conditions of size and taste, that is, to fulfill the purpose for which the planter had purchased them. Ligon likewise employed the ideal of ordered diets to describe the differences among the human inhabitants of Barbados. He wrote, "The Island is divided into three sorts of men, *viz.* Masters, Servants, and Slaves."[19] These divisions were defined in dietary terms: masters ate bone meat no more than twice a week, otherwise consuming potatoes, loblolly (a porridge made from maize), and bonavist (a bean); servants ate no bone meat at all unless an ox died; and "till they had planted a good store of Plantations, the *Negroes* were fed with this kind of food [potatoes, loblolly, bonavist]; but most of it Bonavist, and Loblolly, with some ears of Maize toasted."[20] Prescribing diets for each group served not only as efficient plantation management but also as a method of dividing people into different categories.

Ligon extended this culinary ordering to describe Africans at work collecting and preparing plantains to eat. He created a tableau in which the actions and colors of the people in relation to the plantains produced an ordered, and thus pleasing, scene. He wrote, "But 'tis a lovely sight to see a hundred handsome *Negroes,* men and women, with every one a grass-green bunch of these fruits on their heads, every bunch twice as big as their heads, all coming in a train one after another, the black and green so well becoming one another."[21] Africans are described in terms of their parts, or as a single unit, or "train," that is presented for view alongside the plantains. In Ligon's description, the black and green colors complement one another, the size of the plantain bunches neatly doubles the size of Africans' heads, and the slaves form an orderly, single-file train. As Ligon applied his principle of order to people and objects alike, he established connections between plantations and parts of Africans' bodies based upon relations of proportion and color. The same rhetorical and literary strategies that ordered people and their food into tableaux also supported material forms of order, which placed people into groups of laborers and prescribed different diets for different groups. Good ordering is established at every level of the plantation system, and it thus undergirds not only how natural historians such as Ligon attempted to describe phenomena in the West Indies but also how people from planters to slaves sustained themselves.

These rhetorical and material forms of "good order" were especially crucial in the case of cassava, a staple of enslaved Africans' foodways. Ligon carefully arranged his discussion of the various elements of the "small tree or shrub, which they call *Cassava*," for he placed the edible root in the category of "*Meat and Drink for supportation of life*," while placing the "manner of his growth" later in the text, in a section on "Trees and Plants in general."[22] This ordering of the tree's parts and uses was mirrored in the practices with which cassava was processed and consumed, for, as Ligon noted, order was crucial to making the root edible. He explained, "This root, before it come to be eaten, suffers a strange conversion; for, being an absolute poison when 'tis gathered, by good ordering, comes to be wholesome and nourishing."[23] The poisonous root had to be transformed into flour and, eventually, into bread through a "strange conversion" that involved "good ordering," as enacted by a process of washing, cleaning, grating, and drying the root. Ligon explained that the planters "trust" the "*Indians*" to make the flour "because they are best acquainted with it."[24] Indeed, as I explain in the section below, many Europeans believed that cassava was best converted into flour by indigenous peoples, whose knowledge of cassava was extensive and centuries old by the time Ligon wrote.

Cassava and Its Atlantic Routes

It is not surprising that Ligon emphasized the value of order when it came to processing and consuming cassava, given the root's fatally poisonous qualities. But his emphasis on Indian—that is, people indigenous to the Caribbean—labor obscured African and Afro-Caribbean knowledge of cassava, a knowledge that was crucial to enslaved Africans' foodways. Cassava is a New World plant, unique to the Americas, but it quickly became a global staple in the fifteenth and sixteenth centuries. Probably observed by Christopher Columbus in 1492, cassava attracted the notice of Spanish explorers, who described the ways that indigenous women prepared the root for consumption by chewing it to extract a fatally poisonous juice. They then dried the root and converted it into flour with which they made bread or hard cakes. All varieties of cassava have "powerful toxins related to cyanide," most dangerously, cyanogenic glycosides (which yield HCN through digestion), but soil nutrients, drought, and cultivation can influence the strength or weakness of this toxicity.[25] These poisonous qualities notwithstanding, cassava was and remains a major source of subsistence for several reasons: it can be harvested and cultivated in any season without impacting its yield, it adapts easily to poor soils, even when other crops fail, and it withstands drought and pests, such as locusts.[26] Moreover, the roots can remain in the ground for years without rotting, meaning that harvesting practices can be flexible.

The plant was transferred to Africa as early as the sixteenth century by Portuguese and Dutch travelers and traders who sought resources with which to feed European settlers, ships' crews, and the enslaved Africans who worked on plantations in Africa and who were transported to the New World.[27] Cassava traveled in multiple directions and on multiple routes throughout the Atlantic: to Africa from the Americas via explorers' ships, back to the Caribbean as slave traders and ship's captains employed it as a "secure source of nourishment for the Africans making the voyage to the New World," and to Europe in natural historical descriptions and samples.[28]

Europeans who lived in Africa quickly made cassava part of their diet, but determining the extent of Africans' use and knowledge of cassava before the nineteenth century—and thus to what extent Afro-Caribbean knowledge of cassava was shaped by influences from Africa—remains difficult. As cassava's Atlantic circulation shows, the root was certainly part of the globalization of "biological resources."[29] Most scholars date this globalization to the "Columbian exchange" that began in the fifteenth century.[30] Cassava was present in West Africa throughout the eighteenth century, and it was associated with that region to the extent that one European philosopher even claimed that the root originated there.[31] J. D. La Fleur argues that farmers in Africa sometimes "employed their own ingenuity to develop cassava as a food crop for themselves without any tutelage by foreigners who knew how to plant and process the poisonous plant."[32] Moreover, depending on the region from which enslaved Africans were taken, they may have had exposure to cassava but not to other crops such as corn or rice, or vice versa.[33] By the nineteenth century, Africans were certainly cultivating cassava in ways very similar to practices employed in the West Indies.

It is also possible that, even if cassava cultivation was not widespread in Africa in the eighteenth century, the Atlantic slave trade facilitated the circulation of knowledge about cassava and how to consume it safely, and that Africans in both the New World and in Africa possessed this knowledge. James McCann argues, "The new infusions of West African cultures in large numbers, especially via women, brought generations of experience and ideas about the preparation of food from African culinary practice, which had adapted to include the numerous New World crops imported there, to the original home of staples like cassava, cocoyam, maize, and capsicum peppers. The Atlantic system, again, was in fact far less a simple exchange than a circulation of both ideas and material goods."[34] It is unlikely that Africans' knowledge of cassava exactly replicated that of people indigenous to the Caribbean, and it is probable that agricultural and culinary knowledge related to cassava traveled piecemeal from Africa to the Caribbean. Moreover, Africans probably drew upon and adapted existing practices transferred from Native Americans or planters to develop strategies for using cassava. Thanks to these factors, they possessed practical knowledge of how to cultivate and consume cassava, and, as I show below, they employed this knowledge both to ensure their survival and to disrupt planters' and natural historians' systems of "good ordering."[35]

Poison and Food

In eighteenth-century natural histories, writers developed Ligon's strategy of effacing Africans' knowledge of cassava by erasing altogether the agents who processed the root for consumption and by separating descriptions of cassava from the context in which it

Women were often the carriers of culinary knowledge from Africa to the New World. *Woman Beating Cassava*, by William Berryman. Courtesy of the Library of Congress, Prints and Photographs Division, reproduction #LC-DIG-ppmsca-13413.

was observed. This erasure extended practices of good ordering by ensuring that slaves would remain firmly in the category of chattel or objects to be observed, not agents with useful knowledge. Moreover, such a rhetorical practice allowed readers to focus only on the natural object and its qualities in relation to other, similar objects and to ignore the contexts of slavery that made natural historians' work possible. For example, Ligon's decision to place cassava among other elements that provided "*Meat and Drink for supportation of life*," or "Trees and Plants in general" allowed readers to compare cassava with other foods or trees and thus to identify the qualities that made the root unique.[36] Similarly, in his 1707 *Voyage . . . to Jamaica,* physician Hans Sloane described cassava and its conversion into an edible flour without mentioning the individuals who processed the root. He wrote:

> What is used for Bread here, by the Inhabitants, is very different from that in *Europe:* that coming nearest our Bread is *Cassada.* The Root dug up is separated from its outward, small, thin Skin, then grated on a Wheel, or other Grater. After searcing,[37] the powder is put into a Bag, and its juice squeez'd out, the ends of the Roots are kept for other uses.[38]

With his use of the passive voice, Sloane avoided identifying who performed the digging, grating, and squeezing of the root, actions that ensured that the poisonous juice was removed from the root. It is very likely that he observed Native women or men doing this work, but it is also just as likely that he observed Africans preparing the root for consumption. However, he effaced this knowledge, its sources, and its origins from the natural history by focusing his description solely on the root itself, making this object, not human actions and agency, the focus of his description. Like Ligon's accounts of separate diets and his description of Africans in terms of their body parts and skin color, Sloane's impersonal report of cassava restricts Africans to their position as laborers—that is, as people valued for their work rather than for their minds—by effacing their knowledge of Caribbean plants, foods, and medicines. This rhetorical practice likewise suppressed cassava' local history and uses by failing to include the African (and indigenous) people who gathered trees or plants and who possessed knowledge of Caribbean flora and fauna on which natural historians relied.

Yet natural histories also expose the fact that Africans employed their knowledge of cassava to disrupt practices of good ordering: both the system of plantation slavery and the rhetorical strategies that sought to define Africans as non-agents. Their effacement of Africans' contributions to their knowledge notwithstanding, natural historians sometimes included accounts of this resistance in their natural histories, with the goal of maintaining order on plantations by casting Africans' knowledge as dangerous and illicit. In *Voyage to . . . Jamaica,* Sloane included an account he had received from planter Henry Barham, who told of Africans employing cassava to poison planters. Sloane wrote that Barham "says also, that the Powder of the Maggots bread from the Corruption of the Juice of this Root put under the Nail, given to drink, poisons the Person taking it, therefore on such Accidents they suspect Negroes with long Nails."[39] Barham's natural historical manuscript circulated among men of science before it was posthumously published, and he noted that Africans subtly employed cassava to endanger others: "They dry these worms or maggots, and powder them: which powder, in a little quantity, they put under their thumb-nail, and, after they drink to those they intend to poison, they put their thumb upon the bowl, and so cunningly convey the poison; wherefore, when we see a negro with a long thumb-nail, he is to be mistrusted."[40] Significantly, Sloane located information about the potential dangers of cassava in a supplement to *Voyage*, with the result that Africans' acts of resistance are rhetorically separated from the body of the text and from the appropriate uses of cassava as bread. Although Sloane and Barham do not identify whom Africans poisoned with the juice of cassava, another natural historian, Griffith Hughes, stated explicitly that slaves sometimes poisoned their masters in this manner, writing, "A certain Slave, conceiving herself injuriously treated, poured into her Master's Chocolate about a Spoonful of this Juice: Immediately after he had swallowed it, he felt a violent Burning in his Throat and Stomach; and suspecting he was poisoned, he strove, and with good Success, to vomit, and having taken after this seasonable Discharge, a regular Emetic, his Stomach was, in a great measure, suddenly cleansed of the Poison, tho' it cost him a long time to Perfect the Cure."[41]

These accounts of Africans' expertise with poison should be read with caution, for planters frequently used the term "poison" along with "witchcraft" to label Africans' knowledge as illicit and in need of punishment. Especially during times of unrest, poisonings became an obsession of planters fearful of rebellion (as shown by fears during the Haitian Rebellion of the alleged poisonings said to have been directed by the slave Makandal).[42] Moreover, the term "poison" had "multiple, coexisting" meanings and definitions in the West Indies for "African or Creole slaves, local planters or metropolitan physicians."[43] Thus, while natural historians' alignment of African knowledge with rebellion and poisonings certainly casts Africans' uses of Caribbean plants as inappropriate and in need of surveillance, these moments may also shed light on the ways in which Africans employed their knowledge of foods such as cassava not only for subsistence but also to resist planters' "ordering" and thus their own enslavement. What natural historians perceived as the work of "cunning" or revengeful slaves was likely, for Africans, a means of applying their knowledge of cassava's consumable and dangerous properties to reorganize the categories with which Europeans ordered natural objects and humans alike. Indeed, Africans' use of cassava as "poison" suggests not only their awareness of planters' fear of rebellion but also their knowledge of the ways that planters used food to enforce order on plantations. Placing cassava in planters' drinks required planters to consume the same potentially poisonous materials that slaves did and to admit that Africans' foodways included viable strategies of survival and of resistance. Moreover, natural historians and planters admitted that they could not always distinguish between poisonous and healthy drinks: beverages that appeared to be drinks for sustenance were instead invisibly converted into elements dangerous to planters' lives. The difficulty of determining the cause of such danger is indicated by Sloane's reference to "Accidents," a term that suggests that the symptoms following the consumption poisoned liquids were not easily ascribed to one person or event but appeared inadvertent and random.

Africans' use of cassava as alternately food and poison likewise disrupted the categories natural historians constructed to maintain order in the Caribbean. First, the accounts of poisonings make clear that Africans possessed knowledge of cassava and indicate some of the uses to which they put this knowledge. Slaves' acts of "poisoning" motivated natural historians to include African agents in their accounts of Caribbean foods and to represent the ways that African knowledge shaped the material and modes of consumption on plantations. No de-humanized account of cassava's conversion from root into flour, these descriptions admit that human agency and knowledge are behind planters' poisonings. Even as Sloane, Barham, and Hughes attempted to define African knowledge in terms of its dangers to the plantation, their accounts make clear that Africans knew how to extract poisonous juice from cassava and thus that they were familiar with the "conversion" the root must undergo to make it edible.[44] Second, Africans disrupted the classification of cassava as "*Meat and Drink for supportation of life*"[45] or as "Bread" with their use of cassava as poison. This shows the fabricated nature of natural historians' categories.[46] In the case of Sloane and his relegation of the poisonings to the supplement, Africans' use of cassava disrupts the decontextualized account of cassava in the natural history proper, for the poisonous traits of and uses for cassava are always capable of overturning the category of "bread" with which Sloane attempts to define cassava. Africans' knowledge does not merely contradict natural historians' classification of chattel slaves as things, it also posits an alternative system of "ordering," one in which Africans determine the uses for and qualities of foods.[47] Africans' actions of resistance made it difficult—if not impossible—to determine how to classify cassava: as poison or as flour, as dangerous to planters or as necessary to maintain an enslaved labor force.

The slippery space between food and poison occupied by cassava disrupts natural historian's categories for ordering both food and people. Africans exploited these unstable boundaries as they processed cassava for flour and extracted its poisonous elements, in order to eat and, at times, to resist their enslavement. As the natural histories that attempt to order both cassava and Africans show, the archive developed to document the Americas and to support planters' control of plantations certainly attempted to enforce and justify order over enslaved peoples. But the very documents with which writers aimed to order Africans' foodways also reflect the strategies that Africans developed to obtain food from local, New World sources and to employ the properties of that food to resist slavery. Africans' material practices and practical knowledge, while represented incompletely, nonetheless infiltrated the colonial archive and exposed its strategies, even while providing insight into the ways that Africans drew on their foodways for suenance and resistance.

CHAPTER 2

Native American Contributions to African American Foodways

Slavery, Colonialism, and Cuisine

ROBERT A. GILMER

The history of African American cuisine is indicative of cultural persistence, creative adaptation, and identity, but it is also bound up in histories of slavery, violence, and colonization. In Adrian Miller's book *Soul Food: The Surprising Story of African American Cuisine, One Plate at a Time*, Miller credits Stokely Carmichael with a resurgence of interest in African American foodways by connecting it with the Black Power movement during the Student Nonviolent Coordinating Committee's campaigns in Mississippi. Eating soul food became not just a matter of economics or habit, but also a symbol of cultural identity. The act of food preparation and consumption became a political act grounded in asserting and reclaiming African American traditions and identity. In the process, Miller argues that Carmichael narrowly defines soul food as the cuisine of Mississippi's Black Belt—and as distinctively, and solely, Black—while the reality of its history and contemporary practice, like most aspects of cooking, are in fact a lot messier.[1]

What makes African American cuisine distinctive is the blending of techniques, ingredients, and consumption patterns that developed through the Columbian exchange and the intertwined processes of colonization and slavery: specifically, the combination of African, European, and Native American foodways—exchanges that occurred not only within the southern United States, but also in Africa and the Caribbean. In this essay, I attempt to unpack a portion of this complicated history by focusing on Native American contributions to African American cuisine. While numerous works discuss the transference of foods and culinary skills between Native American and African American peoples, the precise manner in which this transference occurred is often elided or the role of mutual cross-cultural exchanges are overemphasized.[2] These zones of contact—how exactly the foods themselves and the knowledge of preparation techniques were shared between African American and Native American peoples—are what I hope to uncover in this essay. In what follows, I attempt to synthesize bodies of literature on the Indian slave trade, Native American ownership of African slaves, and the African slave trade to explain how these contacts most likely occurred. I argue that these zones of contact are intimately tied to the history of colonization and slavery in the Southeast and occurred through indirect means (primarily through European or Euro-American slave traders and plantation owners), through direct contact between enslaved Africans and free Native Americans, as well as through direct contact between enslaved Africans and enslaved Native Americans.

One of the major challenges in tracing how these exchanges occurred is the paucity of source materials that specifically address culinary interactions, and in many cases, interactions in general, between African American and Native American peoples during the early colonial period. Both groups were largely non-literate peoples, meaning that what sources we do have often come either from the archaeological record or from European or Euro-American sources. While both groups were central to European colonization as trade partners, allies (and sometimes enemies), or laborers, they were also typically viewed as being on the margins of colonial society, further limiting the amount of sources available. Documents such as ship manifests, plantation records, and written accounts by colonists can frequently tell us what foods were being eaten and by whom, but the source material is often silent on how exactly they came to eat those foods and how culinary exchanges developed. My goal in this essay is help fill in some of this gap by suggesting how and when opportunities for these kinds of exchanges occurred.

While my primary focus in this essay will be on culinary traditions within what is now the United States, telling that story involves using a more global approach. Some of these exchanges, as I argue later in the essay, likely did occur within the borders of what is now the United States, but many would have occurred first in the Caribbean, in Africa, or in Latin America and were later introduced into African American cuisine in the United States. Encounters based on mutual respect and curiosity undoubtedly did happen, but I suggest that the majority of these exchanges occurred under far less idyllic circumstances: either through European intermediaries, through African American contact with Native American slave owners, or finally between Native American and African American slaves, toiling side by side and forced into contact through the rise of the plantation system.

The importance of Native American foods to the development of African American, southern, and American cuisine, more broadly, cannot be understated. Perhaps no single food has more profoundly shaped African American and southern cuisine than maize, or corn. While not exclusive to the South, maize has become so closely identified with southern food that the Southern Foodways Alliance (SFA) adopted the name "Cornbread Nation" for their newsletter (it was later changed to "Gravy"), and it is currently used as the title of a book series edited by John T. Edge, the director of the SFA.[3] Corn was first domesticated in Mexico at least six thousand years ago and was introduced into what is now the United States between three thousand and one thousand years ago.[4] Native American cooks developed a number of recipes based on corn that were later adopted by African Americans. Aside from simply eating corn on the cob, they also mixed corn kernels with lye to produce hominy. Both hominy and unprocessed corn were ground up to varying degrees to make dishes like *sofke* (a corn-based drink or soup) and grits or to make flour that was used for breads like corn or ash pone. Frequently, corn flour was, and continues to be, mixed with chestnuts or beans and then boiled to make bread similar to Mexican tamales. Tamales were also produced in the Mississippi Delta by African Americans and sold in northern cities during the Great Migration. While these were likely introduced either by earlier Mexican immigrants to the South or through the experiences of American soldiers during the Mexican American War, one possible theory is that these recipes were adapted from neighboring

Indian peoples. In either case, whether they were introduced via contact directly with Mexico or were adapted from recipes such as bean bread or chestnut bread, delta tamales demonstrate the complex ways that indigenous recipes were adopted into African American cuisine.[5]

The cases of ashcakes and tamales illustrate precisely how difficult untangling the history of culinary transferences can be. While Indigenous peoples in the Americas originally cultivated maize, it was also introduced to West Africa shortly after contact, where it became a major staple.[6] Additionally, the process of wrapping food in leaves and either boiling or cooking them in coals was also already practiced in Africa, suggesting that African cooks could have applied their own preparation techniques to the introduced ingredient.[7] So while we can be certain that Native American ingredients are later being used in African American cooking and prepared in a manner similar to that of Native American cooks, the preparation techniques themselves could have been developed independently in both Africa and the Americas, or, further complicating matters, could be the result of independent development in some cases and a direct transference of techniques in others.

Interviews with former slaves that were recorded as part of the Works Progress Administration's Federal Writers Project captured some of the continuing influences of Native American cuisine on the diets of African Americans during the nineteenth and early twentieth centuries. In one interview, Millie Evans described a number of recipes that indicated strong Native American influences. She described making ash pones from cornmeal by wrapping the ingredients in cornhusks (or collard greens) and covering them in hot coals for ten minutes. In an additional interview, Allen Sims described eating ashcakes as the "best bread [he] ever" ate. Evans also included several recipes for persimmons, including making a persimmon cornbread, persimmon pie, and persimmon beer. Persimmons are a late-ripening tree-born fruit; they can be dried to preserve them as well as eaten fresh. Persimmons were commonly gathered in the Southeast and frequently baked into breads by Cherokees and other Native American peoples, in much the same fashion that Evans relayed in her interview. Cherokee women typically either would dry persimmons for later consumption or would "seed, pound, and knead [them] into cakes" that would be barbequed into bread.[8]

In addition to corn, one of the foods most closely associated with African American cuisine is pork, and particularly pork barbeque. While pork itself was introduced into the Americas through Spanish colonization, the word "barbeque" likely comes from a Taíno (one of the most populous indigenous peoples in the Caribbean at contact) word the Spanish recorded as *barbacoa*. The word originally meant a wooden structure that could either be used for preparing meat, storing corn, or even as a sleeping surface.[9] William C. Witt, in "Soul Food as a Cultural Creation," suggests that the process of smoking meat itself may have been borrowed from Native Americans.[10] Thus, while the ingredients used in pork barbeque were introduced into the Americas, Native American vocabulary and methods of preparation continue to exercise a profound influence on African American cuisine.

Many other foods that are still staples in African American cuisine, as well as ones that are no longer commonly eaten, were originally cultivated by the Indigenous peoples of the Americas. Oysters were dried for use in stews.[11] Peanuts were also cultivated.[12] Greens such as pokeweed, swamp marigold, and milkweed; herbs such as sassafras; fruits; and vegetables such as pumpkins, squash, numerous varieties of beans (including pole beans, kidney beans, lima beans, snap beans, butter beans, and string beans), sweet potatoes, tomatoes, and peppers[13] were all originally grown by Native American peoples and were incorporated into African American diets. The cuisine of Native Americans within the Southeast became adopted so thoroughly by both African Americans and Euro-Americans that its indigenous origins almost became invisible. As Rayna Greene states in her essay "Mother Corn and Dixie Pig: Native Food in the Native South," if a restaurant opened today specializing in the foods of the Indigenous South, it would be "shockingly familiar, albeit a tad underseasoned, to all good Southerners."[14]

This process, however, went both ways. African ingredients and methods of cooking also greatly changed the diets of Native American peoples. For instance, black-eyed peas were originally cultivated in West Africa.[15] They became so popular in some Native American communities that they were once thought to be indigenous to the Americas.[16] Techniques for preparing foods, in addition to ingredients, were also exchanged between Native American and African cooks. While barbequing meats and possibly boiling and baking cornmeal in husks were introduced to African American cooks, African cooks are credited with introducing the frying of foods in fats as a means of preparing dishes.[17] The combination of Indian cornmeal and the African technique of frying led to the creation of the hushpuppy.

Numerous scholars have written on the prevalence of Native American ingredients in African American cuisine, but the question of how exactly this transference occurred has been left largely unanswered. Scholars have suggested various possible influences, but so far no work has brought all of these discussions together to form a coherent picture of how these culinary traditions came to influence one another. Part of the difficulty in establishing how these culinary exchanges occurred is the lack of source material describing peoples who are living on the margins of colonial society. We know that such exchanges occurred because of the end result, but frequently scholars have resorted to statements such as "for the New World crops they didn't know, the enslaved relied heavily on local Native Americans for guidance" or simply mentioned that foods came from Indigenous peoples without delving into how that process occurred.[18]

At times scholars also have depicted these interactions as stemming from chance encounters or a sense of camaraderie arising from their mutual oppression under European colonization. For instance, in her essay "Excavating African American Food History," Anne Yentsch suggests:

> Among the woodlands, meadows, swamps, forests, marshes, creeks, and open bays, black folk possessed a modicum of independence. There networks forged with Native Americans provided additional knowledge of the terrain and its resources. Families came into being that included both black and Indian; children had parents and relatives among both groups with vested interests in making sure the youngsters were enculturated to Native American norms. The techniques they were taught and the training they received infused food collection and preparation within slave and maroon communities.[19]

Or as Jessica B. Harris states, in her book *High on the Hog: A Culinary Journey from Africa to America*, "I like to imagine that on one or more occasions—at a stall on the outskirts of a market, walking along a dusty country road, foraging in the woods at the edge of a thicket— black man would spy red man, red man would spy black man, start, smile, and recognize a kinship."[20] I highlight these selections to suggest not that these kinds of encounters did not occur, but rather that these were not the sole or even primary methods through which these exchanges likely transpired.

In fact, there are numerous cases where relationships such as these developed and led to the creation of multiracial communities within what would become the United States. In the Northeast, where Harris began her discussion by describing her attendance at a Wampanoag feast, intermarriage between Native American and African peoples was quite common during the late eighteenth and early nineteenth centuries. Relatively high rates of African American men being kept as slaves and a higher percentage of Native American women than men living in the area appear to have contributed to frequent intermarriage.[21] Another prominent example is that of the Seminole in Florida, who frequently harbored runaway slaves. African Americans often married into Seminole communities and played a critical role in Seminole resistance against the United States. Seminoles also kept African Americans as slaves, though slavery within the Seminole nation tended to grant slaves much more freedom than in the United States.[22] Other prominent examples include pockets of Indian populations within the Carolinas and Virginia, which frequently led to the communities intermarrying with surrounding populations.[23] The influences of these kinds of unions on the changing cuisines of the populations involved are likely varied and diffuse. While the inclusion of large numbers of African Americans within Indian communities would likely lead to changes in the diets of those communities, the effect on the foodways of African Americans more broadly is more difficult to determine. Such connections would have initially tied African American and Native American communities closer together in areas such as the Carolinas, Virginia, and New England, where those communities were surrounded by American settlements; but in cases like the Seminole, who lived apart from large American populations until much later in the nineteenth century, this likely would have had very little impact, or at least a substantially delayed influence, on the diets of those outside Seminole territory.

What is likely the most frequent, but least direct, conduit for culinary exchange is the intermediary role of Europeans and Euro-Americans. Many Native American crops were already being grown in Africa by the early 1600s as a result of their introduction through European traders. As Judith Carney argues in her essay "African Rice in the Columbian Exchange," within decades of Christopher Columbus's voyages, maize was being planted in Africa, followed by "manioc, sweet potatoes, capsicum peppers, tomatoes, peanuts, cashew nuts, pineapple, pumpkin, squash, and tobacco."[24] Shannon Lee Dawdy also suggests that tomatoes and peppers (which were originally cultivated in South America) were commonly being grown in Africa by the mid-1600s and likely were introduced into Louisiana from Africa.[25] Slave ships often purchased African crops such as millet, sorghum, yams, and rice, foods that were indigenous to other parts of the Americas, and introduced them into North America, changing the diets of African, Native American, and Euro-American peoples.[26] Plantation owners also exercised varying degrees of influence over what foods crops were cultivated and, thus, what slaves were able to eat. While some plantations offered slaves more freedom in determining their meals, the food preferences of planters frequently played a critical role in deciding what crops, whether indigenous, African, or European, were readily available for slaves to utilize.[27]

Another zone of encounter and culinary exchange between Native Americans and African peoples likely occurred through the trade in Indian slaves across North America during the seventeenth and eighteenth centuries. This trade both forced Native American and African peoples together within what would become the United States and also shipped Native American slaves to the Caribbean to work on plantations, where they likely shaped the foodways of the African peoples who worked alongside them. This trade initially began through the capture and sale of American Indian prisoners of war, with early examples occurring in both the Northeast during the Pequot Wars and in Virginia during the wars against the Powhatan Confederacy.[28] Native American captives were generally sold out of the colonies and into the Caribbean, where they worked, lived, and ate with both imported African slaves and enslaved Indigenous peoples from the Caribbean.[29]

Although prisoners of war accounted for a fraction of the early trade in Native American peoples, a much more widespread and destructive trade developed out of colonial Charles Town that sent far more Native American slaves to the West Indies. Charles Town was initially colonized by people from the West Indies who brought a familiarity with both plantation agriculture and race-based slavery that was put into practice from the beginning of the colony.[30] While, previously, Native American captives had been taken and sold into slavery during war, Carolina traders began arming their Indian allies—initially, the Westos and then, later, Chickasaws and other Native American nations—to scour the Southeast in search of potential slaves.[31] This trade, which existed from roughly 1670 through 1717, had wide-ranging consequences. It contributed to the rise of the plantation system in the colony, caused a sharp increase in violence and warfare throughout the Southeast, and potentially contributed to the decline of Mississippian chiefdoms, which, due to their large, sedentary populations, would have been convenient targets for slave raiders.[32]

The bulk of these Native American slaves, which numbered into the thousands and possibly outstripped the number of African slaves being imported during that same period, were sold off into the West Indies or into northern colonies, but many also remained behind and were kept as slaves in both Carolina and Virginia.[33] The roughly fifty-year period during which the Indian slave trade thrived undoubtedly played a profound role in shaping the foodways of African American peoples. The enslavement of Native American peoples in Virginia was, at least initially, viewed as distinct from African slavery. Native slaves were often employed in non-agricultural work as guides or hunters and were subjected to greater attempts toward cultural conversion and assimilation than African slaves.[34] However, in later periods in Virginia as well as throughout the bulk of the Indian slave trade's existence in Carolina, Native American slaves were employed in agricultural labor alongside African slaves. Despite the vast numbers of Indigenous slaves who were shipped out of Charles Town, as many as 1,400 Indian slaves were living in the Carolina Colony in 1708. (At the same time, approximately 4,000 African slaves and an equal number of European colonists lived in the colony.) These plantations offered a direct opportunity for the fusion of African and Native American cuisines to take place. Additionally, over 6,000 free Indians lived in the surrounding area and, at least early in the Carolina colony's history, would have had access to planation areas and could have contributed to the exchange of African and Native American foodways. While some exchanges could have occurred in the Caribbean, the contributions of Native American slaves from North America would have been limited by their separation from their homelands and the enforced nature of the transportation to the islands. Within the southeastern colonies, however, Native American peoples, even kept as slaves, would have had knowledge of the indigenous flora and fauna, making the transmission of that knowledge much more feasible.[35]

While the Indian slave trade through the Carolina colony was a major source of contact between the culinary traditions of African and Indigenous peoples, a simultaneous trade in Indian slaves was occurring from the Southwest and into French Louisiana. A thriving trade in Native American women and children developed across the plains and the Southwest during this period, whereby the Comanche, in particular, would seize captives and transport them into colonial Louisiana, where they were frequently purchased by French colonists, particularly along the borders of French territory. At the same time, large numbers of African slaves were being imported into Louisiana, who, again, often lived and worked in close proximity to Native American slaves. Historian Juliana Barr credits the growth of a new population of people in Louisiana with Native American, African, and European ancestry, particularly after the onset of Spanish rule in the territory, which prohibited the enslavement of native peoples. While in many cases these Native American slaves were being shipped far from their traditional homelands, the preponderance of women within this trade, combined with traditional European gender roles that stressed feminine responsibility for cooking, likely contributed to an infusion of Native American cuisine into the diets of African and European peoples living in colonial Louisiana.[36]

As the enslavement of both African and Native American peoples in the Southeast contributed to the shaping of their foodways, it also contributed to increased suspicions by Euro-Americans that these two groups would find common cause in other areas as well. In the Carolina colony, officials began to view the Indian slave trade and the large numbers of Indian and African slaves working side by side with alarm.[37] While there were earlier calls for a halt to the trade, it took the Yamasee War (1715–1717) to finally bring it to an end. During the war, which was brought on in part because of the tensions flowing from the Indian slave trade, Yamasee Indians freed African slaves living on nearby plantations and encouraged them to flee with them to Florida, from whence they continued to raid the colony over the next few decades.[38]

Even before the outbreak of the war, but especially after it, authorities within the Carolina colony began to push for ways to drive a wedge between Native American and African peoples. Free Indians were banned from entering plantation areas, and people of African descent were barred from working in the Indian trade. In many cases Indians were hired as slave catchers, and, increasingly, treaties between the British and, later, the American government called for Indians to return any runaway slaves. Black slaves were also sometimes armed by British colonists to help fight against Indians, which contributed to the divide between the two peoples. Gradually this process led to the adoption of Euro-American racial hierarchies within Native American communities and simultaneously gave rise to the practice of plantation agriculture and the ownership of African slaves among Indigenous peoples throughout the Southeast.[39]

Ironically, what began as an effort to drive Native American and African peoples apart from one another likely contributed to another avenue of culinary exchange between them. For Indian nations in the Southeast, the incorporation of African slaves initially began as a form of kinship slavery, where slaves would frequently live, eat, and work with, as well as marry, free members of the community. During the first half of the nineteenth century, this system was largely replaced by a system of chattel slavery common elsewhere in the South, but both forms would likely contribute to a blending of culinary habits between both groups. By the outbreak of the Civil War, the total population of slaves in Indian Territory likely numbered as many as ten thousand and ranged anywhere from 10 percent to 30 percent of the total population of the Five Tribes.[40] While this total was dwarfed by the number of African American slaves emancipated at the end of the Civil War, it likely would have had a profound, if localized, influence on the foodways of those slaves, their descendants, and neighboring communities. The previously mentioned interview with Millie Evans, which included a substantial number of persimmon recipes, was in fact conducted in Arkansas, adjacent to the territory of the Five Tribes. While Euro-Americans also adopted persimmons into their diet, it is quite possible that Evans's recipes may have originated, however indirectly, in nearby Indian Territory.

The processes of colonization and slavery provided numerous avenues for culinary exchange to occur between the Indigenous peoples of the Americas and African and, later, African American cooks. Foods such as corn, peanuts, peppers, tomatoes, wild greens, numerous kinds of beans, potatoes, sweet potatoes, and squashes were all originally cultivated by Native American agriculturalists and later became central to the diets of African American peoples within the United States. Preparation methods such as barbequing meats, boiling and baking stuffed cornmeal breads, and frying foods were all products of the fusing of African and Native American culinary traditions. While many of the specifics about how these transferences occurred may not ever be fully understood due to the limits of available sources, the goal of this essay was to identify zones of contact that could have facilitated these kinds of exchanges.

In teaching US southern history, one of the topics that frequently elicits the strongest reactions from students is discussing how the foods they eat are products of cultural and material exchanges that have occurred between peoples from throughout the globe. In a very real way, the foods we eat, the methods we use to prepare them, and, hopefully, the people we continue to share them with reflect the diversity of cultures that shape the world in which we live. While food has the ability to bring people together and remind us of our shared heritages and traditions, the process through which these exchanges occurred must be remembered as well. Sometimes these exchanges did occur as a result of people finding common cause with one another, coming together to break bread, grind corn, or roast a pig in a spirit of unity and camaraderie. All too often, however, these exchanges occurred under forced circumstances brought on by the process of colonization and the development of chattel slavery. Indian and African foods shaped each other's diets with little or no direct contact happening between the two peoples. In other cases Native American and African and, later, African American peoples were forced together to share meals through their mutual enslavement on southern and Caribbean plantations. And in still other cases, Native American peoples themselves adopted plantation agriculture and bought, sold, and owned African peoples. Even under these circumstances, they likely contributed to the creation of new foodways for both peoples and continue to shape the way both groups eat to this day. While these stories of exchanges brought on by shared enslavement, indirect means, and Native American's enslavement of African peoples are much less unifying and romantic, they caused more extensive contact and likely played a much more significant role in shaping African American cuisine.

CHAPTER 3

Black Women's Food Writing and the Archive of Black Women's History

MARCIA CHATELAIN

The field of black women's history has produced incredible theoretical challenges to how the discipline considers marginalized voices and evaluates the intersection of race and gender as constitutive and essential to producing history.[1] In specializing in "the wholly impossible," historians of black women's lives and labors are constantly building archives and redefining analytical frames.[2] Similarly, the growth in scholarship that examines the role of food and culture, encompassed in the broad title of food studies, has yielded an array of interventions into conversations about the family, technology, and representation, among so many others. Scholars Jessica B. Harris, Rebecca Sharpless, and Psyche Williams-Forson have provided compelling narratives of the gendered nature of black women's labor on the African continent, during slavery, and later as domestics under working conditions far from totally free. Collectively, these studies highlight black women's economic and social opportunities via culinary work.[3] They also demonstrate how centering food in black women's lives can serve black women's history on the whole by opening up new avenues of evaluating the past.[4] In addition to a greater recognition of food texts as windows into black women's history, the analytic tools that were critical to the formation of black women's history—from critical race theory's invaluable contribution of intersectionality to notions of racial uplift and the politics of respectability—can and must be applied to black women's food writing to demonstrate their usefulness to the study.[5] In this essay, I examine how black women's food writing serves as a useful archive for deepening inquiries into black women's life and culture. I analyze three examples of black women's food writing from the Great Migration period to the recent past and demonstrate how reflections on culinary experiences have provided black women a space to articulate themselves and to meditate on and resist sexism and racism. I consider how each woman engaged with her historical context and resisted dominant notions or "controlling images" of black women in the kitchen.[6]

Black women are not absent from the archive of US culinary production, particularly its folktales, ephemera, and material culture. The prominent placement of commercial figures such as the Quaker Oats Company's Aunt Jemima illustrates that visibility is not the central problem in the excavation of the relationship between black women and US food histories.[7] Rather, the distorted representations of black women in Lost Cause–inspired cookbooks, live-action cooking demonstrations at World's Fairs, and the advertisements of the post-Reconstruction era have formed forceful and lasting impressions in the thinking that surrounds black women and food.[8] These portrayals of black women as naturally and joyfully servile, unfit for freedom, and deeply dependent on whites for their sense of self are embedded in national food culture and still resonate in contemporary popular culture. By turning attention toward actual black women's food writing, historians can discover humanizing accounts of the complexity of black women's domestic labor and community work. The figure of the black domestic servant versus the reality of the black woman in self-authored food narratives makes clear the extent of the distance between image and substance, but not without complications.

Black women's appearance in the culinary archive can be demarcated between texts authored *about* black women cooks and texts authored *by* black women cooks. The first category of texts have taken many forms, especially, nostalgic tributes to a "dying" breed of loyal mammies and servants immune to the lures of Emancipation and northern migration out of a deep sense of love, obligation, and devotion toward white families.[9] Mammies populate cookbooks from across the nation, with names like Mandy and Aunt Priscilla. The central figure of these cookbooks was sometimes a real-life person, and her story was authenticated with a photograph or illustration. Other times, she was an amalgam of the cooks who had passed through a household, and the cookbook created a single, almost magical subject. In Natalie V. Scott's *Mandy's Favorite Louisiana Recipes*, the author offered readers the truth behind Mandy's identity immediately. "Mandy, of course, is a composite. My own Mandy's name is Pearl. Bless her earnest face!" Scott continued: "There are the Mandys of all my friends—Mammy Lou, and Phrosine, and Tante Celeste, Venida, Felicie, Mande, Titine, Elvy, Mona, Relie."[10] Although Scott knew all of these women by name, the specificities of their stories and their abilities were irrelevant—black women cooks were interchangeably useful to white employers.

Regardless of their veracity, mammy cookbooks conformed to a standard convention that included black dialect-laden transcriptions of crude recipes—where pinches, dashes, and instinct ruled the process—or sage pieces of advice phonetically drawn out for a white reading audience. These depictions of Mammy signaled to white readers that the cookbook, and the cook's joy, would have been impossible without the loving employ of whites and their steady editorial hand. Newspapers published Mammy's advice in food sections, also authored by white journalists, which ridiculed as it honored Mammy in her "natural" role in the plantation kitchen or standing behind the lady of the house poised to serve.[11]

While some white readers found comfort in these tributes to black subservience, African American writers and activists often resisted these characterizations that grew throughout the late nineteenth and early twentieth centuries. African Americans of means and social status produced etiquette manuals, prideful missives, and other publications devoted to thoughtful, and sometimes hyperbolic, representations of black achievement and race pride. This literature coupled with black social outreach movements formed what scholars call the culture of racial uplift. Black clubwomen were deeply involved in activities and leadership designed to affirm black respectability and possibility to combat racism through assimilation with whites. Scholarship on racial uplift culture has primarily focused on literature and journalistic writing as evidence of this ideological movement. Although it has garnered little scholarly acknowledgment, women-authored cookbooks and culinary memoirs can also give voice to the interests of black women's history, from how black women engaged with reform culture to the gendered nature of their labor history to their struggles for racial understanding.

The texts I highlight in this essay center experiences of mobility —physical, economic, and social—in the life of black women culinarians. The writings span nearly a century of black life, from the movement of African Americans from a Jim Crow South to the years right before the election of an African American president. The places where these women lived and traveled were outside of the core of the Deep South, where some of their most popular dishes originated. Despite their migrations to bustling black enclaves of the urban North, the racially homogenous heartland, and the tourist destinations of the coastal South, they were constantly in dialogue with southern, black identities. Although these pieces do not mark every victory of the civil rights movement or the various waves of feminism, when read together they do demonstrate how black women's food work underwent shifts secured by these activist struggles. Black women's food writing shows us how they have used their food knowledge and food labor to secure employment, settle in new locales, travel, and negotiate class dynamics. It also highlights the stark reality that black women's individual and community success can never fully mediate multiple oppressions.

A Cateress and a Race Woman

The 1939 *Recipes and Domestic Service: The Mahammitt School of Cookery*, a guide for caterers, provides excellent insight into how black women capitalized on their culinary skills. Published by Sarah Helen Mahammitt of Omaha, Nebraska, the book's text spoke to other members of the black middle class, as well as to white homemakers who regularly entertained and employed black help. Mahammitt's career as a caterer continued to flourish after the publication of *Recipes and Domestic Service*, and she was later quoted in advertisements for the Omar Company's baking mixes.[12] Cookbooks, like Mahammitt's, doubled as a chronicle of respectability and progress.[13] *Recipes and Domestic Service* can be seen as piece of uplift literature that provided a counterargument to the mammy who was crudely skilled in the kitchen, lacking in the business sense to ever monetize her talents, and always subservient to white families. Readers of *Recipes and Domestic Service* may have imagined Aunt Jemima or Delilah Johnson from the 1934 film *Imitation of Life*, but Mahammitt's emphasis on her successes destabilized ideas about black women's work.[14]

In the foreword, Mahammitt immediately established her authority as a caterer and expert on all matters regarding food, unlike in the texts from an earlier period that relied on white women to verify the author's knowledge or ability (in ways similar to the forewords to slave narratives); Mahammitt did not rely on a white employer to establish her fitness to dispense advice or corroborate her success with white patrons.[15] She instead referenced her thirty years of working as a noted caterer, and she described her publication of the book as a public service to her people. "If the best in cookery is to be attained, we must share our knowledge and not be like the cook of whom her friends remarked, when she had passed to the Great Beyond: 'Here lies a wonderful cook, who has taken so much pleasure of life with her.'"[16] The desire to share recipes with African Americans rather than with her white employers is presented as Mahammitt's duty as a skilled chef, whose training included meticulous study in Paris.

Mahammitt instructed black cooks about which foods to serve at various events, and she believed it essential to know the dishes and tastes of white party hosts. She specified that "a plate of hors d'oeuvres" was "a variety of open sandwiches of caviar, sardines, anchovy, goose liver, stuffed celery, [and] deviled eggs" served during the cocktail hour preceding a proper dinner party.[17] Mahammitt's emphasis on these types of foods was as important as her advice on when they were to be served. The book focused on mostly non-southern fare in her sample wedding, bridge party, and afternoon tea catering menus. Although fried chicken is included in the list of recipes, she prioritized the creation of international dishes and distinguished between Russian and French serving standards. Williams-Forson has argued that National Association of Colored Women club members often held negative feelings about fried chicken and other foods stereotypically associated with poor blacks or southern slave culture.[18] Mahammitt's writing demonstrated a similar self-consciousness. Mahammitt and other black women seeking legitimacy in their ability to serve white customers may have felt the need to use their menu plans to shed associations with southern foods, even if they were skilled at preparing them. In writing about food, Mahammitt employed one of the key strategies of racial uplift: the separation of one's identity from trappings of working-class culture or tastes.

Mahammitt used the text's preoccupation with cultivating talent as a way of explicitly asserting the value and worth of her work and that of other black women earners. In enumerating the qualities of a successful caterer, she recognized black women's devalued labor. In her list of must-have attributes of a caterer, she included a need to be "diplomatic" and the ability to be both "alert and observant," in addition to "being a good cook."[19] In her twelve-item list of the qualifications of a "cateress," she added that she "must have a thorough knowledge of the preparation of foods," "must be familiar with all kinds of china, linen, and silver," must "be a good organizer and director," and must be "familiar with the cost of details."[20] In an era where black women's aptitude for education and suitability for careers was constantly in question and barriers existed in almost every industry and field, Mahammit celebrated her accomplishments on her own terms.

In a complete departure from the mammy cookbooks, *Recipes and Domestic Service* also addressed the power dynamics that structured the relationship between black and white women in the roles of employee and employer. Mahammitt cleverly used the example of late-season asparagus and other "foodstuffs which are out of season in your location" to illustrate why the cateress must not only possess "a knowledge of season," but also be aware of the power white women held in ensuring her good reputation.[21] Recognizing precarious interracial dynamics, Mahammitt warned: "Remember be tactful in bringing your superior knowledge into play." The warning intimated that a white woman needed to appear smarter than her black caterer in social situations, and whites' anxiety about how their entertaining style reflected on their position in polite society could work to a black woman's advantage. "You must save her from error in the eyes of her guests as well as save your reputation." In a reversal of the loyalty narratives of black domestics who needed white mistresses to give their work value, Mahammitt approached this relationship in terms of black women's ability to preserve a white woman's social standing, delivering an unspoken but essential service to her because of her knowledge of foods and her own social savvy. Although she never says that she is speaking of white employers, the racial dynamics of the day and her location in Omaha provided some certainty that she was reflecting on how white women treated black domestics. "Many such persons either do not realize or do not admit that the failure was their own, but will be only too glad to drop the blame upon the innocent shoulders of a too obliging cateress."[22] Mahammitt's discussion of the power struggle between black and white women is especially relevant in the culinary world, where white women not only profited from black women's recipes and creations, but sometimes also assumed levels of intimacy and friendship toward their domestics that were never reciprocated. Sharpless has chronicled this type of tension in her research on Idella Parker, a black maid, and her employer, writer Marjorie Rawlings.[23] From her relative position of power—as a long-standing community figure and economic success—Mahammitt took a stand for black women subjected to an array of exploitative and punitive acts.

Mahammitt's book yields insights on black women's search for the best possible labor conditions during the twentieth-century migration of black southerners to northeastern, midwestern, and western cities.[24] Similar to the black women who clamored to become agents of Sarah Malone's Poro Hairdressing Company or to join the ranks of Madame C. J. Walker's army of hair-straightening beauticians, black women cooks who became caterers and restaurateurs transformed the nature of "dirty work," laborious tasks that provided few with such economic security. Sometimes these jobs were able to propel black women from the status of worker to businesswoman. Many of the women who profited from these systems took it upon themselves to share their experiences, hoping to inspire others to do the same.[25]

Rebecca Encounters the World

Upon an initial glance at Rebecca West's 1942 *Rebecca's Cookbook*, a reader could place it in the category of the traditional, dialect-laden cookbooks that Mahammitt's book resisted. The facts that the book's dedication page announced that West wrote this for "her Lady," a long-time resident of Long Island, and relied on a collaborator to transcribe her stories may lead a reader to think that this is another loyal mammy publication. Yet, when the context of West's creation of the cookbook is taken into account, a historian of black women's work during the Second Great Migration can find a compelling account of mobility and self-fashioning. In ways similar to the double identity of *Recipes and Domestic Service*, *Rebecca's Cookbook* invites an alternative reading of her cookbook as a subversive travel narrative.

The book's opening anecdote delivered a multilayered look at a black woman's position in the urban North and white expectations for the mass of migrants who fled the South for greater economic opportunity in northern cities. West's rise to culinary heights occurred in New York City, among the throngs of domestic workers, many of whom started working in kitchens as young girls. Some hoped to escape the "white folks' kitchen" for good upon their arrival to major cities, but they found their employment possibilities limited, even if better compensated than in southern households.[26] West's story began in 1905 with her departure from a Mrs. Hitchcock's employ and her journey to Washington, D.C., to accept a new job. Perhaps revealing a defiant spirit, West decided to detour and visit New York City, where she visited a Macy's department store. Entranced by all the goods in the retailer, West purchased "a hobble skirt ... a pair of 10-cent earrings ... lots of knick-nacks to hang around [her] neck and a big hat with feathers." West, like many young black women at the turn of the century, indulged in the consumer culture of the urban landscape, and these thoroughly modern adornments signaled their transitions from the South into an entirely new world. Although she was well within her right to spend her income, West did not use this story to celebrate her newfound economic and social independence. Instead, the story served to emphasize her ignorance and lack of fitness for city life.[27]

Opponents and critics of black migration—both black and white—often recounted stories of southerners woefully unprepared for their new surroundings. Black newspapers like the famed *Chicago Defender* even published editorial cartoons and illustrated stories, like the long-running "Bungleton Green," to capture the perils of southerners bumbling through their new urban homes.[28] West represented herself among this mass of ill-prepared urbanites in the Macy's story because her desire for finery ultimately caused problems for the young

woman. West encountered her pastor on the street, and he immediately admonished her for wearing a bubble skirt. Later, a friend
warned: "Why don't you try to get yourself a job instead of spending all
your money dudin' around here?" The outfit caused its greatest harm
when West wore it to a job interview, and she recalled that she was so
emboldened by her new look that she forgot her place in the racial and
social pecking order of the day. West failed to rise from her seat when
Mrs. Biddle, the lady of the house, appeared. The white woman asked,
aghast, "And you haven't manners enough to stand up when the lady
appears? Where in the world have you worked before? But it doesn't
matter, you have no manners, and I don't want you around."[29]

The reader is led to believe that West's "uppity behavior" and
her indulgence in nice clothes meant that she was doomed. But, the
next day, Mrs. Biddle needed to prepare a dinner for a special, unexpected guest, and she was forced to turn to West to save her. Like
Mahammitt's fictional hostess who wanted strawberries in winter,
Mrs. Biddle needed to be rescued by the black cook; and, in West's
estimation, the white woman helped West remember her rightful
place as a domestic. West returned to the Biddle household dressed
in her "workin cloes" and thus initiated the critical turn in West's life.
West imparted a valuable lesson to her black women readers about
dealing with white folks "up North." By demonstrating a return to her
rightful role through her dress, she was able to enter a job that ensured
her financial success. For her white readers, West was merely foolish,
and with proper disciplining, she was able to make something out of
herself. For black readers, they may have identified with West's acqui-
escence, but they also saw her unapologetic assertion about her own
desires and identity. West's telling of the incident with the clothes does
not mean she disavowed her passion for consumer goods or fashion,
as she makes reference to her consumption habits throughout the
book. West changed her clothes but did not fundamentally change
her appreciation for things, and she returned later in the text to her
acquisition of things while traveling.

Once the reader was informed how West came to work for the
Biddles, the narrator deferred to West to incorporate her story with
her life's work: "Perhaps now you know a bit about Rebecca. From
now on, with wisdom, with humor, with kindness, and a rare dramatic

instinct, Rebecca will speak for herself."[30] When West indeed spoke for herself, the book's second identity was revealed: it is not only a cookbook, but it is also a travel narrative. West concerned herself equally between sharing recipes and incorporating her tales of accompanying "her lady" across the country and to neighboring islands. West confided that her white employers wanted her writings to focus on what white women wanted out of such a book, more on "receipts . . . that she could give to her cook," and requested that West "quit putting ideas about travelin' [in a black woman's] head." Although West promised not to do so, she weaved in mentions of locations far and wide, including "Long Island . . . Bar Harbor . . . and the Bohommas Island."[31]

West linked her travel stories to her favorite recipes, and she revealed that she sought pleasure and her own adventures while working. A passage about salads reads like a page of a travel diary. "Salads always make me think of Miami, and 'deed I don't know why" opened a story about traveling to Miami and then to the Bahamas, with little reference to lettuce or tomatoes.[32] West wrote about touring Native American reservations as if she were traveling on her own vacation. "The boat for Nassau didn't leave til four o'clock. . . . I went to have a look at Miami. I remember we went to the Indian Village. And there we saw a few funny dressed Indian makin' blankets and a few Indian children asking for pennies. And I bought myself a little basket to put my darning thread in it."[33] Throughout the travel stories, West talked about purchasing souvenirs, and she did not create much distance between her days with Biddle and her younger self; she never lost her taste for shopping. West did not only spend her earnings on indulgences. In the section on frozen dessert recipes, West announced, "I own my own house for 19 years."[34]

West's book left behind a way of seeing how a black woman constructed a set of experiences about her life as a domestic that destabilized notions of what black women's work could achieve in the period. At a time when black people, particularly young women once confined only to domestic labor, were migrating to urban cores in the South, Northeast, and Midwest, West portrayed her own movements across the country and Atlantic Ocean. In claiming her experiences of travel, even while doing so as a cook, West provided a revision to the representations of obedience that characterized the fictional tales of the trademarked Quaker Oats Company's Aunt Jemima and others, whose loyalty represented an apology and justification for the "benign" institution of slavery and later Jim Crow. Her travel stories insert a black women's perspective about encounters outside of the Deep South and urban North and supply historians with another source for pondering black physical and social mobility.

No Smiling in the Kitchen

In her memoir on turning her passion for food into a career, Chef Gillian Clark presented the sometimes chaotic and always racially tinged environments of elite restaurant kitchens, tracing her path from home cook to owning her own Washington, D.C., eatery. Clark's 2007 memoir, cleverly titled *Out of the Frying Pan: A Chef's Memoir of Hot Kitchens, Single Motherhood, and the Family Meal,* demonstrates the distance black women have traveled in their food careers since the days of Mahammitt and West. Clark told her own stories about the food industry, success, and failure, and she represented a cohort of black women who are no longer spoken for in cookbooks or who need to be deferential to white employers to maintain their positions. Despite momentous changes in black women's educational and occupational possibilities, race and gender still complicate their authority and ability to progress in a male-dominated and mostly white industry. Clark was immersed in a world with few black women chefs, and her narrative engaged in some of the same grounding strategies to communicate to readers the level of skill and training necessary to excel in the kitchen. Clark's story began with the years leading up to her decision to leave her career in marketing and to pursue the life of a chef. Before her change in occupations, Clark identified cooking as the only solace from a period of her life that she described as "living on antacids." In these opening vignettes, Clark immediately disrupted some of the most enduring "controlling images" about black women, particularly as they related to food. Clark loves the kitchen and she embraces it as a place of refuge and solace. Unlike generations of black women before her, the kitchen is not inevitable or intolerable.[35]

The way Clark managed her stress at work and in her crumbling marriage first and foremost highlighted her subjectivity. Unlike black women's food writing in the past, Clark's autobiography included family ties, friendships, moments of vulnerability and strength. Clark prepared beautifully planned meals in her own home, not within another woman's kitchen. The assortments of foods she cooked and the recipes included in the memoir are expensive, expertly crafted, and cannot be mistaken for meals made from employers' cast offs or left-overs. She and her community consumed these meals after Clark spent hours "simmering shallots in the butter while white wine steamed" and preparing "stuffed shoulder of veal with sherry and shitakes . . . [and] corn-crusted scallops with apple brandy sauce."[36]

After Clark graduated from culinary school, she worked doing exhaustive line work while attempting to stay financially afloat after a difficult divorce. She confides that she felt overwhelmed by her new role as single mother to two daughters. Clark's life was unmistakably full and multi-faceted, qualities absent from the earlier texts. In one particularly telling passage, Clark used tropes of black women's domestic service to ponder her perceived failures at balancing her family and work responsibilities. "Was I a chef to my children and mother to my kitchen staff?"[37] She questioned the position of a black matriarch again after she was fired from a restaurant in suburban Northern Virginia. She cleverly remarked: "The restaurant was never my baby. Maybe I was just the wet nurse who got a little carried away."[38] Clark's references to mothering and questioning her status as a "wet nurse" referred to the complicated ways that black women cooks and servants nurtured those outside their own biological or chosen families for economic survival and, sometimes, were unable to devote the time and energy they wanted to on their own kin.[39] Clark's insightful questions about where she mothers and whether a restaurant she groomed to success could ever be her baby immediately placed her story into a longer history of black women's racialized and gendered experiences in the slave system and working as domestic help in the decades that followed. By likening herself to a black mammy, Clark recognized the fraught historical legacy of her food work and acknowledged black women's uneasy position in the restaurant and family kitchen. Clark was on her way to becoming a well-known and highly regarded chef in Washington, but she questioned how fully she could claim her power in the home and the chef's kitchen because of the economic demands of her life, which were undoubtedly shaped by her race and gender.

Clark continued to pursue her passion for food after her dismissal, finding work at a slew of chaotic, and sometimes unsanitary, restaurants and banquet halls. Clark compared her earlier career in marketing and her life as a chef in terms of making and hiding her true self, echoing centuries of African American philosophical musings on race and identity. "Pretending I was someone else was a way of life when I was a business executive doing the song and dance for the board of directors or a potential client. But in this new career I had gotten out of the habit of faking it. I wasn't good at it anymore."[40] Again, Clark's critique of life in corporate America not only was about finding her bliss in the kitchen, but also spoke to the double consciousness of being a black woman in the workplace. Her language mirrored the way black women's histories have theorized black women's psychological strategies for survival, including the deflection of boundary crossing from employers and outsiders. Clark's explicit recognition of the toll her previous career took on her emotional life highlighted that she was able to make conscientious choices about her career and her happiness, the types of choices few black women domestics of the past could imagine. Yet the freedom to choose a new path did not fully liberate Clark from demanding work, and the memoir is constantly aware of the irony of a black woman's escape *to* the kitchen.

The final part of Clark's story began with her opening her first restaurant, Colorado Kitchen, a runaway success in Washington, D.C. Colorado Kitchen's décor self-consciously reflected the legacy of images and stereotypes of black women's cooking.

> We used images of classic food advertising. . . . The images of Aunt Jemima . . . Rastus, Mrs. Butterworth's . . . were framed and hung to help customers recall their food memories when entering the dining room. . . . Aunt Jemima's bandana became the symbol of our commitment to feeding people. . . . We bought hundreds of red bandanas to serve as napkins. . . .We hung chef hats and a single bandana as if to say, "They're here."[41]

Clark's use of black advertising caricatures in the restaurant became a source of contention for some customers. One customer asked: "Don't you know that Aunt Jemima is not a positive symbol for black people?" Clark resisted these criticisms because she believed that Colorado Kitchen was her recapitulation of the space of the kitchen, and she defended her aesthetic choices when she finally owned her own restaurant. When Clark was able to care for her "own baby," she tethered her success to black women's labor and commodification. Clark defended her choice of including Aunt Jemima within a larger assertion that some diners simply did not understand what her restaurant was trying to do—reclaiming past food icons, enhancing soul food by using the conventions of seasonal and fine dining, and creating a space that forced diners to contend with a black woman as a trained chef and not a one-dimensional source of nourishment.

Clark's agenda for Colorado Kitchen placed her squarely in conflict with some of her diners and local Washington media. In the winter of 2011, the *Washington Post* published a feature about Clark with a headline that captured the tensions that she discussed in her book: "Gillian Clark: The Chef People Love to Hate?" The article included details of an online conflict between Clark and her collaborator/partner Robin Smith and viewers of a You Tube video in which the pair was captured parodying unreasonable diners. The video, coupled with incidents in which Clark confronted demanding customers in her kitchen, brought attention to Clark's attitude instead of her dishes. Clark responded to questions about her allegedly cool demeanor and expectations by recalling the racialized images that decorated Colorado Kitchen and referenced the long history of black women's work in kitchens: "I'm led to ask, would you buy less pancakes if Aunt Jemima wasn't smiling on the box?" She continued: "Is it because a black person that's doing the service industry [and] not smiling is offensive, because you feel that I'm not that much further from a slave? If I'm doing a domestic or a service job and I'm not smiling, is it triggering some impulse?"[42] Clark's questions revealed how much her career was shaped by the racial dynamics of the past, but her ability to articulate it in her own kitchen or her own restaurant also indicated the incredible progress of black women and the importance of recognizing the many dimensions in their food stories.

At the end of her story, Clark ultimately affirmed her decision despite the racialized and gendered critiques of her style of restaurant ownership and her struggles to balance the demands of a culinary career and a family. Clark ended the book clearly, and she makes us remember the number of black women cooks who may have shared this sentiment but had no space to articulate it: "More gratifying than the hard-earned success is the realization that cooking is ultimately how I found myself."[43]

Conclusion

The subfield of black women's history has produced excellent models of how the attention to both race and gender can transform scholarship and thinking about the intersections of identities and multiple sites of resistance in a given era. From the recovery of women's slave narratives to the growing analysis of social policy and politics, the landscape of black women's history is both rich and still open for more entry points into the field. Historians of African American women must consider the interdisciplinary potential and possibilities of using black women's food writings as revelatory and important sources, as well as pedagogical tools to illustrate the concerns of black women's history. Black women's cookbooks, autobiographies, newspaper reports, magazine columns, and advertisements bridge elements of lived experiences with the social operation of race, gender, sexuality, and class. By adding cookbooks, guidebooks, and food memoirs to the existing canon of black women's archives and placing them alongside slave narratives, clubwomen's papers and publications, and political biographies, scholars can find another vehicle into deepening the conversation around black women's labor and legacies. From Sarah Mahammitt to Rebecca West to Gillian Clark, black women's meditations and guidance around food can bring their historians closer to telling a fuller and more complete story of black women in the United States.

CHAPTER 4

A Date with a Dish

Revisiting Freda De Knight's African American Cuisine

KATHARINA VESTER

There's Magic in a Cookbook

In 1948, Freda De Knight, then the food editor of *Ebony* magazine, published *A Date with a Dish: A Cook Book of American Negro Recipes*.[1] As the subtitle indicates, the text was meant not only to circulate cooking instructions but also to serve as an archive of African American culinary traditions.[2] The introduction calls it "*an authentic collection of very fine Negro recipes*" (author's emphasis).[3] Contemporaneous reviews of the book were friendly. In an article on black Chicago's literary achievements, renowned journalist Roi Ottley lists De Knight's *A Date with a Dish* in one breath with Richard Wright's *Native Son*, Gwendolyn Brooks's *Bronzeville*, and Lorraine Hansberry's *A Raisin in the Sun*.[4] In another place Ottley respectfully calls De Knight an "authority on the Negro's contribution to cooking," referring to her twenty years of research that went into the book.[5] Although *A Date with a Dish* was "likely the first nationally advertised and distributed cookbook" that devoted itself to African American cooking, as Doris Witt writes, and despite the ringing endorsements when it was published, today's academic histories of African American cooking tend to omit *A Date with a Dish* or merely recall it with a nod.[6] Rarely is it acknowledged as an early attempt to define and record African American culinary traditions. Most likely, because of De Knight's work for *Ebony*, in which she endorsed the magazine's general embrace of assimilationist politics, middle-class values, and an ethic of respectability, the text and its political potential have not received the attention they deserved, an oversight I would like to correct here.[7]

In the following I will argue that *A Date with a Dish* is a notable document of American and, specifically, African American cooking in a number of ways. The text creates a positive concept of African American cuisine that honors it as an important part of a black cultural heritage—much like soul food, a politically infused concept of a nationalist African American cuisine that became popular almost two decades later. It also claims a variety of regional foodways as well as fine American dining for this heritage, thus making a much broader and bolder assertion of African American ownership of American cooking than soul food's narrower focus on southern poor people's food. De Knight's 1948 understanding of African American cuisine occasionally references Caribbean cooking and thus also points, I suggest, in the direction of a conceptualization of African American cooking as part of a diasporic cuisine, foreshadowing ideas that appear in other cookbooks beginning in the 1970s. This chapter also shows that to dismiss *A Date with a Dish* as merely assimilationist is to overlook its divergences from other 1940s cookbooks written for a mainstream (silently implied, white) audience. In her text De Knight occasionally defied and challenged white middle-class ideology, mainly when it came to the construction of gender in relation to cooking and to entrepreneurship, as well as in her presentation of home economics, which betrays an unusually lucid sensitivity for the time to the underlying, gendered power relations inherent in nutritional instruction. *A Date with a Dish* is not an overtly political text in the same way Vertamae Smart Grosvenor's *Vibration Cooking* (1970) or *The Historical Cookbook of the American Negro* (1958) are, but its selection of recipes and its recording of the voices and experiences of black cooks, as well as De Knight's alterations to the genre of the mainstream cookbook, make the text an unusual and interesting example of 1940s culinary writing, American food history, and African American liberation.[8]

How Great Can One Be?

In 1946, De Knight, a trained home economist and former caterer, became *Ebony's* first food editor, the following year creating the monthly column "A Date with a Dish." Within the constraints of the magazine that limited the column to one page, half covered in photos, located near the end of the magazine, De Knight presented content that often promoted a pronouncedly apolitical middle-class lifestyle, concentrating on educated consumption and celebrity gossip. De Knight's column commonly featured the favorite recipes of mostly African American celebrities together with seemingly exclusive glimpses into their private lives. Readers learned that Nat King Cole championed "Tamale Pie for New Year's Eve," Lena Horne served East Indian chicken for her Valentine party, and saxophonist Andy Kirk liked baked fish.[9] Not all her columns concentrated on the entertainment industry, however. De Knight also promoted African American success stories, such as that of "insurance executive" Norman Houston or "New York's highest paid public official," Justice Francis Rivers, who, as De Knight proudly reveals, made $17,500 a year in 1948.[10] All of these stories reflected the *Ebony* line—a picture magazine conceived as a lifestyle guide for a growing African American middle class after World War II. The magazine's creators believed delivering positive coverage of African American success would be inspirational to readers. Convinced that purchasing power could be a tool for political change, *Ebony's* editors embraced, mostly uncritically, middle-class consumption.[11] Only occasionally did "A Date with a Dish" feature regular people, such as in "Budget Meals for Vet Wives" in September 1947.

The column was similarly middle-class driven when it came to the representation of gender. A 1947 *Ebony* photo editorial, "Goodbye Mammy, Hello Mom," outlined the magazine's gender politics, which were also reflected in De Knight's columns: "World War II caused a kitchen revolution. It took Negro mothers out of white kitchens, put them in factories and shipyards. When it was all over, they went back to kitchens—but this time their own."[12] As in white culture, the fact that the wife and mother did not have to work was a sign of middle-class prosperity that allowed one potential adult wage earner to stay at home to devote herself to unpaid labor. At the same time this defined unpaid cooking and kitchen labor as part of hegemonic feminine performance. In De Knight's cooking column women, even celebrities, were depicted in the kitchen, apron-clad and cooking, serving as models for middle-class femininity and social upward mobility. The men featured in the column were typically shown eating and drinking but rarely preparing food.[13]

De Knight's columns also endorsed national myth-making, but occasionally with a twist. In her first Thanksgiving advice on the preparation of turkey ("the main attraction since Plymouth days" "as long as Americans gather to count the national blessings"), she bought into a heritage that has traditionally excluded many from sharing the national blessings.[14] But for her second Thanksgiving column as food editor, De Knight suggested serving gumbo, thus gently infusing the nationalist feast with an acknowledgment of ethnic and regional differences.[15]

Unlike her column, the cookbook De Knight published in 1948—also called *A Date with a Dish*—featured only a few celebrities and instead gave space to recording different traditions of African American cooking. The dishes and cooks the reader was invited to "date" came from around the country. They were lay and professional cooks, each of whom was said to have earned a reputation for culinary creativity. The recipes in the first chapter, "Collector's Corner," focused explicitly on African American cooking. The recipes were accompanied by short biographical sketches of their cooks, occasionally in their own voices, painting in broad strokes a panorama of African American experiences in the middle of the twentieth century: "My father died when I was two and, because my mother was a traveling nurse, I was sent to live with the Paul Scotts in Mitchell, South Dakota"; "Her climb to cooking fame has not been easy . . . [and] she spent several years as a teacher. . . . Today, Lucille Smith has her own cooking program on the radio"; "No, college was not for me because the money could not be spared, but my zeal and curiosity afforded me much pleasure in the preparation of many dishes that satisfied even the most finicky appetites"; "As a girl, Ruth Jackson started her career as a 'top notcher' in the Cooks and Baker Class. Later she married a minister and became one of the pillars of her community when it came to good food"; "Being progressive, Ranny Waters has brought all the modern touches possible into the [catering] business, but still carries out all the traditions and standards set by his Dad"; "In Boston, the Casa Mañana featured Chef Madison in their newspaper ads"; "At the age of twelve she started working in the school lunchroom, and during the summer months as a stock girl for a chain of restaurants"; "It is no simple matter trying to raise a family of ten."[16]

As a rule these stories were optimistic in tone, showing their protagonists overcoming adversity and achieving success, loosely in line with the *Ebony* commitment to positive examples. But the success stories De Knight presented in her cookbook were different from the stories of African American politicians, judges, businesspeople, and entertainers she featured in *Ebony*. She praised the accomplishments of farmers who maintained beautiful homes, young girls who kept orderly households while their mothers worked, and mothers who were able to raise ten children, thus expanding the traditional definitions of success in US society promoted in more traditional American Dream stories. Changing the metrics of what constituted achievements worthy of being printed allowed De Knight to recognize the labor of women and working-class people even if it had not made them rich or famous. It also established cooking as an accomplishment that kept families and communities together, recognizing family cooking not only as essential labor but as cultural work, too.

By collecting these stories, De Knight foreshadowed later authors who would use the cookbook as an ethnographic record, for instance, Norma Jean and Carole Darden, who in 1978 published *Spoonbread and Strawberry Wine,* a family history told in recipes.[17] But beyond recording the diversity of African American voices, De Knight's catalog of African American cooks had the additional effect of undermining stereotypes that often accumulated around the "mammy," an iconic figure within a revisionist telling of southern history in which enslaved women could grow fat and happy while devoting themselves to the well-being of white families. Naturally, the mammy was often imagined as a cook, thus perpetually frozen in the act of nurturing. A cook without training, who, so the idea went, had an instinctual talent for cooking good food that she prepared for white families as much out of love as economic necessity. This image has been so powerful that, as Rafia Zafar writes, "for a twentieth-century African American female publicly to announce herself as a cook means that she must engage with the reigning ghost of American racism."[18] De Knight presents a parade of African American cooks who in their diversity counter-act the stereotypical image of the mammy: old and young men and women, often professionals such as restaurant chefs, railway cooks, and caterers, as well as housewives, farmers, and a couple of paid domestic cooks. These images reflect a vivid diversity within the culinary ranks, defying any simplification by describing individuals with lives, tastes, and specific experiences. They project professionalism, thus working against the stereotypical depiction of the uneducated but intuitive African American cook. In this way De Knight also asserts the value of black culinary expertise, often intentionally omitted in other American cookbooks, reminding her readers that black professional cooks have shaped American cuisine since its beginning. Showcasing black culi-nary expertise, De Knight presented African American authority over American cooking in a modern and more self-determined way (but, as I will show below, she was not always successful in avoiding essentialism).

The Older the Recipe, the Better the Dish

In *A Date with a Dish*, De Knight claims chitterlings, pig's tails, pig's feet, "Sweet 'Taters," collard greens, "Hopping John," and "'Possum and Sweet Potatoes" as part of traditional African American fare, all dishes that by the mid-1960s would be canonized as African American cui-sine through the emergence of soul food.[19] But in 1948, recipes for chitterlings or pig's tails in print were rare (even during the war years that saw a revival of the consumption of less popular animal parts).[20] In *A Date with a Dish*, however, they were but one facet of a culinary kaleidoscope—unlike in soul food cookbooks.

When the concept of soul food emerged in the 1960s it accom-panied the Black Power movement and a shift in activism from the cultural and political hegemony of the North (especially the histor-ical centers of Chicago and Harlem) to the heart of the civil rights movement in the South, from high art such as poetry to the vernac-ular, from a politics of respectability to black pride. All of this was reflected in the making of soul food and the conceptualization of a single African American cuisine. Soul food is, strictly speaking, an invented tradition, as it presents a strategically simplified narrative of African American cooking that served the goal of unifying diverse and numerous communities into a political (and cultural) whole, evoking a sense of pride and achievement in its members.[21]

The narrative of soul food emphasized historical agency, as it told African American history as a story of resilience, determination, and creativity. The authors of soul food, such as Amiri Baraka, Bob Jeffries, and Jessica Harris, traced ingredients and methods prevalent in soul food cooking back to African traditions. They also stated that the dishes recorded the experience of hardship under slavery. Pig's feet, tails, and intestines were what were left to the slaves after a hog was butchered on a plantation, and thus they became central to soul food narratives.[22] These and other dishes using salvaged ingredients such as greens or opossum were said to be a testimony to the ingenuity of enslaved cooks who supplemented their meager rations in creative ways. The lowliest ingredients became comfort foods in the hands of the cooks, who skillfully transposed them from meals created out of sheer necessity to morsels of hope and resistance. Thus soul food served as a successful strategy in acknowledging the little agency slaves had, celebrating not only people's survival under hostile circumstances, but their dignity and grace. Soul food, cookbook writers claimed, made it possible to incorporate a sense of tradition and belonging into contemporary African American families, honoring the heritage in the act of eating, passing down history to the next generation. In all these regards soul food was an important step in mainstreaming the Black Power movement, translating some of its core ideas into a non-threatening quotidian cultural practice.[23] Simultaneously, soul food was from its conception criticized for a number of issues: Eldridge Cleaver called it bourgeois radical chic, romanticizing poverty. Dick Gregory alleged that it was unhealthful and endangered the people eating it. Edna Lewis found it a nostalgic and simplified northern construct of African American history that did not do justice to the rich traditions of southern cooking. Others criticized soul food explicitly for privileging a single narrative of African American cuisine and therewith experience over other experiences and black cuisines.[24]

Before soul food became the hegemonic narrative of African American cooking in the 1960s, African American cookbook authors had published cookbooks that reflected varied regional culinary practices and different registers of culinary skill that went beyond the scope of soul food. *A Domestic Cookbook: Containing a Careful Selection of Useful Receipts for the Kitchen* from 1866 is now thought to be the first cookbook published by an African American woman. The author, Malinda Russell, a former pastry shop owner who lived in Michigan when she wrote her book, tells her readers that she was originally trained in a Virginia kitchen.[25] But her recipes are not classic southern dishes. Instead they are hybrids of several regional practices with ingredients that were available in Michigan when she set them down in print, thereby recording Russell's life story and the cooking practices of the regions she knew. As she moved, Russell adapted her recipes and methods to new ingredients and tastes, thus actively shaping Midwestern cuisine, rather than preserving the cooking practices she was raised with and trained in.[26] *Useful Receipts for the Kitchen* is an example of how African American cooks have historically participated in creating diverse regional culinary practices. The *Kentucky Cook Book* from 1912, whose author is identified only as "a colored woman" and a cook "of many years' experience," does not present southern dishes alone, nor even Kentuckian dishes as the title suggests.[27] The cookbook offers recipes for "Indian Bread," "Hominy Muffins," "Boston Brown Bread," "English Plum Pudding," "Maple Mousse," "Charlotte Russe," "Spaghetti Italian," "French Mushroom Sauce," "Fricassee of Squirrel," and "Lobster Salad," to name only a few, thus representing the great versatility, regionally, but also in terms of the register that an African American domestic cook in the early twentieth century was able to master.[28]

These and other texts by African American authors may not have reflected what black cooks cooked at home or what African American families ate in general.[29] But they certainly reflected the impact African American cooks had on the formation of American cooking all over the country and particularly on American fine dining. In *High on the Hog*, Jessica Harris showed how after the Haitian Revolution at the beginning of the nineteenth century, French West Indian immigrants who started catering firms in Philadelphia introduced French cuisine and educated the American middle class that could not afford French cooks. "Tastemakers," Harris calls restaurateurs such as the Augustin family that ran one of the first haute cuisine restaurants in the United States.[30] The Haitian immigrants also brought patisserie and the knowledge of how to use sugar in many elegant dishes with them to the United States, thus making American cuisine one of the sweetest in the world. Black culinary entrepreneurs served as trendsetters in other parts of the country, too. Philadelphia caterer Thomas Downing, for instance, caused an oyster craze in New York City in the 1820s.[31] But African American cooks not only had an impact on how the wealthy ate, since in some parts of the country they also dominated street vending and food markets as well.[32] The few known African American–authored pre–soul food cookbooks are records of this sweeping culinary impact. And De Knight's *A Date with a Dish* is no exception. The text recognized southern cooking as a central part, but only a part, of a far more complex and wide-ranging African American culinary heritage.

Versatile in Any Dish

De Knight, who was born in Kansas, lived for a part of her childhood in South Dakota, went to high school in Minnesota, and then started a catering career in New York City, presented an encompassing concept of African American cuisine. "It is a fallacy, long disproved," De Knight writes in her preface, "that Negro cooks, chefs, caterers, and housewives can adapt themselves only to the standard Southern dishes, such as fried chicken, greens, corn pone, hot breads and so forth. Like other Americans living in various sections of the country they have naturally shown a desire to branch out in all directions and become versatile in any dish."[33] A 1948 advertisement for *A Date with a Dish* promised "greatly loved Negro dishes from all 48 states."[34] Supporting her claim, De Knight included recipes from many different places in the United States (and a few from other countries), comprising regional signature dishes such as Boston baked beans, for which she gives three different recipes, thus paying tribute to black cooks in New England:

> As long as there has been a Cambridge, Mass., there has been a member of the Wright family who knows the traditional and exciting New England dishes. So it is no wonder Nadine Wright Goodman could look back through old papers and discover old recipes. She gladly consented to give us her own version of the

traditional Boston baked beans, brown bread, and fish cakes that were cooked in the traditional ashes and brick ovens.[35]

Boston baked beans belong to the African American cook as much as to the white cook by right of many generations of practice that go back to the colonial era. Nadine Wright Goodman, looking back on her family's history, can assert ownership not only of Boston baked beans but also of the "tradition" that produced them (and which De Knight invokes three times in the one paragraph above). In such a fashion De Knight re-inscribes African American cooks into the American culinary tradition from which they had been historically omitted.[36]

A Date with a Dish also included international dishes, or as an article about the cookbook in *Ebony* put it: "Negro recipes influenced by the finest in English, Italian and East Indian eating."[37] *A Date with a Dish* participated here in a new national self-confidence fueled by victory in World War II that expressed itself in a rekindled curiosity for other cultures and a fresh feeling of entitlement to other countries' culinary resources.[38] The sacrifices endured during the war, together with new wealth and status many felt as their country became a major player in world politics, encouraged middle-class cooks to try their hand at recipes that had still been considered elite or gourmet just before the war. De Knight's inclusion of Italian, Spanish, and Indian dishes made the case that the African American cook has as much right to these culinary resources (and the cultural capital that accrues to those who can master them) as any other American cook. But unlike other cookbooks of that time that concentrated mainly on European, and occasionally on Chinese and Indian cuisine, *A Date with a Dish* also included Caribbean and Latin American foods. Hattie McDaniel, for instance, is credited in the text with a taste for Mexican cuisine, thus expanding American middle-class curiosity to new frontiers while asserting African American middle-class participation in US global engagement.[39]

Not only did De Knight help create an interest in other people's cuisines, *A Date with a Dish* also carries evidence that De Knight thought of black cuisine beyond nationalist terms. Among the cooks De Knight names in her text, some were born outside the United States. For example, Fred Knight, who was raised in Bermuda, brought with him the culinary skill and knowledge he acquired in his youth when he immigrated to the United States. Memorialized in the "Collector's Corner" is also the life story of Marianne Abramson Perez, a cook born in the West Indies, trained in England, and eventually employed in the United States. She is presented as an example for how her many culinary influences come together in ingenious ways in her own cooking. Through her voice, De Knight claims "Carne Mechada," "Spanish Omelet," and "Rellenos" for her collection of "Negro recipes."[40] De Knight, who had married into a Puerto Rican family and often remarked that she was influenced by the cooking of her mother-in-law, was an active promoter and teacher of Caribbean cuisine during her lifetime.[41] She was also one of the first cookbook authors to mention similarities of African American cooking traditions in the Western Hemisphere. In *A Date with a Dish*, she records that she encountered in Cuba the dishes of "a Negro chef" that resembled those she considered "typically Southern."[42] Here, as in the examples above, De Knight's writing is an early instance of placing African American cooking within a diasporic frame.[43]

Don't Be Afraid to Season Foods

A Date with a Dish is a text that is wary of essentialism and suspicious of the idea of "authenticity" but ultimately is not able to leave either behind. "Authenticity" in De Knight's text is above all a struggle over ownership. As the text presents a challenge to traditionally assumed white ownership of American cuisine, it is no surprise that De Knight contests the validity of authenticity in general. About New Orleans cuisine she writes:

> No two people seem to have the same recipes for the same dish, yet each is sworn into the category of authenticity. . . . Their way is as authentic to them as your way to you. When it comes to food and recipes, it becomes almost impossible to place a criterion on authenticity because of various likes and dislikes . . . each person feels his way is correct.[44]

De Knight emphasizes her rather postmodern understanding of authenticity by repeatedly giving various recipes for the same dish, complicating ideas such as original or authentic. But while she seems to argue through most of her book that dishes prepared by African

American cooks belong to them as much as any other cook who pre-pares them, she still feels prompted to engage in the question of what may define a specifically African American cuisine. In her preface she tries to circumnavigate the entrapments of a biological argument or falling back into the stereotypical depiction of African American cooks, but eventually seems unable to escape them:

> There are no set rules for dishes created by most Negroes. They just seem to have a "way" of taking a plain, ordinary, everyday dish and improvising it into a creation that is a gour-met's delight. Whether acquired or inherent, this love for food has given them the desire to make their dishes different, well-seasoned, and eye-appealing.[45]

Here she is repeating a depiction of black cooks' success not being a result of training and hard work but of intuition and improvisation (an argument that is also, mostly uncritically, repeated in some soul food narratives). In another place she declares: "Negroes and Latin races are famous for spicy foods. . . . Many Negroes have never had the pleasure of reading spice hints, but they most certainly have the knack for adding the right spice at the right time to the right food."[46] Here, too, a racialized culinary difference is asserted, avoiding any expla-nations that are overtly stereotypical or biologist, but still trapped in them. Undercutting her own statement, her recipes do not use more varied, greater quantities, or different spices then those presented in the 1943 edition of the culinary bible of twentieth-century American mainstream cooking, *The Joy of Cooking*.[47]

While De Knight may not succeed in avoiding essentialism when it comes to race, she certainly tries. This is not true when it comes to gen-der, where she engages mostly uncritically in generalizations: "It is the delight of every little girl some time during her first twelve years to play house and cook," she states with great authority on the first page of her book.[48] This kind of gender conservatism was not unusual for a 1940s cookbook, a decade in which gender norms were challenged through the necessities of war, but the rhetoric of the day often bluntly denied the lived realities and enforced conventional gender roles. Postwar cookbooks, especially, engaged in representations of a nostalgic domes-ticity that attempted to lure middle-class women from war jobs back into their kitchens. But in comparison to texts such as *How Mama Could Cook!* (1946)—an enthusiastic endorsement of late Victorian femininities, mildly spiced up with some docile suffragism—*A Date with a Dish* presents women who work and have careers, not only for the duration and not only before they were married.[49] Although De Knight calls women who "stay at home" "fortunate," she addresses the "business-wives," too.[50] Her panorama of African American female culinary voices depicts women who are self-employed or work as cooks, caterers, nurses, farmers, and teachers and who draw great pleasure and self-confidence from their successes. At the same time the text presents men who cook, although mostly professionally. In the "Collector's Corner" men and women cooks are represented equally in their professional success and their ability to cook.

A Date with a Dish refreshingly diverges from other cookbooks of its time by keeping nutritional and organizational advice to a minimum. De Knight was, like many cookbook authors of her generation, a trained home economist. But unlike many of her colleagues, she does not feature nutritional tables and scientific information, instead suggesting that her readers, when it comes to healthy nutrition, should rely on their "common sense" and above all enjoy their meals.[51] In other popular cookbooks of that era, such as Adelle Davis's *Let's Cook It Right,* entire chapters were devoted to topics such as "Good Health Comes from Good Cooking," "Keep the Flavor and Nutritive Value in Your Vegetables," and "Make Your Desserts Contribute to Health."[52] Advising women to pay attention to their own enjoyment and to trust their own common sense is different from advice in many cookbooks of the time that cast family cooks as the gatekeepers of national health, family meals as matters of national security, and hosting parties as a way to live the American Dream. *A Date with a Dish* is not a text that is free from middle-class bias or an imperial appetite for other cultures' resources, but by sharing authorship, telling life stories, and suggesting readers should rely on their own wits, it is on the more democratic end of the ideological spectrum for cookbooks. In this way De Knight not only uses the cookbook as a vehicle for her own political agenda, she uses the authority bestowed upon her as a nutritional and culinary expert to strengthen her readers' self-confidence rather than to intimidate them.

Foods Have Feelings

In contrast to her column in *Ebony*, De Knight used the editorial free-dom the cookbook offered her to create a space to define an African American heritage and to honor the culinary achievements of black cooks in print. The African American culinary heritage De Knight outlined was based on the recipes of African American cooks all over the United States who fed their families, who worked in domestic ser-vice, in restaurants, in boardinghouses, on trains, and on street cor-ners, and who imagined, re-interpreted, adapted, refined, executed, decorated, served, and ate these dishes. *A Date with a Dish* recalibrated the American culinary landscape by re-inscribing African American authorship. Some of the recipes she claimed as African American refer to black traditions beyond US borders, thus bursting national con-straints in defining a black heritage. She struggled but failed when it came to defining race in non-essentialist terms, but in the process she showed that older racial narratives had started cracking. Finally, De Knight challenged some of the rules of mainstream cookbook writing in the 1940s. Not only by re-inscribing the black cook into American culinary history, but also by reformulating the expected standards of cookbook writing, foregoing rhetorical figures of authority typical for the genre, and educating her readers by empowering them, she made careful use of the authority the cookbook endowed her with.

In 1962, *A Date with a Dish* was republished as *The Ebony Cookbook: A Date with a Dish*—a year before De Knight died of can-cer. As the *Ebony Cookbook*, the text now acquired some of the *Ebony* ideology, including the elimination of the "Collector's Corner" that had recorded the voices of average African American cooks, thereby erod-ing the attempt to define a distinct African American cuisine in all its sparkling facets. But the effort to make the book more palatable for a mainstream market only highlighted what an unusually foresighted document De Knight's original contribution had been. Anticipating many of the strategies future authors of African American cuisine were about to engage in, De Knight's *A Date with a Dish* challenged the way in which American culinary history traditionally had been told.

CHAPTER 5

What's the Difference between Soul Food and Southern Cooking?

The Classification of Cookbooks in American Libraries

GRETCHEN L. HOFFMAN

Introduction

Finding library materials about African American cooking and food-ways seems like a simple process. A library user types a few search terms in an online catalog and receives a perfect list of titles in the collection. In reality, searching a library catalog for specific subjects is imperfect and messy. Library users and authors use language differently, and these differences can make searching library catalogs a difficult and frustrating process. Library catalogers help library users find library materials by assigning subject headings and classification numbers that describe what the materials are about. Their work is guided by many complex standards for subject access developed by the Library of Congress, especially those found in the *Library of Congress Subject Headings* (LCSH) and the *Library of Congress Classification* (LCC). These standards "control" language through the use of approved words and phrases that best represent knowledge. Like a back-of-the book index directs readers to the knowledge in a book, library standards direct library users to the knowledge contained in libraries. Language, however, is difficult to control, and subject headings and classification numbers do not represent knowledge perfectly. These standards have the power to provide access to library materials, but they also have the power to limit access.[1] Subjects in each standard are constructed by librarians who determine which words are authorized and unauthorized, which subjects to include, and which subjects to exclude. Although standards strive to help library users, some knowledge, concepts, and groups may be favored, and library users may not see themselves or their interests reflected in library catalogs.

How library standards have constructed African American cooking and foodways affect access to materials about these subjects. The purpose of this essay is to discuss how the *Library of Congress Subject Headings* and the *Library of Congress Classification* construct African American cooking and foodways and to show how this construction affects access in libraries. To provide a context for this discussion, each library standard will be described. Then, cooking subject headings and cooking classification numbers will be examined. Finally, the treatment of foodways in each library standard will be explored.

Subject Access in Libraries

Libraries provide access to subjects to help library users find library materials. Every library in the United States uses at least one standard list of subject headings and one classification scheme to provide subject access to its collection. Two standards used in most American academic libraries are the *Library of Congress Subject Headings* and the *Library of Congress Classification*.

The *Library of Congress Subject Headings* is a list of approved words and phrases used to describe broadly what library materials are about.[2] LCSH was developed in the early 1900s, and the first edition was published between 1910 and 1914.[3] It was developed originally to provide access to the Library of Congress's collection, but today it is used in most academic libraries in the United States. Subject headings are constructed with one "authorized" form of a subject, concept, group, and such (e.g., "Food"), and this heading is used consistently in the library catalog. If needed, topical, chronological, and form subdivisions are added to bring out aspects of the subject (e.g., "Food—United States—History—19th century"). Only one authorized form of a subject heading is allowed, so cross-references are used to control language. They bring together variations of a subject's name and show relationships. Cross-references direct library users to authorized headings (e.g., instead of "Collard greens," use "Collards"), show how subject headings are related hierarchically (e.g., for "Pork," see also the broader term "Meat" and the narrower term "Bacon"), and show how subject headings are related non-hierarchically (e.g., for "Cauliflower," see also "Broccoli"). LCSH uses technical terms over popular terms (e.g., "Cowpea" instead of "Black-eyed pea"), and it is meant for use in general research collections. LCSH is not a universal representation of knowledge. Subject headings are created based on "literary warrant," which means a subject heading is not created until something, usually a book, has been published about a subject. Subject headings tend to reflect knowledge in books, because libraries do not index serial publications.[4]

The *Library of Congress Classification* (LCC) is another standard for subject access in libraries.[5] It is a classification scheme that uses alphanumeric notations to represent subjects. It brings together works on the same subject and organizes libraries by subject. Like LCSH, it was developed in the early 1900s to provide access to the Library of Congress's collection, but today it is used in most academic libraries in the United States. The first editions were published irregularly between 1901 and 1948.[6] The scheme is divided into twenty-one main subject classes based on letters of the alphabet (e.g., H for social sciences, Q for science, T for technology), and each main class is maintained and published separately. Subjects in LCC are arranged hierarchically into general and specific categories. Each main class is divided into several subclasses that are subdivided into specific subjects. An example of the hierarchical structure of LCC is shown in figure 5.1, which shows the classification of "Cowpeas."

FIG. 5.1.
Classification of "cowpeas" in the *Library of Congress Classification*

T: Technology
    TX1-1110: Home Economics

TX642-TX840: Cooking
TX801-TX807: Vegetables (Preparation)
TX803.A-Z: Special Vegetables, A-Z
TX803.C68: Cowpeas

LCC works closely with LCSH, and a classification number is assigned to most subject headings. Like LCSH, LCC is based on literary warrant. A classification number is not established until a book has been published on a subject, and a subject heading is established before a classification number is created.[7]

LCSH and LCC are not objective systems of knowledge. They are socially constructed, artificial, representations of knowledge. Librarians at the Library of Congress decide what knowledge warrants inclusion in each standard, what should be excluded, what to name subjects, and so on. These standards are supposed to represent subjects, but the decisions made at the Library of Congress construct subjects as well, and there are cultural and racial assumptions inherent in the standards.[8] LCSH and LCC are constructed to meet the needs of the majority of library users, so all viewpoints are not reflected equally. Subjects, concepts, and people not in the majority are treated as exceptions. For example, subject headings exist for "Nurses" and "Male nurses" but not "Women nurses." The assumptions are that nurses are women, and male nurses are the exception to the norm. Another example is the subject heading "Executives." Although it is a broad term that should encompass all groups, there are separate subject headings for "African American executives," "Women executives," "Gay executives," and such. This assumes that white, heterosexual men are executives, and everyone else is an exception to the norm. There are assumptions inherent in the subject of food as well. Food has been socially constructed, and these constructions may or may not reflect the subject accurately and may affect access to materials on food.

Focusing on the majority means that these standards may exclude and marginalize subjects, concepts, and people that do not fit into them.[9] Because of this focus, LCSH and LCC have been criticized heavily for reflecting inaccurate and culturally insensitive views of concepts and people, for being biased toward American, white, male, and Christian views, and for being slow to change.[10] An example of this is the subject heading "God." Until 2006, "God" meant the Christian God. All other religions were qualified, such as God (Judaism). This subject heading was identified as problematic in 1971 because it privileged Christianity and made other religions exceptions to it.[11] Yet, it took the Library of Congress thirty-five years to change the subject heading to "God (Christianity)." This change is significant, not only because it no longer privileges Christianity, but also because the Library of Congress rarely makes large structural changes in the standards. It is difficult to keep pace with knowledge and changes are expensive for libraries, so the structure of knowledge in each subject area can be rigid and locked into place. Subject headings and classification numbers may not reflect current knowledge, and this can affect access to library materials.

How library catalogers apply LCSH and LCC in practice affects access as well. Catalogers do not index library materials exhaustively. The Library of Congress directs catalogers to add several approved subject headings from LCSH and one classification number from LCC to describe broadly what a work is about, and the classification number represents the *first* subject heading assigned to a work.[12] Although the standards can be rigid, subject analysis is a subjective process. No two catalogers will assign the same subject headings and classification numbers. It depends on the cataloger's background, subject knowledge, interpretation of a work, and knowledge of the standards. Determining what a work is about is not easy. Works do not always fall neatly into one subject heading or classification number. For multifaceted works, catalogers are instructed to classify the most "dominant subject" or whatever subject is listed first, so catalogers must make judgment calls about the most important aspects of works.[13] Catalogers often have to force works into subject headings and classification numbers that do not represent them well.

Cooking Subject Headings

How library standards have constructed African American cooking affects access to library materials about this subject. The *Library of Congress Subject Headings* contains many cooking subject headings that are assigned to cookbooks and works about cooking. The cooking subject headings were developed in the early 1900s and included in the first edition of LCSH, published over several years, between 1910 and 1914. The structure of the subject was developed at that time. Cooking is divided into subject headings for national and ethnic cuisines (e.g., "Cooking, Spanish," "Cooking, Basque"), ingredients (e.g., "Cooking (Okra)"), recipes for special diets (e.g., "Low-fat diet—Recipes"), and special aspects of cooking (e.g., "Gumbo (Soup)," "Baking"). These types of headings are used still today. Although the Library of Congress changed the name of the subject from "Cookery" to "Cooking" in 2010, the structure of the subject has not changed in over a century.[14] The Library of Congress just creates a new subject heading when a cookbook is published about a new national/ethnic cuisine, ingredient, type of diet, or such. This structure may not reflect the dynamic nature of cooking today because it forces cookbooks to fit into these categories. This is especially problematic for subject headings about national and ethnic cuisines, because cookbooks do not always fit neatly into one national or ethnic category. A cookbook may include recipes from many different nationalities, ethnicities, and styles of cooking, and the cookbook cannot be reduced to one or two subject headings.

American cooking falls into the national/ethnic cuisine category. American cooking is a mix of various national, ethnic, and regional cuisines, but the subject headings are limited to place. "Cooking, American" is the main subject heading and there is a subject heading for each regional style of American cooking (e.g., "Cooking, American—Southern style"). Cookbooks about states are assigned a subject heading for the state (e.g., "Cooking—Georgia"). The focus on place limits access to American cookbooks. Cookbooks not about a particular place are assigned only the broad subject heading "Cooking, American," which does not explain specifically what a cookbook is about. Cookbooks about national ethnic groups in the United States are focused on place as well, but they are not included in American cooking. They are assigned the subject heading for the national cuisine. A Chinese American cookbook, for example, will be assigned the subject heading "Cooking, Chinese," even if the cookbook contains recipes developed in the United States. This practice excludes national/ethnic cuisines from American cooking, minimizes the influ-ence of other cultures on American cooking, and does not reflect the rich cultural heritage of American cooking.

Southern cooking is considered a regional style of American cooking, but the southern cooking subject headings have developed haphazardly. There has been no attempt to create subject headings that reflect the subjects. "Cookery, Creole" is the oldest subject head-ing related to southern cooking; it was published in the first edition of LCSH. The main subject heading, "Cooking, American—Southern style," however, was not established until 1986. The Library of Congress just creates subject headings as needed. The lack of planning and structure means the subject headings do not reflect everything related to southern cooking. Cooking in Louisiana is favored; there are many subject headings, such as "Cooking, American—Louisiana style," "Cooking, Creole—Louisiana style," "Cooking, Cajun," "Cooking—Louisiana," "Cooking—Louisiana—New Orleans." Yet, there is no subject heading for Floribbean cooking, a style of cooking influenced by native foods in Florida and the Caribbean Islands, although cook-books have been published on the cuisine.[15] LCSH provides uneven access to southern cooking and favors cooking in Louisiana over other forms of southern cooking.

The focus on place in American cooking affects access to works about African American cooking, too. The authorized subject heading "African American cooking" is used to describe African American and soul food cookbooks, and it has changed names many times. The first form of the subject heading was "Cookery, Negro," established between 1948 and 1957. In 1975, the subject heading changed to "Cookery, Afro-American" when the Library of Congress changed the "Negro" subject headings to "Afro-American." The heading flipped to "Afro-American cookery" in 1991 and changed again to "African American cookery" in 2000 when the Library of Congress changed all "Afro-American" subject headings to "African American." In 2010, the subject heading was changed to "African American cooking." There are two issues with the subject heading that affect access.

One issue is that "African American cooking" is treated differ-ently in LCSH because the subject heading cannot be reduced to a place in the United States. In addition, subject headings for national and ethnic cuisines begin with the word "Cooking" (e.g., "Cooking, Italian"), but naming the subject "African American cooking" instead of "Cooking, African American" means that the subject heading files under "A" instead of "C." This excludes the subject heading from other cooking subject headings and treats African American cooking as an exception to other types of cooking.[16] Also, as shown in figure 5.2, there is no cross-reference for "Cooking, African American" to direct library users to the authorized form of the subject heading. Library users may have a difficult time finding African American cookbooks.

FIG. 5.2.
African American cooking subject headings in the
Library of Congress Subject Headings

AFRICAN AMERICAN COOKING

Used for: African American cookery
Used for: Afro-American cookery
Used for: Cookery, Afro-American
Used for: Cookery, Negro
Used for: Soul food cooking
Broader term: Cooking, American

Another issue is the cross-reference "Soul food cooking," which was added in 1980. Soul food refers to African American cuisine that originated in the southern United States, and it has a rich and diverse heritage.[17] Frederick Douglass Opie explains, "Soul food is African American, but it was influenced by other cultures. It is the intellectual invention and property of African Americans. Soul food is a fabulous-tasting dish made from simple, inexpensive ingredients. Soul food is enjoyed by black folk, whom it reminds of their southern roots."[18] Soul food (and African American food in general) is tied strongly to US history and culture, especially in the South. Jessica B. Harris states, "[African Americans] have created a culinary tradition that has marked the food of this country more than any other. Our culinary history is fraught with all the associations with slavery, race, and class that the United States has to offer."[19] Yet, despite the influence of soul food on American and southern cooking, the Library of Congress added "Soul food cooking" as a cross-reference to "African American cooking" instead of establishing it as a separate subject heading. Therefore, a soul food cookbook must be assigned the subject heading "African American cooking." This makes "Soul food cooking" and "African American cooking" equivalent headings, even though they do not mean exactly the same thing. Although soul food is African American cooking, not all cooking performed by African Americans is necessarily considered soul food.

In addition, because "Soul food cooking" is just a cross-reference, there is no way to show it is related to southern cooking. This excludes "Soul food cooking" from southern cooking, even though soul food is related closely to southern cooking. This assumes, too, that white people cook "southern" food, while black people cook "soul food," not "southern" food. This assumption is not accurate and does not reflect the influence of soul food on southern cooking. In a practical sense, it also puts the responsibility on a library user to perform multiple searches and on a library cataloger to know enough about soul food to assign "Cooking, American—Southern style" to a soul food cookbook. This would not happen unless a cookbook stated explicitly it contained "southern" recipes.[20]

Cooking Classification Numbers

Classification numbers are supposed to match subject headings, but unlike LCSH, the classification of cookbooks in the *Library of Congress Classification* is quite limited. General cooking is in the "Home Economics" subclass (TX) of the main "Technology" class. Cooking for specific diets or diseases is in the "Therapeutics and Pharmacology" subclass (RM) of the main "Medicine" class. LCC follows the structure of LCSH. The general cooking classification is divided into national/ethnic cuisines, ingredients, and special aspects of cooking. Like LCSH, this structure was developed in the early 1900s and has not changed much since that time. Today, only 199 numbers are used to classify the world's cookbooks. This small range of numbers may have been adequate in the early 1900s, but there are not enough numbers to classify cooking today. Many subjects are classified at the same number, which makes browsing library collections difficult, and the classification does not reflect all national and ethnic cuisines. Just twelve whole numbers represent the cuisines of the world, and there is a distinct Western bias in the classification. Nations in North America and most of Western Europe, for example, are assigned separate classification numbers, but the Middle East, Australia, and Africa are classified together at one number.

The American cooking classification is limited as well. It has two classification numbers, shown in figure 5.3. The general American cooking number is TX715, and American regional styles of cooking are classed at TX715.2, with a number added for a particular region. For example, "Southern style" cooking is classed at TX715.2.S68 and "Louisiana style" cooking is classed at TX715.2.L68. Canada and Greenland are included in American cooking by necessity because there are not enough numbers in the cooking classification.

FIG. 5.3.
American cooking classification in the
Library of Congress Classification

LCC—AMERICAN COOKING CLASSIFICATION

TX715: General Works

    TX715.2A-Z: By Style of cooking, A-Z

    TX715.2.C34: California style

    TX715.2.L68: Louisiana style

    TX715.2.M53: Midwestern style

    TX715.2.N48: New England style

    TX715.2.P32: Pacific Northwest style

    TX715.2.S68: Southern style

    TX715.2.S69: Southwestern style

    TX715.2.W47: Western style

TX715.6: Canadian

TX715.8: Greenlandic

Because the classification's structure favors regional styles of American cooking, it cannot accommodate cookbooks that do not fit neatly within a particular region of the United States. If a cookbook cannot be reduced to a region, then it will be classed at the general TX715 number, and thousands of cookbooks are classified at this number.[21] The classification also excludes national and ethnic cuisines in the United States. LCC follows LCSH in that cookbooks about national ethnic groups in the United States are classed with the nation. For example, an Italian American cookbook will be given the subject heading "Cooking, Italian" and will be classed at TX723 for Italian cookbooks. Like LCSH, the classification excludes national and ethnic groups in the United States, even if the cookbooks are distinctly American.

This practice affects the subject heading "African American cooking" as well. This subject heading cannot be reduced to a specific region in the United States so it is classed under the general American cooking number at TX715. "Soul food cooking" is related to southern cooking and could be classified at TX715.2.S68, but because "Soul food cooking" is just a cross-reference to "African American cooking," soul food cookbooks cannot be classified at that number. Like LCSH, LCC excludes soul food cooking from southern cooking and privileges white southern cooking. African American and soul food cooking are assigned the general American cooking number. Practically, this means that African American and soul food cookbooks are scattered on library shelves and access to them is limited. Library users cannot find them easily because they are not shelved together at a specific, dedicated number. A similar problem exists for "Cooking, Cajun." Because the subject heading does not include a region, it is classed under the general American cooking number at TX715, even though Cajun cooking is related to Louisiana-style cooking and could be classified at TX715.2.L68. Creole cooking is another issue. The subject heading "Cooking, Creole—Louisiana style" includes a region, so it is classed at TX715.2.L68 for Louisiana-style cooking. However, the subject heading "Cooking, Creole" does not include a region so it is classed at TX715, the general American cooking number. This is problematic because "Cooking, Creole" is used to describe Creole cooking outside of Louisiana. Cookbooks about Creole cooking in other places in the world are classed under American cooking as well.

African American Foodways

The construction of African American cooking in LCSH and LCC is not perfect. There are issues that affect access to these materials in libraries. Yet, room has been made for cooking in both standards; catalogers can catalog and classify cookbooks without difficulty. Works about African American foodways, however, are difficult to catalog and classify because there is no room for them in either standard. "Foodways" does not exist as a subject heading or a classification number. The authorized subject heading is "Food habits." The first form of the subject heading in LCSH was "Man—Food habits," and it was created sometime between 1941 and 1944. It changed to "Food habits" in 1957. The subject heading is classified under eating and drinking customs at a range of numbers between GT2850 and GT2960.[22] "Foodways" was added as a cross-reference sometime between 1981 and 1987. Because it is a cross-reference, a work about foodways must be assigned the subject heading "Food habits." This makes "Foodways" and "Food habits" equivalent headings, even though they do not mean the same thing; foodways is broader than food habits. Works about foodways discuss how food affects society and how food relates to culture, gender, economics, history, and so on. They tend to be inter-disciplinary and cross many subject boundaries in LCSH and LCC. Yet, there are no subject headings or classification numbers that reflect foodways adequately. Catalogers must assign a variety of subject headings to bring out different aspects of foodways works because existing subject headings do not describe these works well. Proper cataloging and classification depend on the subject knowledge of the cataloger. A cataloger must understand what a work is about and must know the types of subject headings available to bring out different aspects of a work. The classification of foodways materials is complicated as well. Works about foodways can be classified in many different places depending on the first subject heading assigned to the work. If the first subject heading is not accurate, then works about foodways may be classified at numbers that do not represent them well.

Several examples illustrate the difficulty with cataloging and classifying foodways. One example is *A Mess of Greens: Southern Gender and Southern Food*, by Elizabeth S. D. Engelhardt.[23] The cataloger had to assign seven subject headings to bring out different aspects of the book, shown in figure 5.4.

FIG. 5.4.
Subject headings assigned to *A Mess of Greens: Southern Gender and Southern Food*

1. Food habits—Southern States—History
2. Food—Social aspects—Southern States—History
3. Cooking, American—Southern style—History
4. Women—Southern States—Social life and customs
5. Southern States—Social life and customs
6. Southern States—Social conditions—History
7. African American cooking—History

Because the first subject heading is "Food habits—Southern States—History," it is classified at GT2853.U5 for eating and drinking customs in the United States (there is no number for southern states). Although this is the appropriate subject heading and classification number for foodways, it neglects other important aspects of this book, such as gender. The subject headings cannot show this book is about the relationship between southern gender and southern food because no subject headings exist. The cataloger had to construct the subject headings creatively within the boundaries of LCSH.

Building Houses out of Chicken Legs: Black Women, Food, and Power, by Psyche A. Williams-Forson, is another example.[24] To bring out the various aspects of this book, the cataloger had to assign eight subject headings, shown in figure 5.5.

FIG. 5.5.
Subject headings assigned to *Building Houses out of Chicken Legs: Black Women, Food, and Power*

1. Chickens—Social aspects
2. Meat—Symbolic aspects
3. African Americans—Food

4. African American women—Social conditions
5. African American cooking
6. Cooking (Chicken)
7. Food habits—United States
8. Food preferences—United States

Because the first subject heading is "Chickens—Social aspects," the cataloger classified the book at GT2868.5 for eating and drinking customs related to meat. This book, however, is not just a discussion of the social aspects of chicken. The subtitle, "Black Women, Food, and Power," explains what this book is about, yet the cataloger made the decision to focus on the "chicken" aspect of the book because there are no subject headings that can show the relationship between black women, food, and power.

Another example is *African American Foodways: Explorations of History and Culture*, a collection of essays edited by Anne L. Bower.[25] It contains seven essays about African American foodways and culture, but the cataloger assigned one subject heading, "African American cooking," and classified the book at TX715, the general American cooking number. Although recipes are discussed in some essays, this collection is not a cookbook. The cataloger did not assign the subject headings necessary to bring out different aspects of this collection. The cataloger may have thought foodways and cooking are synonymous terms. Because of the cataloger's decision, the book is not shelved with similar materials. Instead, it is shelved among the American cookbooks. Until subject headings and classification numbers exist for foodways, these works will be poorly cataloged and scattered throughout a library's collection.

Conclusion

The *Library of Congress Subject Headings* and the *Library of Congress Classification* construct African American cooking and foodways based on assumptions that affect access to these materials in libraries. Understanding the assumption in each standard can help library users search for cooking and foodways materials more effectively. It also can help librarians create subject headings and classification numbers that represent these subjects well. The Library of Congress has the power and responsibility to provide better access to African American cooking and foodways materials. Small changes could improve access greatly. For example, "Soul food cooking" should be a separate subject heading related to "African American cooking" and "Cooking, American—Southern style." African American cooking should be assigned its own classification number so that all African American and soul food cookbooks are classed at a specific number. Subject headings and classification numbers should be created for Creole cooking outside of Louisiana and for newer forms of southern cooking, such as Floribbean cooking. Perhaps most importantly, foodways is a growing subject but there is no room for it in LCSH or LCC. The Library of Congress needs to create subject headings and classification numbers specifically for foodways. This would be a significant amount of work, but it must be done to provide better access to foodways materials. Foodways researchers should consider working with the Library of Congress to establish foodways as a separate subject area in LCSH and LCC. Librarians do not understand foodways as well as researchers in the field. By working together, foodways researchers can help the Library of Congress facilitate access to foodways materials in libraries.

PART II ▪ Representations

CHAPTER 6

Creole Cuisine as Culinary Border Culture

Reading Recipes as Testimonies of Hybrid Identity and Cultural Heritage

CHRISTINE MARKS

> *In understanding the relationship between commodity and person, we unearth anew the history of ourselves.*
>
> SIDNEY MINTZ, *Sweetness and Power:*
> *The Place of Sugar in Modern History*

Eating is an agricultural, ecological, and political act. It draws us into the histories of the objects we consume, as we literally bite into the material manifestation of the many ecological and social exchanges that shape the cultivation and circulation of the culinary product. Eating practices must be regarded as signifying acts embedded in cultural discourse. Mary Douglas has suggested, "If food is treated as a code, the messages it encodes will be found in the pattern of social relations being expressed. The message is about different degrees of hierarchy, inclusion and exclusion, boundaries and transactions across the boundaries."[1] Many of these degrees are recorded both explicitly and implicitly in cookbooks, which makes them a rich archive of cultural messages and expressions of power relations inherent in food and eating practices. Cookbooks can be instruments of both maintaining and erasing cultural heritage, and they allow the reader to trace foodways and preparation methods as well as gender, race, and class relations played out in the kitchen.

American cookbooks have a comparatively short history, with the first publications appearing in the late eighteenth century. From its very beginning this history is one that reflects the United States' diverse past, as American cuisine quickly absorbed Native American, African, and European cooking techniques and ingredients. In this chapter, I read New Orleans Creole cookbooks of the late nineteenth and early twentieth centuries as artifacts that bear testimony to their authors' pride in regional culture and negotiate a conflicted heritage that is a unique product of colonial history. The desire to create American art forms, showcased in the formation of the Hudson River School in the 1820s and the beginnings of new American literary traditions with writers like Edgar Allan Poe and Walt Whitman, also manifested itself in nineteenth-century culinary culture. Creole cuisine maintained its European roots but was at the same time deeply connected to the ecological and cultural conditions of the American South. The history of Louisiana, in particular, is one that entangles the lives of African Americans and Native Americans with those of white settlers, predominantly from France and Spain. I read three examples of Creole cookbooks—Lafcadio Hearn's *La Cuisine Creole: A Collection of Culinary Recipes from Leading Chefs and Noted Creole Housewives, Who Have Made New Orleans Famous for Its Cuisine* (1885); *The Picayune's Creole Cook Book,* first published in 1900; and Célestine Eustis's *Cooking in Old Créole Days: La Cuisine Créole a l'Usage des Petits Ménages* (1904)[2]—with a particular focus on transatlantic and regional continuities and ruptures, especially with regard to the differing degrees of cultural retention discernible in these texts. Creole cuisine is composed of ingredients and cooking methods from both African American and Native American cultures; however, the former's influence is frequently obfuscated, while the latter is granted more visibility and recognition. This uneven representation of cultural heritage in Creole cookbooks is indicative of the increased anxiety over race relations in the post–Civil War South as well as a move toward romanticizing Native American culture in the aftermath of the fulfillment of America's "Manifest Destiny" and the resultant stylization of Native Americans as a "vanishing race."

Many cookbooks convey ideologies explicitly through prefaces and introductions to ensure that the recipes are framed and, therefore, received appropriately. In this chapter, I will focus on the more implicit messages contained in the recipes themselves—the essence of culinary literature. What do the ways in which the preparations and origins of ingredients are described tell us about race relations in post–Civil War America? What stories do the ingredients themselves have to tell? If the kitchen, as Kyla Wazana Tompkins has argued, is the place from which the servant "threatens to speak" and "infuse[s] the food she produces ... with the stifled political affect that the walls of the kitchen are supposed to contain," how much of her message remains legible in these recipes?[3]

Louisiana Creole cuisine may be one of the most contested and diverse American cuisines, and it occupies a special place in the American imagination: a blend of the exotic and the local, it may evoke feelings of southern nostalgia and comfort. Yet the ingestion of Creole food inevitably implicates the eater in a complicated history of production and consumption that is rooted in both oppression and resistance. As Jessica B. Harris has highlighted in *Beyond Gumbo*, Creole food is a fusion food. Early Creole cookbooks, while at times deliberately obscuring the nonwhite origins of their recipes, ultimately bear witness to the "tangled histories of the Americas" through the ingredients and food preparations they exhibit.[4] This reading of Creole cuisine exposes the intersection of multiple foodways, underlining notions of hybridity and following Paul Gilroy's call for a "theorization of creolisation, métissage, mestizaje, and hybridity" in contravention of "overintegrated conceptions of culture which present immutable, ethnic differences as an absolute break in the histories and experiences of 'black' and 'white' people."[5] Creole food is the product of multidirectional adaptations, and the anxieties generated by such fusion of various cultural elements surface in its representations in cookbooks.

Creole, in the widest sense, stands for people of non-American ancestry—both from Africa and Europe—born in North or South America.[6] Jessica Harris traces the etymology of the term "Creole," making very obvious the racial tensions that have shaped various meanings over time—Creole could mean anything from a white French person born in Louisiana to a person of Eskimo and Russian mix in Alaska.[7] She goes on to propose a further definition of Creole, one that takes into consideration linguists' interpretation of Creole as a language that, while a product of different origin languages, ultimately becomes the speaker's mother tongue. This, as Harris argues, is a useful way of considering Creole food, as "it allows for the coming together of diverse elements to create a vital, vibrant new entity."[8] While many publications today celebrate the vitality of the many cultural forces conjoined in Creole cuisine, post–Civil War society certainly struggled with this new entity, as it wasn't equally at ease with all elements of this new "mother tongue." Seemingly embracing the multicultural composition of Creole food, the cookbooks were still deeply embedded in a racist discourse that promoted a nostalgic view of the Old South, turning to food and eating as a means for regulating social relations.

As Ania Loomba notes in *Colonialism/Postcolonialism* (1998), "One of the most striking contradictions about colonialism is that it needs both to 'civilise' its 'others,' and to fix them into perpetual 'otherness.'"[9] Both civilizing and othering are ideologies that get undermined in Creole cuisine. While the "mistresses" of the household, as well as the authors of the cookbooks, may do their best to claim authority over their kitchens and their products, the civilizing process is multidirectional in a hybrid cuisine; and through the absorption of African and Native American traditions, white subjects lose the ability to "fix" the other at a safe distance. Creole cuisine can be considered a culinary border culture, a "contact zone," in Marie Louise Pratt's sense: a social space "where cultures meet, clash, and grapple with each other, often in contexts of highly asymmetrical relations of power."[10] The symbolic contact zone of Creole culinary culture is mirrored by the actual contact zone of the kitchen: it is the space in which the labor of cooking is performed, the space which the authors of cookbooks attempt to regulate through precise instructions and measurements. The kitchen is a site of mediation between the public and the private, and "the central space where the threatening porosity between bodies—most specifically between ruling-class and subaltern bodies—is most apparent."[11] I read Creole cookbooks as (often involuntary) testaments of this porosity, a place of mixing much in the sense of Gloria Anzaldúa's borderlands. The intimacy of food, its crossing from the outside to the inside of the body, destabilizes the dichotomy of self and other as they are inseparably connected through material and symbolic exchanges.

The need to fix the other in perpetual otherness was felt with particular acuity by the white Creoles in eighteenth- and nineteenth-century Louisiana. The first slave ships arrived in the state in 1719, and as early as 1727 a census determined that white settlers were outnumbered by slaves (1,561 versus 1,460).[12] Susan E. Dollar describes the process of miscegenation that created Louisiana's first racially mixed Creoles of color when Louisiana was a French colony, which became even more diverse when Spanish colonization began in 1763 and Spanish colonists entered the blend, further complicating racial relations and unsettling dichotomy of black and white that white American settlers tried to maintain.[13] The increased apprehension over interracial mixing—both a result of the colonial developments in Louisiana and the rise of scientific racism in the nineteenth century—likely caused a shift in the dominant definition of "Creole" in Louisiana, turning it into a term reserved for white people only.[14]

This idea of "cultural superiority and racial purity of Creole society," as Daniel Usner argues, had a great influence on writers' representations of French and Spanish Louisiana.[15] Accounts of Creole identity after the Civil War often pursued the goal of whitening the past by denying interracial mixing.[16] And the authors of cookbooks grappled with a similar unease with the hybrid constitution of Creole culture. Ralph Bauer and José Antonio Mazzotti refer to a compelling case for the interrelated forces of creolization and othering (which they, however, reject as they view the tendency toward the creation of racial binaries as a "dialectical and often rhetorical response to environmental determinism"): "It has been suggested elsewhere that the early modern invention of racial essence and purity as well as the identification of peoples in categories such as white and black were, paradoxically, the very products of a creolized subjectivity."[17] This tension arising from creolization and hybridity is palpable in the pages of the Creole cookbooks in the late nineteenth and early twentieth centuries.

One product of culinary creolization is gumbo, the heart of southern Creole food. While this stew exists in near endless varieties, made of ingredients like chicken and sausage or seafood, its distinguishing characteristic is what gives it its particular texture: alternatively, one may choose okra, filé powder, or roux as a thickening agent. These three ingredients represent three major cultural influences on Creole cuisine:

African, Native American, and French. The way in which recipes portray the origin and function of these components transports a message about the authors' conceptions of the cultural heritage as presented through their recipes. Okra and filé powder are prominent in the cookbooks investigated here, testifying to the central role of African and Native American cultural heritage in the formation of this cuisine.

The term "gumbo" itself means "okra," and okra has been the predominant ingredient in Creole cooking from its beginning. While the exact origin of okra is unclear, it presumably materialized first either in present-day Ethiopia and parts of Sudan and Eritrea, Senegambia, and the West African forest-savanna ecotone, or in Central Africa.[18] It is also not certain how and when exactly the plant was first brought to the North American continent, yet it is likely that either slaves took it with them on the Middle Passage or it was shipped over as cheap food for slaves.[19] Harris calls okra "emblematic" of southern food and "virtually totemic for all Africans in the diaspora."[20] She reflects, "Everywhere that okra points its green tip, Africa has been."[21] In Creole cuisine, okra, besides serving as a thickener, also makes frequent appearances in soup, fritters, and other vegetable dishes. There is presumably not a single Creole cookbook that has no reference to okra, and by the end of the nineteenth century the plant had, in fact, made its way into cookbooks throughout the United States.[22] Tracing the spread of okra reveals that the African American culinary influence indeed extended far beyond southern kitchens. The incorporation of this African staple food infused American culture with a taste of the oppressed, as African culinary culture emerged from these cookbooks in its irreducible materiality that tied its consumers to the history of slavery and exploitation.

La Cuisine Creole

Lafcadio Hearn, in his *La Cuisine Creole: A Collection of Culinary Recipes from Leading Chefs and Noted Creole Housewives, Who Have Made New Orleans Famous for Its Cuisine* (1885), regularly emphasizes the economical use of food. He praises the soup for its "economical way of using up the remains" of any kind of meat that's left over in the kitchen.[23] While the emphasis on thrifty application of all culinary elements was certainly promoted in cookbooks in other parts of the world, in the American South this was most strongly developed through slaves' practice of making use of leftover and undesired pieces of meat to sustain themselves. When giving instructions on dressing a turtle, Hearn inserts in parentheses, "If preferred, open and clean the chitterlings and intestines also—some use them."[24] The value of such animal parts that many considered waste likely emerged from the survival skills of African American slaves. Today, pig chitterlings are a staple dish of African American cuisine, another testament to the creative power of black cooks who managed to turn discarded parts of animals into dishes that are now consumed throughout the nation.[25] Hearn's parenthetical statement epitomizes the complicated relationship between white culture and black culinary achievement: a reluctant acceptance of the merit of making use of all parts of the animal, a move from the "other" to "some," a guarded and concealed opening toward slave food tradition.

In his instructions on soup making, Hearn stresses, "Okra alone is vegetable enough for a gombo."[26] He recommends using either okra or "filee" (today usually spelled filé), a powder made from dried sassafras leaves, as a thickening agent in gumbo, but some of his recipes also ask for roux. Filé powder was adapted from Native American cuisine and seems to have been an integral part of the culinary culture of the Choctaw Indians in the South. Hearn includes eight different recipes for gumbo, including everything from oysters to crab to chicken, and a variety of different vegetables—the only common ingredients for all recipes are either okra or filé. Like in most recipes for gumbo, he suggests rice as an accompaniment to the stew.[27] The following is the recipe "Simple Okra Gombo": "Chop a pound of beef and half a pound of veal brisket into squares an inch thick; slice three dozen okra pods, one onion, a pod of red pepper, and fry all together. When brown pour in half a gallon of water; add more as it boils away. Serve with rice as usual."[28] This sample is representative for the majority of all recipes in Hearn's book in its simplicity and rather vague instructions (other recipes, however, at least call for salt and pepper). Hearn seems to trust his readership to possess some basic cooking skills to complement his directions.

While Hearn does not give any hints about either okra's or filé's cultural significance, he explicitly credits Native Americans with inventing jambalaya, which is likely the second most prominent dish in Creole cuisine. In the "Salads and Relishes" section, Hearn presents a jambalaya recipe made with fowl and rice, which has little in common with our contemporary notion of jambalaya and which he claims to be an Indian dish ("very wholesome and palatable") that southern children are fond of.[29] Today, jambalaya is usually made with rice, celery, peppers, onions, chicken, sausage (often Andouille), and seafood, and because of its resemblance to paella it is often presented as a Spanish Creole dish. The origins of both the dish itself and its name, however, are subject to debate, which serves as an indicator of the confusion that the blend of cultural heritages apparently creates in people trying to decipher its message. The etymology of the word has been traced back to a mixture of French *jambon* or Spanish *jamón* and Spanish *paella*, while the *Oxford English Dictionary* claims jambalaya to be of Louisiana French origin and Karen Hess regards jambalaya as a variant of Provençal pilau.[30] The indecisiveness attached to the making and meaning of jambalaya is symbolic for Creole cuisine as a whole, and its portrayal in recipes is shaped both by the authors' cultural contexts and their political agenda. The fact that Hearn presents jambalaya as an "Indian" dish suggests an openness toward Native American culture that he does not display toward African American culture. Pointing out its nutritional value and its popularity among southern (likely white) children further amplifies his endorsement of the acculturation between white and Native American cultures. As a further concession to the significance of Native American elements, Hearn also includes several recipes containing corn or cornmeal, such as "Indian Breakfast Cakes," "Indian-Meal Griddle Cakes," and "Succotash," a mixture of corn and shelled beans widely popular among Native American tribes. Corn and beans (which, together with squash, formed the "three sisters") were integral parts of a Native American diet.[31] And Native Americans were first to cultivate corn on the continent.[32]

The Picayune's Creole Cook Book

The Picayune's Creole Cook Book, first published in 1900 and republished in new editions throughout the twentieth century, is maybe most conspicuous in its racist glorification of a past in which racial relations were clearly structured in a master-servant hierarchy.[33] The Picayune authors acknowledge the labor that was needed to produce Creole food, yet they present the African American cooks as mere instruments—as essential to a successful culinary enterprise as fresh produce or the various kitchen utensils needed, but without creative agency, which makes it necessary for the "white Creole mistresses" to monitor and guide their actions.[34] Like Hearn, the anonymous authors of *The Picayune's Creole Cook Book* also acknowledge Native American heritage in their recipe for gumbo filé while omitting any reference to the origin of okra in spite of its many uses in the recipes:

> First, it will be necessary to explain here, for the benefit of many, that "Filé" is a powder manufactured by the remaining tribe of Choctaw Indians in Louisiana, from the young and tender leaves of the sassafras. The Indian squaws gather the leaves and spread them out on a stone mortar to dry. When thoroughly dried, they pound them into a fine powder, pass them through a hair sieve, and then bring the Filé to New Orleans to sell, coming twice a week to the French Market from the old reservation set aside for their home on Bayou Lacombe, near Mandeville, La. The Indians used sassafras leaves and the sassafras for many medicinal purposes, and still sell bunches of the dried roots in the French Market. The Creoles, quick to discover and apply, found the possibilities of the powdered sassafras, or "Filé" and originated the well-known dish, "Gumbo Filé."[35]

There is a marked difference here between the attention paid to the origin of okra and mention of filé. While okra is omnipresent, there is no mention of its symbolical and practical significance to African Americans in any of the examples presented. Filé, on the other hand, is deemed worthy of a culinary history, including its use for medicinal purposes by the Choctaw Indians.[36] This may be at least partially due to the fact that filé is a traded commodity rather than a crop that has already been repossessed and securely placed within white ownership.

The recognition of Native American cultivation techniques as autonomous processes stands in stark contrast to the *Picayune's* portrayal of African American subjectivity. Instead of an acknowledgment of African American heritage, the *Picayune's Creole Cookbook* is at best an exercise in ventriloquism. The authors utilize a mammy figure, "Tante Zoé," to paint a nostalgic picture of the "typical Creole kitchen where 'Tante Zoé,' in the early morning hours, in her quaint, guinea blue dress and bandana 'tignon,' is carefully concocting the morning cup of CAFÉ NOIR."[37] In this kitchen imaginary, the servant's voice is void of threat, as she is only allowed to speak the words put into her mouth by the cookbook authors. In this case, Tante Zoé's task is to explain to the reader the intricacies of Creole coffee ("And she will tell you. . . . She will tell you, too").[38]) This, however, is still in need of editorial commentary: "By the best ingredients she means."[39] In a further instance of mammification, the cookbook's recipe for "Calas" starts with a reminiscence of "ancient old Negro women" selling rice cakes in the French Quarter.[40] Again, the authors evoke the stereotypical mammy figure wearing bandana tignon and blue dress with white apron.

> The olden Creole cooks would rush to their doors to get the first fresh, hot Calas to carry to their masters and mistresses with the early morning cup of coffee. The Cala women have almost all passed away, for . . . there is a "new colored woman" in New Orleans, as elsewhere in the south, and she disdains all the pretty olden industries and occupation which were a constant and genteel source of revenue to the old Negro mothers and grandmothers. Only one or two remain. . . . Once in a while, like some ghostly voice of the past, one starts up in bed of an early morning as the weak old voice faintly penetrates your chamber. In a second more it is lost in the distance, and you turn over with a sigh for the good old times and the quaint customs of old Creole days, which gave such a beautiful and unique tinge to the life of the ancient quarter. But the custom of making Calas still remains.[41]

While at the time this may have been intended as a gesture of appreciation and an appraisal of African American culinary tradition, the nostalgic mourning of a lost time in which black women's highest desire was to serve was an endorsement of slavery and the racial hierarchies of the Old South. The "new colored woman," with her unmanageable and unreasonable rejection of her appropriate position in society, turns the white ruling class into Proustian figures who desperately yearn to revive the past through the sweet taste of calas—the racist version of tea and madeleine.

As in other cookbooks of the nineteenth century and early twentieth centuries, one senses in the *Picayune's Creole Cook Book* the anxiety of a ruling class that feels threatened by the unruly powers of its servants penetrating the pages. Frequently, there are direct guidelines aiming to ensure the proper control of servants, to minimize the danger of inefficient or even rebellious behavior. At the same time, the authors seek to contain the permeability between bodies by stressing ideas of regulation and cleanliness. In order to work against ideas of contamination and contagion, the authors of the *Picayune's Creole Cook Book* instrumentalize the mammy figure, the "clean, tidy, old negresse, with neat guinea blue dress, white kerchief and bandana tignon," as an agent of cleanliness who ensures to maintain the kitchen as a "well-regulated" and clean space.[42] They stress that "the slovenly, untidy, unkempt cook has no place" in the kitchen. Covering the individual body of the black cook in the stereotypical costume of the mammy reinforces the notion of containment and cleanliness as well as lack of subjective agency that the authors wish to promote.

Cooking in Old Créole Days

Célestine Eustis's *Cooking in Old Créole Days: La Cuisine Créole à l'Usage des Petits Ménages* (1904) is a bilingual collection that combines French and English recipes, songs, and illustrations. It features an English introduction by the physician S. Weir Mitchell, in which he hearkens back to a glorified vision of the Old South, and a French introduction by Célestine Eustis. Likely because they expected a larger English-speaking audience, there are more English than French recipes in the collection. Most of the gumbo recipes Eustis presents call for roux or filé as a thickener, and only one out of five gumbo recipes uses okra. Unlike Hearn, however, Eustis does include okra in her jambalaya recipe:

JUMBALLAYA A LA CREOLE

Add to a cupful of rice, which has boiled five minutes, a rich brown chicken fricassee, put it in a saucepan, not closely covered, let it dry slowly, turn with a fork. The Carolinians make different perlous prepared in the same way by adding cooked tomatoes and butter. Green peas with a little butter is delicious. Okra and tomatoes fried together and added to rice. Oysters a little fried in butter. Hopping John is made in the same way with small pieces of ham, fried sausages, to which you add some cow peas that have been partially boiled. The St. Domingo Congris is like the Hopping John.[43]

This recipe's many references to variations and overlaps with dishes originating in other parts of the South and Eustis's undecidedness regarding possible ingredients are indicative of Creole cuisine's fusion status and its permeable relationship with other southern cuisines. Hopping John and St. Domingo Congris, like okra, are dishes that have been traced back to West Africa, further highlighting the inextricable connection between black and white cultures in Creole cuisine.[44]

Instead of simply ignoring the origin of okra, Eustis's *Cooking in Old Créole Days* actually designates full authority over the plant to the colonial powers. Eustis not only neglects to mention the African heritage of okra entirely, but in effect promotes an absolute appropriation of the crop by the colonizer. Under "Hints for Housekeepers," Eustis adds an entry called "Okra Hibiscus": "De Brazza, the great explorer, told me that in his expeditions into Africa whenever they stopped for a few months the first thing they planted was Okra Hibiscus, because they considered that vegetable to be so wholesome and nutritious."[45] This passage exemplifies one of the great ironies of Creole cuisine: while cherishing the nutritional value of okra and therefore embracing it as an integral part of Creole cuisine, Eustis, rather than acknowledging the African heritage of the plant, actually rewrites the story to reinforce colonial ideology. Not enough to highlight De Brazza—an Italian explorer who helped establish French colonies in the Congo— she also turns him into the agricultural architect responsible for the growth of the nourishing plant.

Perhaps surprisingly, in relation to this conspicuous denial, Eustis explicitly points to the Native American origin of "Gumbo Filé."[46] This she describes as "a powder prepared by the Indians. When the leaves of the sassafras tree are very tender and green, they gather them, dry them, pound them and put them in bags."[47] She also gives credit to Native Americans for the preparation of "Gofio," "corn meal dried in the oven and salted. It is an Indian preparation. They put it in a bag and eat it on their tramps, or when they go out hunting."[48] Eustis seems more comfortable with the visibility she grants Native Americans, not just in illustrating their contributions of ingredients, but also in acknowledging their mastery of preparing the food. Eustis's acknowledgment of independent Native American cultural processes is interesting to read together with her praise for the African American servant Nanette's skills in the kitchen. In a section entitled "Art and Science of Salad Making," she writes: "But Nanette [the cook], in her line, is an artist who has acquired the simple stroke that produces the masterpiece. Occasionally there arises a genius in lay ranks who snaps her finger at experience and arrives at Nanette's degree of skill by inspiration. But geniuses are few."[49] While Eustis uses Nanette to demonstrate that anyone is capable of producing a masterpiece, she distinctly emphasizes that this is the result of work experience, not genius. While there may be achievement in the creation of a salad, this process seems safely embedded in the controlling frame of white discourse, whereas the Native American cooking techniques are allowed to exist independently and enter Creole cuisine from the outside.

Conclusion

The cookbooks' different representations of African American and Native American cultural influences are exemplary for the growing disparity in race relations in the American South in the late nineteenth and early twentieth century. The iconic photograph *The Vanishing Race*, published by Edward Curtis in 1904, visualized the myth of Native American tribes that would dominate the twentieth century: with the elimination of any real threats of resistance, white America was now embracing a romanticized image of Native American culture that also surfaced in the cookbooks' acknowledgment of Native American cultural traditions.

Creole cookbooks, while appropriated by the white imagination, nevertheless provide insight into African American and Native American food traditions and cooking practices. Recipe collections are written testimonies to the various social differences and contradictions making up the dishes they record. The history of the Creole is marked by racial anxiety, and "across the nineteenth century black bodies and subjects stick in the throat of the (white) body politic, refusing to be consumed as part of the capitalist logic of racism and slavery as well as the cultural and literary matter that they produced."[50] No matter how much of an effort is put into voiding the impact of African American culture on Creole cuisine and denigrating and infantilizing black cooks, the product of their work persists and enters the culinary imagination untamed.

What speaks most strongly, in the end, are the ingredients themselves, acting as tools of "self-expression, self-actualization, resistance" that unsettle the racist frame of the text.[51] Rather than simply adding a taste of racial otherness to offer a spiced up experience to the white palate—as bell hooks has observed in contemporary white supremacist society—ingredients like okra can be read, as Andrew Warnes proposes, as "a potentially hazardous signifier of irrepressible Africanism" and "unwanted evidence of black cultural autonomy."[52] Ultimately, these recipes reveal the interconnectedness of the histories of African Americans, Native Americans, and white settlers in Louisiana, and these histories will continue to manifest themselves in the many Creole dishes served throughout the nation.

CHAPTER 7

Feast of the Mau Mau

Christianity, Conjure, and the Origins of Soul Food

ANTHONY J. STANONIS

When musician Louis Jordan wanted to address the poor state of race relations in the United States in 1949, he turned food into a metaphor and cut a record to make his point. His "Beans and Cornbread" told a tale of tension between two staples of the African American diet. One dark and one light, Beans and Cornbread spar for supremacy. Though, as Jordan has it, Beans literally tells Cornbread that the tension is one-sided: "You always getting mad at me, I ain't mad at you." After trading barbs and punches until Cornbread is almost dead, Beans halts the assault in recognition that the two foods "go hand in hand." Beans shouts, "We should get up every morning and hang out together like sisters and brothers." What follows is a litany of ingredients to an inter-racial feast. Beans and Cornbread go together like wieners and sauerkraut, chittlings and potato salad, liver and onions, red beans and rice, molasses and hotcakes, or some other combination of dark and light foods. Jordan celebrated fellowship and abundance as if straight from a church picnic. But the power within Jordan's dishes came from a secret ingredient, another African American religious tradition known as conjure. For some believers, the careful preparation of foods of dark or light shades could exert supernatural influence over people of black or white skins. A skilled conjurer could make foods speak to the races.[1]

Writings about "soul food" rarely acknowledge that the pot used to cook collard greens might also be used to boil a black cat. The same cayenne pepper bottle used to flavor a gumbo might also be used to speed the effect of a trick bag. Scholars of African American culture, as Yvonne Chireau argues, often overlook that "Christian ministers and religious practitioners sometimes doubled as proprietors of magic and occult businesses." Similarly, Carolyn Long's study of the commercialization of conjure during the twentieth century traces the continued enchantment of "innocuous herbs like cinnamon and mint" as businesses and mail-order catalogs catered to African Americans, especially as the Great Migration increasingly urbanized the black population. Advocates of soul food in the 1960s emphasized the figurative power of a unique black culinary aesthetic in order to promote cultural nationalism and racial pride. Yet, in doing so, they obscured an important legacy; African American cooks had maintained culinary traditions in which ingredients possessed actual power over people and events.[2]

Scholars in African American and culinary studies have provided intricate explorations of African influences on foodways in the New World, the blending with European and Native American customs, and the importance of soul food as a racially unifying force for African Americans during the 1960s. Yet the concept of soul food, rooted in a deeply religious culture, remains underappreciated, though much has been written about the efforts by Black Muslims since the 1960s to discredit soul food as symbolic of poverty and slavery.[3] Soul food referenced a religious idea while specifically uplifting African American pride. Furthermore, soul food ingredients united African Americans not only in terms of their shared culinary history, dating back through slavery, but also in their shared religious heritage, rooted in Christian faiths adopted under slavery and folk spiritualties carried over from Africa. Food items mixed correctly equated, in some instances, to delicious meals and, in cases such as a trick bag, to powerful forces against oppression. In either form, soul food cast a spell against racism.

Though culinary scholars have viewed "soul food" as a term that emerged in the 1960s, the phrase had long been embedded in African American Christianity. Christian ministers and their laity since at least the nineteenth century emphasized the importance of soul food for the strengthening of faith. Black and white Christians noted the separation of soul from body and, for each, recognized the need for regular nourishment. According to a poem published in the *Anti-Slavery Bugle* from New Lisbon, Ohio, in 1855, emancipation would allow each slave to "gather for her thirsty soul, food, fitted / For her spirit's wants." Again and again, well into the twentieth century, Americans related church attendance, prayer, biblical readings, charity work, or some other such action to soul food that provided spiritual enrichment—a concept all could easily understand given the relationship of actual food to the maintenance of a person's physical body. Advocacy of civil rights was a particularly soul-affirming commitment for African Americans. A faculty member at Payne Theological Seminary of the African Methodist Episcopal (AME) Church disdained the segregation he experienced while traveling from Ohio to Texas on a family visit in 1895. The degradation caused by the Jim Crow cars along his rail journey stirred outrage: "Some people now are like the people in Christ's time; if they can get the bread for the body, they care nothing for the soul's interest, so far as soul food is concerned." He condemned blacks who accepted such conditions as "stuffing the material body and starving the soul."[4]

Nurturing the soul and body remained a key theme before the emergence of soul food as a cuisine. The black press recorded an AME conference "rich in mental and soul food" for those in Cleveland, Ohio, in 1919, especially noting the importance to locals who were straining to accommodate the poor black migrants from the South. Religious classes offered by Kansas City, Kansas, churches were described in 1923 as "full of soul food and many are feeding off of these spiritual feasts." An advice column from 1945 even stressed the need to enliven homes with bright colors since African Americans were "starved for soul food."[5]

Understanding the religious context for soul food helps us understand the aims of the African American community in later championing their foodways under the phrase. The important role of Christian churches and ministers in providing the faithful with solace while also energizing support for civil rights mirrored the comfort and sustenance offered by soul food dishes that allowed African Americans to resist the dehumanizing effects of segregation. Soul food celebrated faith, family, and racial fellowship. The low-on-the-hog meals concocted by blacks since slavery heralded the triumph of their human spirit under inhumane conditions. Food and religion were intricately linked. With Bibles commonly the sole book in a house, one passed from generation to generation, these became ideal for recording heirloom recipes in some families.[6] Furthermore, revivals since the nineteenth century were as much social as religious gatherings that could last for days. Historian Frederick Opie explains how a revival served "as a spiritual fueling station for the soul and a refuge from racism." Food was a key component of these religious gatherings. For example, the *Guide*, an African American newspaper in Oklahoma City, heralded a nearby "general camp meeting for Oklahoma and southern Kansas" in summer 1899. "Plenty of eatables and soul food will be provided," announced a preacher.[7] Robert Graetz, a white Lutheran minister working in Montgomery, Alabama, in the 1950s, recalled an interracial Bible camp where meals provided a vital means of fellowship, in violation of state customs and laws.[8] African Americans even came to call chicken, according to one historian, the "'Gospel bird,' as a traditional sacred food," for its prominent place in Sunday meals or religious gatherings.[9]

The bond between African American Christianity and food was reinforced by the emphasis on home life. A home grounded in a Christian morality allowed African Americans to refute whites' suspicions of black savagery and ignorance. The kitchen centered the Christian family home that African Americans struggled to create after emancipation. In a racist world, the kitchen offered African Americans a sense of community, a place for family unity, and a barometer of their financial condition. Legendary singer Isaac Hayes commented, "The real heart of the house was Mama's kitchen." "As in many families, our main gathering place was the kitchen," remembered W. Ralph Eubanks of his childhood in post-1945 Mississippi. The family farm provided a cornucopia of produce that equated to security. The kitchen not only hosted all family meals but also guarded the family "from unwanted influences that would tell us we were inferior because we were black." D'Army Bailey recalled visiting his relatives in 1950s Memphis, where he spent "love-filled days" at the kitchen table "feeling safe." In the kitchen, black Christians demonstrated sacrifice as well as faithful persistence in an adverse world. The celebration of soul food during the 1960s paid respect to African Americans' triumph over racism and poverty—a triumph galvanized by refrains of Christian preaching and song.[10]

The emergence of soul food as a secular term for African American foodways reflected both the success of the civil rights movement and the rise of Black Power. White civil rights workers from the North often acquired their first taste of soul food in campaigns across the South and pursued those tastes in black-owned restaurants after returning home.[11] Bringing attention to soul food as a cuisine made African American foodways more palatable across the color line, as reflected by the proliferation of cookbooks and homages to soul food eateries beginning in the 1960s. White gourmets were now encouraged to sample this uniquely African American cuisine. At the same time, as historian Doris Witt argues, writers of early soul food cookbooks constructed "their cookbooks as a form of resistance to white appropriations of black culinary traditions."[12]

Yet when we turn to discussions of soul food within scholarship, cookbooks, or the various other commentaries about African American foodways, a stunning silence is heard about the influences of conjure. Champions of soul food repeatedly tied the cuisine to the black cook's intuition, a spiritual endeavor reflecting personal craft. Soul food, according to one scholar, was "located within the black body," a style that could never be fully appreciated by the rote demands of cookbooks. Soul food emerged from oral tradition, born of illiteracy and a need to preserve cooking secrets to ensure employability within the Jim Crow South. The spiritual powers believed to influence that black body thus shaped African American foodways.[13] Gospel legend Mahalia Jackson stated a similar sentiment in her published cookbook: "Courage, fervor, and action convey the feelings (that's really what it is) of *cooking soul*."[14] But who were these black cooks? And what lay within those cooks' souls? Drawing on Doris Witt's call to develop a "systematic analysis of black music and food," we must listen to the history of foodways, music, and African American religion to recognize the secret powers influencing soul food.[15]

Slaves adapted white Christianity to their own condition. In the aftermath of the Great Awakening in the mid-1700s, white plantation owners began Christianizing slaves. Masters conflated bondage with a divine mission to bring Christianity to their human property, though the ability to read and write was strictly denied. The owners stressed earthly obedience. However, those in bondage stressed divine judgment of their oppressors and the coming of freedom as part of a divine plan. Just as slaves maintained food customs in order to enrich their diet or supplement their meager rations, those in bondage held tightly to empowering spiritual traditions brought from Africa. Illiterate, they safeguarded their oral traditions. Considered property under the law, slaves retained spiritual, medical, food, and other customs that provided security, a sense of their humanity, and an occasional feeling of power over their oppressors.[16]

Publicly, Christian Americans of both colors sharply criticized any remnants of African religious beliefs, even if they sometimes secretly turned to such discredited practices when needed. Christian spokespersons of both races argued that folk traditions were at best ignorant and at worst blasphemous. In the popular national imagination, religious practices such as conjure or hoodoo—spiritual exercises that blended African folk beliefs with Protestant elements—became synonymous with voodoo, a more organized religious faith that mixed African religious traditions with Catholicism. White Americans conflated the varied practices under "voodoo" because of their anxieties about black savagery in Haiti, the first independent black republic in the Americas. The alien nature of Catholicism in the largely Protestant United States also made voodoo a more comprehensible target from the nineteenth into the early twentieth centuries, especially as Catholic immigrants from Ireland and Italy flooded the ports. Whites typically used voodoo to emphasize blacks' ignorance and the need for white supremacy. Blacks, especially devout Christians and the rising middle class who pursued integration and racial uplift, sought to escape the stigma.[17]

The focus on voodoo within popular American culture rested on associations of both Catholics and Africans with cannibalism. Catholicism's mystical transubstantiation of wine and bread into the blood and body of Christ suggested a cannibalism that Protestant Americans could easily relate to tales of African cannibalism. Writing in 1834, William Craig Brownlee of the Reformed Dutch Church decried how Catholics, through transubstantiation, "eat and swallow down *human flesh*! If that make them not cannibals, then words have lost their meaning; and men have lost their reason, their judgment, and their senses!"[18] One Methodist critic of Catholicism asked in 1915: "Is divinity digestible? Are souls ranked as food?"[19] Indeed, temperance advocates on the march toward Prohibition in 1920 made much of the Catholic celebration of alcohol, given the importance of wine to the faith. In *Rum, Rags, and Religion: Or in Darkest America and the Way Out*, from 1892, Olin Marvin Owen considered Catholicism's emphasis on alcohol a perversion of Christianity that lowered the standard of civilization among believers to "below those in 'Darkest Africa.'"[20]

Such descriptions are remarkably similar to white Americans' views of Africans, Haitians, and African Americans. An encyclopedia from 1888 described "tribes in . . . Africa along the equator from east to west, who habitually practice cannibalism in its most repulsive forms, even to the length of buying and selling human flesh for ordinary diet." These included "some of the most advanced and advancing of negro races."[21] Indeed, defenders of slavery and Jim Crow regularly harped on African cannibalism to justify white supremacy and point out the dangers of racial equality. Horace Fulkerson celebrated the civilizing process of slavery. His 1887 study of potential racial regression due to emancipation led him to talk of cannibalism in West Africa: "Dried African and African on foot! What a field for Armour, the great meat king, and a packing establishment." Other prominent works, such as *The Negro: A Menace to American Civilization*, from 1907, likewise warned that African Americans were "but a day removed from savagery and cannibalism."[22] It was in Haiti, however, where the cannibalism of Catholicism and Africa wedded into grotesque voodoo rituals—horrors that warned white Protestant America of how each would corrupt the republic. Paul Barringer, in his 1900 study entitled *The American Negro: His Past and Future*, noted that the "young negro of the South, except where descended from parents of exceptional character and worth, is reverting through hereditary forces to savagery." For the consequences, he turned to Haiti. Barringer quoted a fellow scholar: "The religion, nominally Christian, is largely Voudoux, or serpent-worship, in which actual and horrible cannibalism is even now a most important element. Instead of progressing, the negro Republican has gone back to the lowest type of African barbarism." Barringer saw a similar retreat of civilization in Guadeloupe and Martinique.[23]

Comments from African Americans regularly echoed whites' disgust with voodoo and, thus, conjure in whatever form. In the 1880s, the *Washington Bee* linked two African American advocates of racial separation with "political cranks, society mutual association deadbeats, travelling humbugs, hypocrites, frauds, voodoo doctors, fortune tellers, [and] 'hand-writers on the wall,' [who] should all be put in the same category." The *Wisconsin Labor Advocate*, in an 1886 article on voodoo in New Orleans, decried the ignorance of the faithful yet also linked the practice to evil: "To be sure, the superstition is most prevalent among the negroes, nearly all of whom are believers in the power of the 'voudoo' man for evil, but there are many white people—of the least intelligent class, of course—who hold the charms of this peculiar evil genius in great awe." Like the white press, black publications in the 1880s linked any African American folk spiritual beliefs, such as those practiced near Tuscaloosa, Alabama, to "mysterious voodoo."[24]

Black critics condemned the popularity of fanciful voodoo rituals on mainstream stage and film. The white and black middle class only viewed black spirituals as the exemplar of black arts within American popular culture until the mid-twentieth century. The popularity of jazz and blues affirmed white perceptions of black decadence. "But the perpetual presentation of African voodoo and esoteric jungle influence is becoming a bit sordid," remarked Rudolph Dunbar of the Associated Negro Press in 1936.[25] Others in 1937 condemned a "March of Time" newsreel about Harlem for depicting "all of the colored residents of New York as voodoo worshippers." Whites' representations of African Americans as prone to savagery and superstition led blacks to disavow conjure while embracing more mainstream forms of Christianity.[26]

However, jazz and blues music, popular among the black working class, gave voice to spiritual beliefs denied by racial spokespeople of the black middling and upper classes who often mimicked white societal standards. As an African American cookbook from 1969 argued, "The word 'soul' comes out of the church, of course, but jazz and blues brought it out into the non-black world."[27] This "soul" celebrated by black musicians was not only the soul food long spoken of by Christian spokespersons but also the soul food crafted by conjurers. According to the authors of the *Integrated Cookbook*, published in 1971, soul food mimicked black music: "Like jazz, it had a solid base, but the rest was improvised, varied to suit deep down feelings." In other words, soul food possessed a mixed religious heritage. Pioneering jazz clarinetist Sidney Bechet of New Orleans recalled a family tale of "witch women making brews" in his description of jazz's origins in voodoo rituals.[28] As the recording industry emerged in the early twentieth century, producers of so-called race records scoured the countryside for tunes that struck a chord with the largely poor, rural African American population and their relatives migrating to cities in the South and North. Emerging art forms such as jazz and blues referenced unique religious customs and foodways.[29]

Musicians frequently described conjure. W. C. Handy's "Sundown Blues," written in 1922, told the story of Arkansas conjurer Aunt Caroline Dye, who instructed spurned women to bake "Hoodoo in his bread." Lizzie Miles of New Orleans described having a "black cat bone's a-boiling" in "Shootin' Star Blues" in 1928. Memphis Minnie's "Hoodoo Lady Blues" from 1936 talked of a conjurer who could turn water into wine. Performers gained success by voicing the daily struggles of the black working class. Profiting from their appeal to this market, these singers could shun the criticisms leveled at blues and jazz by white and black elites.[30]

By the mid-twentieth century, black and white performers, such as Screamin' Jay Hawkins of Ohio and Dr. John of Louisiana, respectively, openly embraced African American conjuring, thereby subverting negative critiques long used against blacks. Pauline Coggs, the first black woman to head the Washington, D.C., Urban League and later appointed to the Wisconsin Civil Rights Commission, published a poem entitled "Black Power" in 1967. She noted, "Voodoo is black magic," but "Black is not bad." Toward the conclusion, she stresses, "Blackness can offer protection."[31]

Studies of conjure reveal the close ties between food and African American spiritual practices. Hortense Powdermaker, in a pioneering anthropological study of Indianola, Mississippi, during the 1930s, identified widespread belief among blacks and whites that a person could be influenced "by putting something" in his or her food. More importantly, Harry Middleton Hyatt, an Anglican minister from Illinois, spent decades gathering evidence of conjure within black communities during the early and mid-twentieth century. One New

Orleans conjurer offered a recipe of steel dust, rotten egg, sugar, and sweet olive oil carried in a bottle to win sympathy from the police. "[Sugar] makes people kind," explained the conjuror.[32] Another New Orleanian offered numerous concoctions to ward off police or win at cards and dice. These required brown sugar, horseradish, beef tongue, table salt, black pepper, and cayenne pepper.[33] A conjurer from Algiers, Louisiana, told of powers provided by the proper use of lemons and coconut.[34] A believer from Florence, South Carolina, divulged a tea made from fig tree bark and nine black peppercorns that, when the words "In de Name of de Father, de Son an' de Holy Ghost" were spoken over the boiling water, would make the drinker break out in hives. A mixture of nine spoons each of graveyard dirt, table salt, sulfur, and cayenne pepper sprinkled evenly around the house while speaking in the name "of de Father, de Son an' Holy Ghost" would ward off police.[35] Madam Collins from Memphis offered a cure for skin diseases that involved mixing a quart of wine, a half box of mustard, a quart of rainwater, and a quart of boiling water. The sufferer was instructed to place some in the bath for four straight days, on the last of which to also consume a pint of milk spiked with a tablespoon each of mustard and sugar.[36] Basil, caraway seed, crab, garlic, onion, potatoes, nutmeg, parsley, peanuts, rice, and numerous other items common to the kitchen possessed supernatural powers waiting to be unleashed by the right recipe.[37]

Different foods carried unique powers based on their look, odor, or taste. Sugar sweetened a person by making him or her kinder and more amendable; the heat of pepper, whether black or cayenne, acted as a catalyst that hastened the effects of a spell. The lightness or darkness of a food could direct a spell against either whites or blacks, respectively.

Smells of particular foods received attention from believers in conjure. For instance, onions, with their pungent, tear-provoking odors, represented turmoil. A Memphis conjurer stressed, "Yo' don't 'sposed tuh leave cut onion in yore house no kinda way." Leaving a chopped onion exposed invited domestic tensions. The conjurer explained, "When yo' peel onions in yore home, yo' supposed tuh put sugah an' salt—sugah an' salt on it [the peelings] an' put it on de stove an' burn it. Dat's keepin' down de fuss [in the house]. An' if yo' havin' fuss dere, put salt on de onion an' burn it up." A native of Florence, South Carolina, emphasized that burning the onion peel not only warded off turmoil, but promoted good fortune by neutralizing the powerful aroma: "See, yo' cookin' a pastry or sompin an' yo' use de onion, an' de outah peel yo' cut off de onion. Yo' take dat an' sprinkle salt ovah dat, an' wrap it up in a papah, an' put it in de stove an' burn it." "Bring luck to de house," explained the conjurer. In Wilmington, North Carolina, a popular belief suggested that carrying a red onion tempered by salt and wrapped in a paper would assist the unemployed in finding work.[38]

The color of food likewise carried important meanings, frequently as a representation of race. To ward off someone who was disagreeable, one conjuror told of writing the person's name on an eggshell thirty times, then breaking the egg in the house. She explained, "Well, now, yo' take a egg—if it's a white person, yo' take a white-shell egg from a white hen; if it's a colored person, yo' take a egg from a black hen."[39] To attract business or ward off enemies, a female New Orleanian called for sprinkling a house or workplace with "brown sugar for colored people—for white people . . . white sugar."[40]

One of the more elaborate recipes for gaining power was the attainment of a black cat's bone. Gaining such a bone involved boiling a black cat alive. However, different conjurers offered different means of finding and using the luckiest bones. Some emphasized the bones that floated. Others suggested boiling the cat while saying the "Lord's Prayer." A native of Brunswick, Georgia, instructed on picking the bone that best fit in the user's mouth. A Virginian described boiling a black cat, mashing the bones to powder, then mixing the dust "in soup, anything with vegetables," in order to win the eater's affections. According to one Memphis conjurer, the cat should be boiled with "sugah an' oil of bergamot an' oil of cinnamon."[41]

Cookbooks on soul food rarely mention the importance of conjure to African American culture. The centrality of Christianity has marginalized folk religion. Though people may well practice, they rarely publicly state belief in conjure. Zora Neale Hurston, in her pioneering anthropological study of conjure, published in 1935, wrote, "Nobody knows for sure how many thousands in America are warmed by the fire of hoodoo, because the worship is bound in secrecy. It is not the accepted theology of the Nation and so believers conceal their faith." The practice was shrouded in "profound silence."[42] Hyatt confronted this silence during interviews with Floridians in 1970. Asking an African American woman about the degree to which his whiteness made practitioners hesitant to discuss hoodoo, the woman replied, "In some cases, but they's a lotta colored people ain't gonna give no black or white no info'mation." Alice Walker, in her short story "Strong Horse Tea" from 1973, noted the reluctance within the African American community to acknowledge traditional home remedies—conflated with conjure—as nothing more than "nigger magic" symbolic of a desperate people.[43]

The preponderance of church-published cookbooks—facilitated by templates provided by publishers such as Fundcraft since 1942 and Morris Press since the early 1980s—partly explains why conjure receives no mention.[44] Within secular cookbooks, the popular technique of using recipes to recall African American family life, which often emphasize Christian piety, works against recognition of conjure. Furthermore, fundraising efforts and festivals are, in the words of one scholar, an often Christian-oriented "public stage" for participants "to share religious messages or to express personal belief in the Lord."[45] Yet, unwittingly or not, Freda De Knight, who published the classic African American cookbook *A Date with a Dish* in 1948, recognized the power within a cuisine crafted by illiterate men and women of color who cooked from oral tradition and personal senses. She entitled the introduction "There's Magic in a Cook Book."[46]

The rare exceptions that mention or demonstrate conjure go far in explaining how embarrassment and racial stigma served to obscure the relationship between conjure and foodways. In San Francisco, Mary Ellen Pleasant, popularly known as Mammy Pleasant, became a powerful force within city affairs from the 1850s until the 1890s. Pleasant was renowned for her catering skills. Investing wisely, she built a fortune of millions with assistance from her white partner, Thomas Bell, by feigning, according to one scholar, a charade of "master and mammy."[47] Within popular culture, Pleasant's success and inversion of white supremacy gave rise to popular rumors about her skilled use of conjure. Helen Holdredge, an author who wrote two biographies and a cookbook about Pleasant between the 1950s and

1970s, even alleged without much evidence that Pleasant developed her spiritual powers while residing with Marie Laveau, the famed New Orleans voodoo queen, before traveling to California. Laveau, who well understood how to unleash the forces latent within ingredients, turned Pleasant "into an accomplished cook." Holdredge's interpretation diluted Pleasant's skills (as well as Laveau's) into a fanciful tale that reflected racist misunderstandings of black foodways and conjure. The dismissive nature of Holdredge's studies reveals much about why African Americans publically shunned conjure.[48]

Yet at the grassroots, conjure remained a powerful force against poverty and discrimination. Richard Dorson's 1959 study of folklore within the United States noted how African American accounts of conjure continued to influence daily life within black communities: "Fictional tales, true experiences, and popular beliefs continually cross into each other's territory. The belief in the spirit or the hoodoo leads into a true story of black magic or spirit visitation; and the supernatural folktale may be told as a real occurrence." The spiritual power of foods thus remained a force in African American life. Published in 1969, for instance, the *West Oakland Soul Food Cook Book* gathered recipes and home remedies from neighborhood charities and community outreach programs within the African American community of Oakland, California. After presenting recipes, the book concluded with a telling list of home remedies that bordered on conjure. To cure a headache, sufferers were instructed to "put an old stocking over your head, covering your forehead . . . or dip a brown paper bag in vinegar and salt and put over your head." A nosebleed could be stopped by placing "some keys on the back of the neck," allowing the blood to "drip into some ashes," or tying a "string on both little fingers of the person." Killing a goose and rubbing the fat on a person's chest cured colds, while mixing sugar with three drops of turpentine solved other forms of sickness. To stop alcoholism, readers were told to place a "fresh piece of beefsteak in a glass of whiskey" and allow it to rest for five days before consuming the drink. What may appear as superstitions were powerful remedies for an African American community that endured the inequalities of modern America.[49]

Like Louis Jordan, musician Screamin' Jay Hawkins in 1963 and 1969 used song and food to relate another tale of struggle between black and white. The song, "Feast of the Mau Mau," ridiculed long-standing white suspicions of African barbarism while referencing the Mau Mau's unsuccessful anticolonial struggle against British rule in Kenya during the 1950s. The feast, after all, was a "test for the best for who stays." Hawkins lampoons cooking baboon, raccoon, fly, fleas, bulldog, and finally human. He warns in the first verse: "Take your time, ain't life for good cookin' / Cause the rest of this mess ain't good lookin.'" The song concludes with a lengthy description of cannibalism. He describes eyeballs as "heathen olives." Requesting a rib, he rejoices in getting to "bite on that cat's bone"—a likely pun referencing the power of feline bones within conjure. In the midst of this meal, however, Hawkins asks, "Gimme some more of that inside soul, yeah / That—what you mean you ain't got no more soul?" The imperialist view of Africans as savage cannibals evaporates as Hawkins conjures a mess of images that notes the ridiculousness of white stereotypes of African culture. But the soul—the human spirit—could not be so easily boiled down to a lampoon. Released at the peak of the civil rights movement then re-recorded at the height of the Black Power movement and the first emergence of soul food cookbooks, Hawkins's "Feast of the Mau Mau" recalls how conjuring and cooking were both vital to the survival of African Americans; they manifested efforts by people of color to challenge white supremacy around the globe. As Hawkins sings, "Sure tastes good, man."[50]

CHAPTER 8

The Sassy Black Cook and the Return of the Magical Negress

Popular Representations of
Black Women's Food Work

KIMBERLY D. NETTLES-BARCELÓN

When you cookin' white food, you taste it with a different spoon. They see you puttin' the tastin' spoon back in the pot you might as well throw it all out, spoon too. And you use the same cup, the same fork, the same plate. Everyday. And you put it up in the cabinet. And you tell that white woman that that's where you gone keep it from here on out. Don't do it and see what happens! When servin' white folks coffee, set it down in front of 'em. Don't hand it to 'em, 'cause your hands can't touch. And don't hit on they chil'ren, white folks like to do they own spankin'. Last thang. Come here. Look at me. No sass-mouthin'. (Her daughter looks away and rolls her eyes. Minnie puts her hand to her cheek and forcibly turns her head so they are looking again eye-to-eye.) No sass-mouth. I mean it! (Minnie smooths out the collar of her daughter's uniform and exhales heavily. Softening her gaze.) Now give your mama a kiss.

"MINNIE JACKSON," *The Help*

In my course *Cultural Representations of Black Women and Food*, we viewed the film *The Help* (2011) to discuss the ways the dominant media continues to provide romanticized images of black women's food work that are rooted in the still-prevalent tropes of Aunt Jemima and Mammy. In the weeks leading up to the viewing of this film, we read and viewed foundational pieces by Patricia Hill Collins, Psyche Williams-Forson, Toni Tipton-Martin, Jessica B. Harris, Patricia Turner, and Rebecca Sharpless. In preparation for our direct discussion of the film, we read the Association of Black Women Historians' "An Open Statement to the Fans of *The Help*" and other critical reviews and viewed a snippet of a recent conversation that took place at The New School between black feminist cultural critic and scholar bell hooks and *MSNBC* host and professor Melissa Harris-Perry. In this piece, Harris-Perry and hooks engage in a rousing, funny, and thought-provoking discussion about the cultural work done by films like *The Butler* and *The Help*:

> bell hooks: What I am tired of in general is sentimentality. James Baldwin said sentimentality is the ostentatious parading of excessive and spurious emotion. It is the mark of dishonesty, the inability to feel. . . . [B]ut why is there this obsession at this historical moment with sentimentality and melodrama? 'Cause you know my favorite melodrama is *Imitation of Life*. [Says in a melodramatic, high-pitched, pleading voice:] "Mama, mama . . . I did love you!! I did love you!" [Pause, audience laughs. And then back in her usual tone:] But again, Mama don't get to hear that 'cause she dead. . . . I mean what are your thoughts on that . . . this upsurge in sentimental portraits of blackness?

> Melissa Harris-Perry: OK, so there's *Django* on the one hand, and then there's *The Butler* and, god help me, *The Help*. [The audience responds with a collective groan.]

> bell hooks: All of which are sentimental.

> Melissa Harris-Perry: Yes, right . . . so I'm just trying to think through this. It certainly felt to me like *The Help* and *The Butler* are popular culture responding to the angst of the possibility of not only black empowerment in the personhood of President Obama, but also the desire for the "magical Negro"

to reappear to make things better. So that the Tea Party can actively, just weeks after President Obama's inauguration, can take to the Mall in anger about a 10 percent unemployment rate. When we know that a 10 percent unemployment rate for black people would be cause for like Juneteenth. . . . [W]e would be happy. So I presume that part of what happens then, why we need *The Butler*, why we need *The Help* . . . and I'm gonna pause and think that maybe this is also why we need to bring back slavery, but I'm not sure. I'll think about it. But maybe the reason we need to engage with them in our fictional and emotional lives is because those Negroes, they solved the problems of America through their willingness to sacrifice for the American project.[1]

After viewing the clip, one of the students said quite loudly and with great gusto, "She's so sassy. I just love it!" I was taken aback by this comment, partly because the student had come in late and missed my spiel to the class about appropriate classroom discussion etiquette.[2] In fact, her in-class engagement style was the motivation for the spiel in the first place.[3] But more importantly, I saw her comment as a distinct minimizing of the depth and thoughtfulness with which both hooks and Harris-Perry engaged the ideas. Indeed, this self-identified wealthy white student's palpable desire to know, consume, and enjoy black culture was often accompanied by an equally passionate (though perhaps unconscious) effort to reduce it to small tasty bites.[4] The complexity of hooks's and Harris-Perry's thoughts boiled down to an exclamation of appreciation of the performance—deemed simply irreverent, funny, and sassy.

> **sassy** \sa-sē\ *adj sass·i·er; -est* [alt of *saucy*] (1833) **1:** impudent, saucy. **2:** vigorous, lively **3:** distinctively smart and stylish.
> **¹sass** \sas\ *n* [alter of *sauce*] (1835): impudent speech
> **²sass** *vt* (1856): to talk impudently or disrespectfully to[5]
> *****
> **sas·sy** [sas-ee]
> adjective, sas·si·er, sas·si·est. Informal.
> 1. impertinent; insolent; saucy: a sassy reply; a sassy teen.
> 2. pert; boldly smart; saucy: a sassy red handbag.
> *Origin:*
> 1830–1835, Americanism; alteration of saucy

Related forms:
sas·si·ness, noun
sas·si·ly, adverb[6]

After class, I reflected on that "sassy" comment for the rest of the evening. I did so in light of *The Help*, in which the character Minnie Jackson is known for her wonderful cooking (especially her facility with pie baking) and for being "sass mouthed." Her skill in the kitchen gets her jobs as a domestic worker in the Jim Crow–era Jackson, Mississippi, where the film is set, but her impudence gets her fired. Indeed, in the pivotal moment of the film Minnie serves Miss Hilly a "special pie" as a payback for firing her and bad-mouthing her to all the other white women.[7] Unfortunately, even in the act of retribution (which was supposed to secretly fulfill her desires for revenge), Minnie is unable to keep her mouth shut in the face of Miss Hilly's continued denigration. Minnie is then met with even more abuse from her husband when he returns home that evening fuming with the news that Minnie had potentially ruined her chances of finding domestic work ever again. He beats her in that moment and then eventually forces her to take their eldest daughter out of school to work as a domestic to earn the money Minnie would have been earning to help maintain the household. In a subsequent scene (quoted at length in the opening epigraph), we see Minnie schooling her daughter on the importance of holding her tongue: "Don't sass!," she admonishes. "Don't eat with the same utensils. Don't let your hand touch theirs when you serve them coffee," and on and on. She's telling/instructing her daughter: know your place.

The Help has been well and thoroughly critiqued by scholars and film/cultural critics for its deeply problematic portrayal of the life of black female domestics and their relationship to their white female employers and charges in the Jim Crow South.[8] These critics have also noted the way in which the film's representation of men is grossly inaccurate in the sense that white men are curiously benign and black men are primarily either shadowy or violent. Furthermore, the critics have bemoaned the antiseptic rendering of the violence of the time, experienced not just "in the streets" (lynchings, beatings, arson, generalized terror) but also in the homes (endemic sexual assault of black women by white men). And finally, *The Help* centers on the narrative of the white female protagonist who appears as catalyst for change and uplift in the everyday lives of the black female domestics. The novel and the film create, as bell hooks and Melissa Harris-Perry assert, a sentimental portrait of this time in our recent history in order to do double work: to soften our look back and to cloud our current vision of the continued violence and inequalities we face as African-descendant peoples.

In this chapter, I want to take a small sliver of this, um, pie. I want to begin by thinking through the Minnie Jackson character to illuminate the degree to which this one particular expression of black women's food work continues to have resonance in our collective imaginations—both lovingly and with disdain. Then I move into a discussion of how one real-life black woman chef navigates this terrain in her representations and self-representations. In both cases, I argue that the representation of black women's food work hinges on a cultural desire to consume the delicious products of that labor while actively obscuring the material conditions under which it is created.

The Sassy Black Cook

When Minnie Jackson is unable to find another domestic job after her run-in with Miss Hilly, she turns (on the advice of her best friend, Aibileen Clark) to the outcast white female, Celia Foote, for domestic employment. The Celia Foote character, a caricature of the Marilyn Monroe persona, plays on a series of dualities of white womanhood: sexy/childlike, naive/wise, vulnerable/strong. She enters into the town and into the narrative of the film as the "poor white trash" girl who marries up. She is unfamiliar with the ways of ladyhood in the middle-class Jackson, Mississippi, community and is naively trying to find her place within it. The sexual rivalry between Miss Hilly and Miss Celia thwarts her movement into society, creating a buffer zone that serves as a safe space of domestic employment for Minnie Jackson.

The relationship that develops between Minnie Jackson and Celia Foote depends upon them revealing a series of "secrets," both large and small, to each other. Miss Celia's largest secret is that she has been unable to maintain a pregnancy and has miscarried multiple times. She refuses to tell her husband, "Mr. Johnnie," and buries the fetuses in a part of the yard off the back porch of their home, marking each grave with a rose bush. The smallest of Miss Celia's secrets is that she is unable to cook or to maintain the large plantation-style home her husband has inherited from his family. Minnie Jackson's smallest secret is that she is being physically abused by her husband and refuses to take her children and leave him. Her largest secret is that after being fired by Miss Hilly, she served her the "special pie" in an act of revenge—what is referred to in the film repeatedly as "the terrible awful."

As many critics have noted, these two characters' interactions provide a great deal of levity to the film, serving as a distraction from the grave situation that black women as domestic workers and blacks as subjugated people experienced during this time. From the perspective of representations of black women's food work, I was also struck by the ways in which these two characters so closely resembled the kinds of representations of the black mammy cook that were prevalent in popular culture and advertisements of that era.[9] Miss Celia is the childlike white woman who turns to the black woman to comfort and guide her into her rightful place in society. Minnie, while critical of the role she is to play in society, responds to it in innocuous ways: back-talking, being humorous, being sassy, finding a sense of comfort and purpose in the cooking of food, and taking her task of molding the white woman into respectability with great seriousness.[10]

In the following scene, Minnie Jackson is teaching Celia Foote how to fry chicken. It begins with Minnie in the kitchen, looking out of the window at the chicken coop, where Ms. Celia emerges with a live chicken in one hand and an axe in the other. Ms. Celia places the chicken on the stump and raises the axe. The camera switches back to Minnie just as we hear the thud of the beheading. Minnie shudders and walks away from the window. When they regroup at the kitchen counter, presumably after Miss Celia and/or Minnie pluck and clean the bird, they proceed with the lesson:

MINNIE: So, what can you cook? (She adds seasoning to flour in a big paper sack on the counter.)

CELIA: Oh, um ... I can cook corn pone, boil potatoes ... um, I can do grits. (Says the last in an excited tone.)

MINNIE: (Laughs, shaking her head.) ... Well, I reckon' if there's anything you ought to know about cookin' is this ... (holds up a can of Crisco shortening), the most important invention since they put mayonnaise in a jar. (She takes the can of Crisco and goes to the stove with Celia following her.)

MINNIE: You got gum in yo' hair? Got a squeaky door hinge? Crisco . . . (as she puts two big spoonfuls of shortening in a hot cast-iron skillet).

CELIA: (Giggles and oohs and aahs as she looks at the pan of quickly melting Crisco.) How pretty . . . (touches the still solid bits of Crisco with her fingers and rubs it between her thumb and index finger). . . . Looks like frosting.

MINNIE: Got bags under your eyes? Wanna soften your husband's scaly feet? Mmm-hmm (murmurs low and melodic). . . . Crisco. But . . . (sighing deeply, softly) . . . it's best for fryin' chicken. (Smiles while shaking her head and looking down at the process of seasoning and putting the chicken in the brown bag). Fryin' chicken just tend to make you feel better about life (pause). At least me anyway. Mmh. . . . I just love me some fried chicken.

In the next scene we see Minnie sitting at the small kitchen table prepared to eat her fried chicken lunch when Celia comes in with her plate and walks decidedly over to the kitchen table. It is a scene that we are led to understand has happened again and again. Seemingly ignorant of their social distance, Celia wants to sit and eat with Minnie. But Minnie knows better:

MINNIE: (Stands up and pushes her chair back.) We done been over this Miss Celia. You supposed to eat in the dining room. That's how it work. Here, let me take your plate back . . . (she reaches for the plate).

CELIA: (Pulls the plate back out of her grasp.) No, I'm fine right here Minnie. (Celia looks Minnie straight in the eye. For the first time not laughing or giggling.)

MINNIE: (Reluctantly sits back down.)

CELIA: (Takes a bite out of a chicken leg and begins chewing the crispy bird. The skin crackles as she eats, and she shakes her head.) I just want you to know I'm real grateful you're here. (She says this with a look of great admiration and relief.)

MINNIE: You gots plenty more to be grateful about than me. And look, I ain't messin' around no more. Now, Mr. Johnnie gonna catch me here and shoot me dead right here on this no-wax floor. You gots to tell him. Ain't he wonderin' how the cookin' so good?

In addition to these scenes playing as a (perhaps) tongue-in-cheek commercial for Crisco shortening, they are also an homage to a particular relationship (whether real and imagined) between white women, black women cooks, and food.[11] It is through the food, rendered somehow uncomplicated by race and class injustice, that these women find connection, friendship, even kinship. Indeed, in another scene in Miss Celia's kitchen, we see her putting a cold compress to a wound on Minnie's temple and advising her to just leave her husband. It is in the kitchen that these two women—"white-trash" girl-woman and troubled black cook—find common ground.[12] In one of the final scenes of the film we see this story-line wrap-up with Mr. Johnnie revealing to Minnie (as she walks to their home with a bag of groceries) that he knows of her working in their household.[13] He expresses his gratitude at her being there and saving his wife's life through her cooking and her care. And when they return to the plantation-like home, Minnie is surprised by the elaborate meal laid out in the main dining room for her—all cooked by Miss Celia. As they encourage Minnie to sit and eat, they assure her that as long as she wants she has a secure place of employment with them and their family. In a voice-over after this scene, we learn that because of this experience of largesse with Miss Celia and Mr. Johnnie, Minnie finds the strength to take her children and leave her abusive husband.

The Minnie Jackson character epitomizes the sassy black cook who shoots off her mouth, wisecracks, has a lot of folk knowledge, is often pleasantly plump, and knows her way around a frying pan. This imagery is carefully crafted, welcomed, and rewarded within a white-dominated media, both historically and contemporarily.[14] If, as many scholars have argued, these "controlling images" have material consequences in the lives of black women in general, what may be the specific implications for black women who cook professionally?[15] In what ways are black female culinary professionals and culinary personalities operating within and against images of their work predominated by Mammy, Aunt Jemima, and what I'm calling "the sassy black cook"?

Chef Carla Hall: Sassy Black Cook
and the Return of the Magical Negress

At the height of the controversy surrounding television celebrity and chef Paula Deen's fall from grace, Carla Hall, co-host and chef on the ABC daytime show *The Chew*, tweeted: "I love you and I support you @ Paula_Deen."[16] Several days later, some members of the cast of *The Chew* gathered together to reflect and respond to the allegations of racism being levied at Paula Deen. The co-hosts sitting around the table on the set of the show each spoke about their experiences with Paula Deen and made efforts to provide a different perspective than the one that had been circulating quite rapidly throughout the media.[17] Each of them talked of how they knew Paula Deen personally and had never experienced her as racist and, indeed, found her to be the most kind and loving person they knew. Chef Carla Hall was the last to speak and offered this reflection:

> Being a black person who was raised and grew up in the south, I . . . knowing Paula . . . and when I heard it . . . I put a tweet out sayin': "I love you and I support you." And that got a backlash. And I think it's about intent. You can say "orange" to me, but if I feel a negative, hateful intent, I'm gonna be hurt. I mean I don't care if it's the "n . . ." . . . I mean I would not like to hear the "n-word" [says this quickly before moving on]. But the other thing is . . . forgiveness is power. And that's what was just in my heart when I read all of this. And basically, I just want to say: How powerful are you? At the end of the day, how powerful are you to forgive somebody and move on? Because unless we can tackle this and move on . . . and forgive it and not stay in a place, then this will always be an issue; it's always going to be this simmering thing.[18]

As the only African American on the show, Chef Carla was positioned as "the voice" of black people. Her reference to markers of black authenticity (being born and raised in the South and not being a stranger to the use of the "n-word") were intended to make her narrative of love and forgiveness more impactful. Certainly, if *she* can forgive and move on, then the rest of us—black, white, orange—can do the same.

As disappointing as Carla Hall's reflections were, her position was not surprising. Indeed, in her meteoric rise from local D.C. caterer[19] to contestant on the popular Bravo television series *Top Chef* to co-host on the ABC-network show *The Chew*, she has been cultivating herself (or has been cultivated) as a spiritual guide and a fun-loving girl guru. During season 5, known as "the season of love," she was dubbed "Kooky Carla" and developed the reputation as the chef who cooked with love.[20] In the reunion show for that season we see a montage of her persona:[21]

HOST: Carla, we got a lot of questions about your food, but we got so many more just about you. Take a look at "Kooky Carla."
[The video begins with vaguely mystical-sounding music and a collage of images of Carla Hall in meditative poses and doing yoga.]

CHEF CARLA: It is so important for me to get centered and truly reaching out to my spirit guides.
[As the voice-over plays, we continue to see her doing yoga poses, sitting with her eyes closed as in deep meditation.
We see a clip from the show when one of the cheftestants (a white male chef) is in the kitchen of their living quarters and she's sitting on the sofa. He asks her: "What are you doing; meditating, Carla?"
She responds, "I was just getting centered." Shrugging her shoulders and shaking her head.
Another cheftestant (a white female) is reflecting on Carla: "She's very spiritual and she's very calming." Cut back to interview with Carla.]

CHEF CARLA: I make food good by putting my heart and love into it.
[Goes to voice-over where we see Carla plating in the professional kitchen.]

[Then cut to a scene at the judges' table, where Carla is explaining why it's not important that her dish did not turn out perfectly.]

CHEF CARLA: My dishes aren't quite what I want them to be, so I'm just going to send out some love with this stuff that I'm giving you.

CHEF TOM COLLICHIO: [With a smirky smile and a tone of confusion] How can your enjoyment impart the enjoyment . . . ?

CHEF CARLA: [Responds with a somewhat southern tang] That is my belief, Tom![22]

The montage goes on to show scenes of Carla singing, dancing, meditating, breaking the tension amongst her co-cheftestants with sing-a-longs and "hootie-hoo" lessons, and ultimately wooing the judges with a combination of her zany personality and solid cooking skills. While she becomes one of the finalists (along with two white male cheftestants) based in part on her ability to cook good food consistently, what propels her onto the national stage is her ability to perform a certain self.[23] As regular viewers of these sorts of season-long reality cooking contests on *Bravo*, *The Food Network*, and *The Cooking Channel* know, the work of the shows' producers is to create characters who the audience will want to watch week after week. Chef Carla became a character who was non-threatening, trustworthy, self-effacing, and loving.

On *The Chew* Carla continues to codify her brand and present as a fun-loving, kooky, zany person.[24] She breaks into song in the middle of cooking demos, she will stop plating a dish to do a dance across the stage, and she is often in situations where she is the brunt of some lighthearted prank that makes fun of her height (tall) or her body (lanky). Even though she does not physically conform to the stereotyped image of a black woman doing food work (she is fair skinned, tall, and thin), her on-camera personality has many shades of "sassy." For instance, on an episode themed "It's a Fried Day," Carla is doing a fried chicken demo.[25] I was initially drawn to her narrative surrounding the demo because it offered a potentially layered representation of middle-class black life. Carla describes visiting her grandmother in New York City and how she would take her to see shows like the musical *Bubblin' Brown Sugar*. But as she mentions this, Carla breaks into the musical's theme song and does a dance before continuing on with detailing her grandmother's fried chicken technique. As a black woman viewer, I would have appreciated less levity in her description of this moment because it offered a potentially different vision of the black grandmother—a woman who is urbane, cultured, and a good cook—than is held in our popular imagination.[26] Instead, Carla tends to present a narrative of self and food that strives to comfort a seemingly predominately white female audience.

I do comfort food. Even though I'm from the south (Nashville, TN) I don't really want be known for Southern food. I like all kinds of food. A lot of the food we gravitate towards is comfort food. I just want to be known for food that hugs you, that inspires you to get back into the kitchen and take your power back. I consider it an honor to cook food for people and I take it very seriously. If I cook something for you, you're saying you trust me to make something good. So what I want to do is inspire. . . . We went through a phase when women were too proud to cook but now we're getting back into the kitchen and with shows like this and the Food Network and Bravo people are starting to experiment more. It's about good food.[27]

It is because of Carla's performance of her food work at these particular intersections of race and gender that her success is, at the moment, well established. Her line of petite cookies (produced out of her company *Alchemy*) are now being sold at the Manhattan upscale Italian food marketplace *Eataly* (which is one of Mario Batali's ventures), at the *Whole Foods* market, and through her own website (CookingWithLove).[28] In addition to the two cookbooks under the *The Chew* imprint, Carla also has two individually authored cookbooks and has appeared on various television talk programs touting her "Philosophy of Love" in the kitchen.[29] She also has an endorsement deal with *Kraft* foods, appearing in print and television ads. And most recently, she successfully completed a KickStarter campaign to fund her new restaurant *Carla Hall's Southern Kitchen*—with 1,550 backers pledging $264,703.[30] So Carla Hall, as a food personality, has entered into the world of celebrity chefs. She has built a brand—herself—that utilizes many racialized and gendered stereotypes of black women and food work: being happy and entertaining, providing sustenance that is emotional, spiritual, and nutritive to her charges, sustaining her cultural heritage through foodways, and doing the work for love—love trumps everything.

But does it?

Carla's Paula Deen tweet, her subsequent performance of racial forgiveness in the scripted *The Chew* conversation, and the ongoing development of her public food persona make sense in this so-called post-race, post-feminist moment. Carla can claim her authenticity as a black southern-born and southern-raised woman, while at the same time disavowing the realities of her own middle-class upbringing and the material consequences of the sort of racism on which Paula Deen's empire has been built. Chef Carla can also allude to women's desire to leave the kitchen as a site of (past) oppression only to encourage them to now reclaim their "power" within it. But which women can do that work?

In the aftermath of the Deen "n-word" controversy, *some* greater scrutiny was given to Deen's exploitation of black women cooks long in her employ.[31] What these reporters and social commentators describe is a contemporary, real-life manifestation of the story romanticized in films like *The Help*, *The Butler*, and the original *Imitation of Life*. It is here where we meet Paula Deen's "soul sister," Dora Charles, who has worked for Deen more than twenty years, playing key creative and technical roles in the kitchens of each of her businesses but, reportedly, receiving very little in terms of compensation and recognition for her labors. So the real story here is about more than the use of racist language, more than assessing intent in using that language, and more than forgiving past mistakes.

Unfortunately, speaking from the position of Carla's carefully crafted public persona, this reality is elided. What we are left with is a sentimental plea to forgive rather than a call to never forget the continued invisible labors of black women cooking in other women's kitchens for their profit and their comfort.[32]

Coda: On Being and Not Being Sassy

In the spring of 2012, reporter Christopher Borelli wrote a piece for the *Chicago Tribune* on the lack of representation of African Americans in the now seemingly glamorous world of professional food production. That article, "Where Are the Black Chefs?," inspired a PBS feature on the same topic where they interviewed fifteen "culinary insiders" to get their take on why black chefs were not frequently represented in mainstream culinary television programming or in leadership positions within top restaurants, even as the numbers of African Americans attending culinary programs has been on the rise. In that PBS feature, under the theme "The Relevance of Color," the following appears:

Embedded within our discussion of *Culinary Masters and Representation* is the subject of race. It's [sic] relevance today is highly debated. There are cases of typecasting in the industry that exist today like Chef Tanya Holland who left her show at a top network because she was asked to be more "sassy." But how large of a role does race play on a person's advancement in the industry? What glass ceilings exist, if any, and is race still a determining factor? The subject of race remains a sensitive topic with varying opinions about its influence.[33]

Although the majority of the culinary professionals and personalities interviewed by PBS were women, the salience of race as an organizing principle, with no mention of gender, is striking.[34] At the same time, Tanya Holland is quoted as saying her reasons for leaving the cooking show she hosted on a top network were linked to her presentation of self—not being "sassy" enough—and this makes it clear that her expected performance of food work was intimately linked to our cultural notions of gender, race, and class.

Black women food workers at all levels in both real and imagined spaces must always contend with the limiting notions of their craft, skill, and presentation of self. Minnie Jackson *and* Carla Hall are fictional representations of an elemental relationship in US culture between black women who cook and the seemingly white public who consume the food and are entertained and comforted by those cooks. Nearly 150 years post Emancipation, it is long past time to amplify our efforts to resist, change, and complicate the Mammy and Aunt Jemima figures in our public imagination in ways that allow for continued appreciation of black women's food work while also recognizing the material conditions of that labor.[35] This is necessary not just for black women food workers (historically and contemporarily) but for the countless numbers of black, Latino, and Asian women and men who labor in our kitchens, restaurants, and fields to bring good food to the table.

CHAPTER 9

Mighty Matriarchs Kill It with a Skillet

Critically Reading Popular Representations of Black Womanhood and Food

JESSICA KENYATTA WALKER

Representations of what constitutes and challenges notions of authentic Black life have always found a home on American mainstream television. From the sitcom household to the college dorm, the spaces where Black life is represented have spread to a wide audience, constructing the viewers' conception of what Black people do and say. Nonetheless, few TV shows have focused on representing or critiquing the culinary practices purportedly representing authentic Black life. Very little attention has been given to the televisual kitchen space for the way it communicates ideologies like domesticity while constructing notions of race, class, and gender through performances of food preparation. This chapter partially fills that gap by examining the television show *My Momma Throws Down* (MMTD), which emerged in May 2012 as the first of its kind, only to be cancelled after its first season.

MMTD distinguishes itself from other cooking competition shows because of its intent to showcase the amateur cooking abilities of Black mothers. This idea presupposes a natural affiliation between Blackness, motherhood, and exceptional cooking. These are tropes that comprise the dominant catchall category for African American culinary expression—soul food. Yet, I argue, it is this slippage between Black motherhood, cooking ability, and soul food that invites a deeper reading into the show's construction of an authentic Black life. MMTD represents an intriguing set of interactions in a Black televisual kitchen new to food programming.

The interstices of race, class, gender, and food are deployed discursively and formally in televisual spaces, shaping narratives around what counts as authentic identity. This chapter critiques how MMTD presents and challenges narratives of Black authenticity through representations of soul food. Of particular concern are the ways Black women, through the logics of mammy stereotypes, are figured as authentic in relation to the food they prepare, the way it is judged, the appearance of their personal kitchens, and the use of emblematic kitchen utensils that identify what counts and doesn't count as soul food and, by extension, authentic Blackness.

In order to disentangle these interconnected concepts, this chapter draws from Douglas Kellner's three-pronged approach to analyzing multiculturalism in media culture.[1] This includes a consideration of the show's production, textual analysis of the meanings it produces and circulates, and exploration of audience response. Using textual analysis of select scenes while situating the emergence of MMTD on TV One, I trace how the varied meanings of mammy, health, and class circulate within the show's limited but noteworthy audience response.

Scenes are read backward from the image to reveal the ways dominant cultural rules and expectations structure the representation of Blackness. This analysis is grounded in Herman Gray's pivotal observation that television is a discursive site through which choices over the meaning(s) of Blackness are pursued.[2] This chapter examines just a few of these choices made in the production of the show, analyzing how they presuppose larger ideological scripts that frame what Black women's cooking practices are supposed to look like. The spectacle of the televisual kitchens begs a reading that Sarah Murray notes includes "cultural or ideological analyses" of "niche food television."[3] In doing so I argue that networks like TV One make claims to Black authenticity through associations between Black women and soul food that both adhere to and diverge from dominant scripts.

The Show

Courtesy of the production team that brought you nonstop gladiatorial battles such as *Iron Chef* and *Iron Chef America*, TV One's *My*

Momma Throws Down (MMTD) promised similar culinary face-offs where "mighty matriarchs [had] to kill it with a skillet and dominate the opposition." Nominated by family and friends, contestants were almost all married, heterosexual, Black women with large families.[4] Comedian and host Ralph Harris introduced the "no holds barred cooking battle" that shows the world how these mamas' "knife skills meet their life skills."[5]

In the premier episode, contestant Mama Thea says that food brings happiness to her family, who "live to eat."[6] But she reminds us not to get into her pots, and that, while she is "fun," she is also "no nonsense." She accentuates her point by hitting a cast-iron skillet against the palm of her hand while staring menacingly into the camera, saying: "I know my way is the best way, and I have to be right all the time. And if I'm right about this time, I'm gonna win this competition!"

Mama Thea's competitive spirit contrasts with the more subdued spirit of her challenger, Mama Marilyn, a mother of two daughters who believes her passion for cooking keeps everyone happy and full. She's not as rambunctious as Mama Thea, but she cautions the viewer not to underestimate her, saying, "You don't have to be loud and outright . . . to be competitive." Yet, when Ralph Harris asks Marilyn if she's going to win, she raises an eyebrow, points to Mama Thea, and jests, "Yeah, no disrespect, but keep it moving!" The introduction of each competitor is lighthearted and jovial, peppered with a palatable showing of sass and self-confidence.

In a series intended to showcase the talents of Black female cooks, both women move within somewhat expected stereotypes of sassiness, down-home vernacular, and motherly pride. This representation of Black food is intimately tied to a scripted notion of soul food's compulsory association with Black womanhood. These scripts rely heavily on "commonsense" narratives that, while offering limited definitional value, are in fact complicated by a close reading of the way the women articulate their food philosophies and interact with kitchen objects and of the standards by which they are judged. Despite the fact that the contestants use their own words, we cannot underestimate the way that introductions presuppose "sass" as simply part of how Black women cooks operate. As Psyche Williams-Forson notes, the effort to represent authentic Black life through food on television and in film (mamas have knife skills, mamas are competitive, mamas brandish knives in kitchens) often reproduces stereotypical cultural logics, so that "authenticity" and racial stereotypes are often intricately entwined in visual representations.[7]

Common Sense and TV One

MMTD was broadcast on a network where the desire to see the "authentic" Black life is negotiated within industry structures that index authenticity through carefully considered niche markets. Developed by Radio One and the Comcast-owned niche mini-network TV One, the show taps into the popularity of food competition shows such as *Top Chef*, *Chopped*, and *Master Chef*.[8] Together, Comcast, Radio One, and TV One illustrate the increased consolidation of smaller media producers into the paradigms of larger media conglomerates. This shift has had significant implications for depictions of social difference. Each outlet must give the appearance of diverse programming that reaches Latino, Asian, LGBT, and Black minority markets, while in reality the programming is developed under the same umbrella corporation. In 2007, the then president of TV One, Jonathan Rodgers, explained how this structure affects Black TV programming, saying, "When all we had was BET, they had to be everything to everybody. Why do we, the people who watch the most TV, have only two channels?"[9] In implying that increasing Black programming choice means increased political representation, Rodgers is affirming a long-held logic that diverts attention away from the false promise of corporations. In offering a broad range of programming choices, TV One bills itself as a corrective to other networks that do not seriously take on the complexity of Black life.

Yet, at the same time that this channel purports to offer diversity, company promotions show a push to reinforce simplified scripts of Black homogeneity. For example, Catherine Pinkeney, executive vice president for programming and production at TV One, said, "I have this theory that whatever show we make, however we choose to tell the story, our viewers know it's someone who cares about their lives and their culture."[10] Here Blackness is homogenous ("their lives . . . culture"), drawing on a commonsense notion of race that defines the way it is discussed in the public sphere. "Common sense," according to David Lyonel Smith (applying Antonio Gramsci's analysis) is a collection of "habit, superstition, fact, hearsay, dissent, (and) prejudice" that conforms to produce a feeling about how we "know who and what is truly black."[11] The relationship between race and cultural products is readily legible, so that we can easily recognize what is made for and by Black people and what is not. Beyond simply doing "a show with black people," as Pinkeney notes, TV One is also relying on a commonsense ideology in order to produce shows that aim "to be honest and authentic."[12] While these concepts are not stable, it begs the question, How does the network's attempt to show authentic Black life translate to the food the mamas prepare on the show?

My Mammy Throws Down

MMTD cannot escape the ever-present "mammy" trope that lurks in the background of the American imaginary that envisions what Black women's kitchen work looks like, including how food is cooked, what food is cooked, who is doing the eating, and how Black women are supposed to feel about the cooking. Her pervasive presence on pancake boxes, trading cards, dolls, cookie jars, and much more means that if we want to investigate the puzzle of how Blackness and womanhood get attached to the preparation of certain food stuffs, we have to look at mammy.[13] However, it would be simplistic and limiting to name the contestants on MMTD as recapitulated mammies. Instead I consider how this icon haunts the legibility of these figures. Mammy is not in the frame per se, but her defining characteristics (sass, amateur cooking ability, nurturing and joyful character) do indeed cast a shadow on this televisual kitchen, translating what we see into a popular narrative of Blackness, womanhood, food, and authenticity.

The show relies upon mammy tropes, common sense, and soul food discourse to show the "authentic" Black life. But this has to be negotiated within industry structures that commoditize authenticity and are supported by commonsense notions of race that circulate in a public sphere and organize social difference. Through representations of contestants' kitchen spaces, signifying battles, and an ever-present sass, the show quickly locates itself within a scripted narrative of soul food that, I argue, is intended to represent authentic Black collectivity through its proximity to a *certain kind* of Black womanhood.

Why Mammy Is Important on MMTD

Mammy is not only a caricature to be vilified, but an important guide-post for how to understand the complicated interconnections of nostalgia, popular media, race, consumption, and domesticity in terms of Black womanhood.

The mammy figure is a versatile and flexible symbol of southern antebellum domestic nostalgia mythologized in the American imagination through the dolls, films, and cookie jars that bear her image.[14] Her pervasive presence after Reconstruction was fueled by the success of Aunt Jemima pancake mix advertisements, introducing her to a new level of mainstream commercial media presence.[15] Not all mammies look alike or were used for the same product, but that doesn't seem to matter as the image has such a "provocative and tenacious hold on the America psyche."[16] Even if the body, sass, and iconic kerchief are not there, the nature of an icon of her caliber is that, like a cheat sheet, she assists in making what we see on TV, in cookbooks, and in magazines comprehensible. However, it would simplistic to name the contestants on MMTD as versions of mammies. Instead I consider how this icon haunts the legibility of these figures, eliciting a tension between discomfort and familiarity.

In an attempt to reach niche markets, executives at TV One may have underestimated the extent to which audiences would both abhor *and* identify with these mamas. Seeming to recognize the slip between mamas and mammy, one viewer called the show's title "ratchet," and another complained that "we [Black people] don't speak like that," while still others found it an authentic celebration of African American culinary traditions.[17] The food on the show, however, is one of many factors that might influence how viewers come to recognize traditional and authentic African American cuisine.

The Uncommon Eggplant: Judging Black Food

While most cooking competition shows have clear rubrics, this show is often unclear about the standard against which the cooks are measured. This is evidenced in the first episode of MMTD when both mothers are challenged to cook a predetermined main dish (squash casserole and green salad), as well as their own signature dish, within a restricted amount of time, while family members, positioned behind the mamas as they cook, look on and cheer. The dishes are then evaluated by four different judges on every show. These judges ranged from food scholars to television and film personalities and Black celebrity chefs. Actresses Nicole Ari Parker, Malinda Williams, Vanessa Williams, and African American foodways scholar Jessica B. Harris served as judges for the pilot episode. While judges from other cooking competition shows evaluate dishes based on presentation, technique, or creativity, the judges for MMTD often had unclear rubrics.

This lack of a clear rubric leaves the judges free to articulate a cohesive, stable narrative of African American food. Asked what she is looking for in contestants' cooking, Harris states, "Well, I'm really looking for dishes that really talk about the rich history of African-American food and who we are and where we're from on the plate."[18] The statement, although short, contains many assertions about what constitutes African American food and what does not. In this view, the history of African American food, although rich, is singular, and the past of all African Americans is unified ("where we're from") into a neat collectivity able to be plated and consumed. Echoing Pikeney, Harris's expectations of the food denote a version of a consumable Black authenticity that can at least symbolically indicate collective origins.

The audience gains a somewhat clearer definition of what constitutes Black food traditions when the mamas present their signature dishes to the judges. While Mama Marilyn cooks baked macaroni and cheese with eight cheeses, green peppers, garlic, and fried onions on top, Mama Thea prepares eggplant Parmesan. Mama Thea tells us that in order to get her now adult sons to eat vegetables she would call the golden-brown rounds of sliced eggplant "big chips." In a showoff that could earn the winner $500 cash, the stakes are high as the judges announce the verdict for Mama Thea. There is not enough sauce for

Harris, while Malinda Williams, having never eaten eggplant before, wanted a little more spice, and Vanessa Williams really loved the crispness. Parker also thought Mama Thea's "chips" were delicious, saying, "I just applauded you for figuring out a way to bring uncommon vegetable to the African-American home and making it scrumptious."[19]

The judge's evaluations frame the culinary repertoire of not just Black women but also heterosexuals, mothers and, by extension, the Black community that they are imagined to feed.[20] Harris's conservative interpretation of a unified African American culinary tradition is quickly reaffirmed by Parker, who, in noting that the foodstuff is "uncommon" in the cuisine, is setting the definitional boundaries for what constitutes it. What ideas informed both Harris's and Parker's expectations of what dishes are common to African American culinary tradition?

The judges are not alone in positing a definition of African American food based on terms that are scripted by the idea of soul food.[21] Popularly understood through the familiar story of enslaved Africans transforming the least of master's scraps into savory, life-sustaining dishes, soul food has an almost mythical origin story, unencumbered by its historical inaccuracies. In some ways, these contradictions matter little to the term's ability to create meaning for those who rely on it.[22] Common sense allows these stories to circulate despite their tenuous grasp on history. This serves to reinforce the familiar—the structures through which we think about soul food, as coming from one place or land, void of vegetables or nutrition, and representing a common tradition.

These commonsense narratives are discursively formed and maintained through everyday actions and choices. "Soul food," for instance, is a term developed in a specific cultural moment with different political stakes for connecting unique Black cultural products to a West African past.[23] In the current moment, the origin story of the term is often obfuscated by the term's dual effect of symbolizing Black collectivity and its popular demonization as an unhealthy style of eating. Parker places eggplant outside of the purview of soul food because common sense does not connect soul food to health. However, as Williams-Forson notes, doing so "makes it difficult . . . to accept any variation on this theme," further highlighting the tension between the show's representation of the healthy possibilities of soul food and a narrow definition of a cuisine that excludes eggplant as authentically African American.[24]

While the show reifies commonsense scripts, it can also be a terrain where it is negotiated. The point of this analysis, following bell hooks, is not to differentiate between right and wrong interpretations but, instead, to embrace a transgressive analytical approach.[25] This approach emphasizes the extent to which, as Stuart Hall notes, "Black popular culture is a contradictory space" full of depictions that challenge as well as reaffirm our expectations of what Black life looks like.[26] So while a judge might name a certain vegetable as outside the purview of Black consumption, another may frame the cooking of such vegetable as a part of the diverse and "rich" ways Black people cook and consume. Indeed, the show oscillates between reproducing commonsense notions of soul food (Black people do not eat eggplant) and showing how the contestants cook dishes unique to their families. What binds these diverse foods together is the heterosexual Black female body that cooks them. Within the popular culture space the show creates, her cooking transcends these distinctions, symbolically indexing Black collectivity through Black motherhood.

Cast-Iron Skillets

Consider, for instance, the demonstrations of authenticity that occur in the dizzying transitions in and out of segments and mini-games within the forty-three-minute show.[27] One of the richer segments of the show includes sharing a "lucky item," usually a kitchen utensil that is supposed to bring the competitors good fortune throughout the competition. When asked what lucky item she brought, Mama Marilyn explained that her cast-iron skillet symbolized much more than a cooking tool: "It was my momma's skillet, and I ate a lot of fried chicken and pork chops and all that good stuff out of that skillet. . . . [S]he was such a great, great woman and cook." Mama Thea also brought a cast-iron skillet, and as she busily mixes ingredients she tells us the skillet belonged to her father, who used to make "so many wonderful things." Ultimately, through these skillets, both women connect to a unified cooking tradition.

These segments exhibit the ways authentic African American cooking traditions are scripted through Black women's position as cultural transmitters while also reminding us that this work is never really done in isolation. Here I am less concerned with the familial traditions these objects represent than with the choice to represent them. The explanation of the symbolic value of this object relies on the familiar script of mothers teaching daughters to cook as well as the foodstuffs (fried chicken and pork chops) that belong to the canonical definition of soul food. Still some unexpected moments emerge. Indeed, the cooking wisdom of Black fathers, not a part of the mammy trope, points to a moment when we realize that Black women in the kitchen—although depicted as the sole mighty matriarchs—are never really alone. Family members occasionally take quick taste tests to reassure or to correct a mama's cooking dish, and the culinary teachers, whether male or female, reveal how seemingly solitary cooking practices are indeed interconnected.

Interrogating the "common sense" at play in the show means that the visual field is never neutral, and so the staged moment when both mamas bring the same lucky item is noteworthy. As both women acknowledge the culinary education they received from their parents, they simultaneously articulate their skillet's ability to bring their loved ones into the space, exhibiting the power of material objects to establish continuity of self between past memories, present existence, and future hopes.[28] This centuries-old cooking implement intertwines mothers and grandmothers as culinary teachers, fried chicken and pork chops, and remembrances of the past. As a central object in the scripts of soul food, a cast-iron skillet is made to last for generations; and, as a tool made for open-fire or hearth cooking, is emblematic of traditional African American cooking, reaching in the imagination as far back as the eighteenth-century plantation South.

Often pictured with a mammy or Aunt Jemima, the cast-iron skillet and mammy are not strangers. The object also evokes Harris's seminal text *Iron Pots and Wooden Spoons*, where her own passionate, nostalgic remembrances undergird the historical foodways she recounts in a book that features a cast-iron or heavy skillet in at least thirty-five recipes.[29] Harris's grandmother, too, is mentioned as an important transmitter of cooking wisdom, resonating with the contestants' connection to traditional African American cooking and womanhood.

The relationship between object, race, gender, and food in this segment is a discursive one. The cast-iron skillet was not created for the Black woman cook, but its affiliation with southern food traditions makes it an undeniably important utensil for the cooking of soul food dishes. These taken-for-granted associations are used to bolster the show's claims toward authentic traditions that speak to the nostalgic and reductive view of soul food, while also adding an unexpected element—the presence of family and fathers "helping" these matriarchs kill it with their skillets.

The show articulates a unified soul food tradition through Mammy—the closest referent in American popular media for articulating Black women's relationship to food. Although the contestants don't become mammies in the process of the representation, the always-in-the-background mammy provides an entry through which the show asserts claims toward Black authenticity. Indeed, if sass, cast irons, and menacing gestures with kitchen knives were not depicted as inherent to Black cooking, then the imagined Black audience of the show would be forced to grapple with its own desire for a constructed notion of authentic Black food through a reliance on this trope of the mammy.[30] In other words, the absence of a figure proximal to the mammy would unsettle the common sense she embodies. Working backward from the image illustrates how Black collectivity is imagined through the symbolic attachment of food to Black womanhood rather than through an understanding that the food comes with always already made meaning.[31]

Cooking Class in the Kitchen

When contestants explain the meaning of their cooking practices in their own words and within their own kitchen spaces, performances of class intersect with discourses on health to further complicate which foods authentically attach themselves to Black identity. As Patricia Hill Collins notes, Black women are uniquely positioned to shoulder the "gender-specific" representations that distinguish "poor- and working-class authenticity and middle-class respectability." On

MMTD these differences are indicated through contestants' investments in preparing healthy foods.[32]

The material objects that fill the contestants' kitchen spaces reveal classed cooking practices. In the third episode, Mamas Natascha Sherrod and Avarita Hanson battle it out, making "Crab Cakes and Green Tomatoes." As the show transitions to a segment introducing the cooks, we see Mama Natascha in her home kitchen, adding seasoning to what looks like three simmering ground-beef patties. The mother of four goes on to explain that she cooks because it makes her family "feel good." The kitchen she works in is moderately sized, with modest cabinetry (a drawer is missing on one fixture) and countertops, two microwaves, and a dishwasher; and she cooks on a flat four-range surface stove using one pan and fork to transform ground meat into a juicy burger. We then see her with her arms wrapped around her young son, who is holding a plate with the burger on a white bread bun with bright red ketchup gushing out of the sides. She asks her son, "Is it good?" Silenced by a mouthful of hamburger, he enthusiastically bobs his head up and down and gives the camera a thumbs up.

Her competitor, Mama Avarita Hanson, is a self-described "real-life Claire Huxtable" who is an attorney by day and a "grandiose" chef for her husband and two sons by night. Footage of her working in her kitchen elicits a sharp contrast to her competitor's space. Tall mahogany cabinetry, crisp white marble counter tops, and stainless steel appliances, including a double oven and a six-burner range with a warming drawer, surround Mama Avarita as she cooks. She narrates the images, describing her interest in healthy cooking as the result of a recent battle with breast cancer. To Mama Avarita "cooking means fellowship," but it is also a hobby to which she has dedicated much time and energy. She reminds us she's there to win, saying, "I've been cooking a long time; I read cookbooks; I have had dinner parties; I do a lot of cooking. In fact, I give my caterers recipes, and so I really like to win."[33]

In contrast to Mama Natascha's use of one pot, utensil, and seasoning to make her meal, Mama Avarita uses two different pots, including a teal Dutch oven. She makes selections casually from a waist-high, pullout spice cabinet containing at least twenty different spices. Her family is seated at a marble island, dressed in business casual as they eat from mini dessert glassware. Although their kitchen spaces denote different class locations, they both perform an intriguing gesture ending the segment. In a kind of visual mimicry, both women slash or jab through the air with butcher knives while posturing with menacing smirks as we hear dubbed audio of them declaring their competitive and tough nature. We are not to mess with them.[34]

These images serve to punctuate the show's emphasis on the natural mothering abilities of these sassy, resilient contestants, indexing traces of mammy's no-nonsense approach to having complete dominion of her kitchen space. This makes one wonder to what extent these images rely upon what Williams-Forson calls a "historical stereotype with modern day currency."[35]

Healthy eating and class position constitute an added dimension that disrupts the soul food script's assumption about common Black cooking practices. Throughout the show, the judges negatively comment on Mama Natascha's use of boxed goods while applauding Mama Avarita's choice to bake instead of fry her green tomatoes. In this way, differences in class position are constructed to also communicate different investments in preparing healthy foods. Health here is not a universal concept but instead is a discursively formed American ideology of physiological and cultural wellness often reserved for white middle-class bodies and defined against the narrative of unhealthy poor Black mothers and families.[36] The cultural formation in which MMTD is located contains an impassioned debate on how food procurement practices of African Americans are perceived versus the nuances of their everyday actualization.

In the current globalized food system, financial wealth often translates into culinary capital, marked by increased access to safe foods and ethnically diverse foodstuffs and participation in high-end food service industries such as catering. Although Black class tensions around food are nothing new, class here adds another cog in the wheel of understanding how MMTD displays affinity with a commonsense notion of unified soul food while at the same time disrupting that very same script by depicting class and the access that comes with it as something that can significantly differentiate the cooking practices of Mamas Avarita and Natascha.[37]

The content and discourse that shape MMTD are contextualized in a specific cultural formation. Although it is important to Black people claiming historical rootedness to locate the origin of soul food in West Africa within everyday practices like cooking, archaeologist Dell Upton reminds us that tradition is forever in a shifting state of invention, where cultural products are both in and outside heterogeneous communities with different social and political commitments.[38] In asserting the richness of reading the televisual kitchen, both for the way it encompasses these tensions and for the way it articulates these negations, I argue that, while there is no right or wrong representation, there are certainly specific conditions connected to representation that cannot be separated from the cultural contexts in which they were developed. MMTD seeks to capitalize on a popular investment in a simplified story of soul food, not to "debunk" this truth, but rather to point to both the tangible and intangible components that constitute food traditions. As Williams-Forson notes, "until most Black people begin to realize that what they perceive as soul food does not define the whole of Black eating habits, then who and what is being misrepresented is subject to particular subject positions."[39] A show like MMTD both attends to and disrupts how we might imagine not only soul food as a discourse but also the stakes of Black women's creative practice. Some, like anthropologist John Jackson, attend to the paradox of authenticity by disrupting hegemonic forms of identity formation and locating the definitions for the authentic in Black vernacular explanations, calling "authenticity" a "rendition of identity."[40] In critiquing the visual field MMTD presents, I argue that one must work backward through the representation to understand how certain renditions get attached to foods and, as is the case with the dominant scripts of soul food, how these renditions continue to be embodied through Black women.

CHAPTER 10

Looking through Prism Optics

Toward an Understanding of Michelle Obama's Food Reform

LINDSEY R. SWINDALL

Since moving into the White House in 2009, food reform has been central to Michelle Obama's agenda as first lady. In that time, Obama has launched Let's Move, a program focusing on nutrition and exercise, broken ground on the White House kitchen garden, and taken her crusade for healthy eating to the airwaves of late-night television and hip-hop music. Understanding the import of her food activism, and the concomitant reaction to it from critics, demands a dynamic approach that employs multiple modes of analysis. The reporting of a story from March 2014 is a good place to begin a discussion of Obama's food reform and its, perhaps unexpected, complexity.

The news item, which was about the resignation of White House pastry chef Bill Yosses, did not initially center on Michelle Obama but quickly devolved into base name-calling that was rooted in racial caricatures. The *New York Times* ran the original piece about Yosses "hanging up his whisk" and moving from Washington to New York. This article opened with a tongue-in-cheek reference to Mrs. Obama: "The first lady, Michelle Obama, is soon to lose her executive pastry chef, Bill Yosses. And she is partly to blame."[1] The story went on to explain that Obama's attention to "the relationship between food and health" had motivated Yosses to devote more of his time to raising consciousness about food literacy. The piece quoted a statement from Obama that said she was "incredibly sad" about the departure of

Yosses, appreciated his past work, and wished him well. The positive working relationship between Yosses and Obama was made apparent throughout the item. However, that was soon to be overlooked as coverage spread.

The story was picked up by various news carriers, most of which essentially summarized the main points of the *Times* article.[2] Yet some outlets that ran the piece began to position Yosses's departure as the result of a dispute between him and Mrs. Obama. Headlines such as this one began emphasizing Obama: "White House Pastry Chef Leaves: Blame FLOTUS?"[3] Abridged versions of the news item asserted Yosses's exit was "all Michelle Obama's fault."[4] It was not long until radio host Rush Limbaugh claimed that Obama had "forced" Yosses out of the White House kitchen.[5] Perhaps most instructive was a brief story that was posted on the website the Daily Caller, which stressed that Yosses was leaving because he did not want to "demonize" ingredients like butter and sugar. Additionally, this piece alleged, Yosses had been unsatisfied when Obama had "forced" him to make more nutritious offerings with smaller portions.[6] Rather than highlighting Obama's positive influence on Yosses regarding healthful eating, these reports characterized her as tempered and bossy. In short order, nearly three thousand comments to the Daily Caller item from readers echoed this negative portrayal of Obama.

The evolution of the media characterization of Michelle Obama in this news piece reveals how quickly any analysis of her food work becomes rather complicated. At one level, the story shows the importance of Obama's message about eating healthful foods and how it helped shape the direction of the White House kitchen. It also demonstrates the positive influence of her advocacy, exemplified by the fact that Yosses now wants to devote more of his own career to raising awareness about nutrition. However, multiple layers to the story appear when one delves further into the reportage. The backlash against Obama is exposed in vitriolic insults aimed at her body of work on healthful eating as well as at her physical body. Many of these swift repudiations turned to the long-held trope of the angry black woman in order to classify her behavior. Yet, the stereotype does not hold because it does not explain or describe her actions in this narrative. Yosses had embraced her ideas on nutritious eating and she sent best wishes for his future endeavors. Thus, this misguided analysis of Obama as an angry black woman strains to position her within an ill-fitting white supremacist framework. The label does not work and the stereotype is unsuitable not only because it is racist and clearly erroneous but also because Obama's advocacy defies the tidy depiction of a single label.

Though her platform about exercising and eating a nutritious diet is vital in an era of widespread obesity, it is not the most significant aspect of Michelle Obama's food reform endeavors. What is even more striking than her message about healthy eating is the way in which her work presents an occasion to conceptualize the relationship between women and food in new ways. Understanding new directions in the relationship between women and food is vital because, in the words of Psyche Williams-Forson, it will help "promote the understanding of black women's lives as cultural work."[7] Additionally, Michelle Obama's advocacy is informed by a long and important relationship between black women and food in the United States. As Doris Witt has pointed out, "the connection between and frequent conflation of African American women and food has functioned as a central structuring dynamic of twentieth-century U.S. psychic, cultural, sociopolitical, and economic life."[8] While Obama's activism is part of this history of women and food, she is also breaking new ground and confounding many of the categories used to characterize women and food. For example, she cares about food issues deeply, but she is not a mammy (she does not even cook!), nor is she an angry black woman throwing chefs out of the kitchen. Furthermore, by supporting food reform rather than eschewing domestic issues she is not the feminist icon that some supporters had hoped.

Analyzing Obama's food activism is like gazing through a multi-edged prism. Looking at the subject directly seems fairly straightforward. But a simple turn of the head deviates the beam of light and disperses it into many wavelengths that the human eye sees as a rainbow spectrum. Because of the "prism optics" of Obama's food advocacy, examining her work solely through the lens of race could miss the simultaneous, overlapping, and sometimes contradictory interplay of gender and class issues. Her activism cannot be essentialized into one category because there are too many bands of light being refracted.

Similarly, her reform activities should not be explored in a vacuum. The reaction to her endeavors must also be considered to aid a broader understanding of the direction of her work and its consequences. This helps to lay bare some of the anxieties in American society's relationship with an Ivy League–educated black woman who is in a position of authority. Indeed, Rebecca Sharpless has cogently argued that women's involvement with food "indicates a great deal about the way a society functions."[9] In order to illustrate the prism optics of Michelle Obama's food advocacy, this chapter will discuss three examples that show how her work defies a simple, clear-cut analysis and calls for new theorizing on women and food for the twenty-first century.

As the story on Bill Yosses's departure from the White House kitchen indicated, reactions to Michelle Obama's food advocacy have summoned the stereotype of the angry black woman, or Sapphire. Sapphire is an "overly aggressive and masculinized" black woman who rules her roost with an iron fist and does not accept disrespect from anyone.[10] This figure has deep roots in both US culture and policy. Her name is based on a character in the long-running radio and television program *Amos 'n' Andy*, which presented denigrating caricatures of African Americans for public entertainment from roughly the 1920s through the 1950s. Sapphire Stevens regularly berated her husband, portrayed as indolent and scheming, for being a failure as a breadwinner.[11] In addition, this trope was invoked in the conclusions of the 1965 Moynihan Report, which pointed to the role of black mothers, instead of long-standing social issues like poverty and institutional racism, as a cause of pathology in black families.[12] Patricia Hill Collins has posited that "labeling Black women unfeminine and too strong works to undercut Black women's assertiveness."[13] The stereotype also worked to reinforce a racial hierarchy by perpetuating the idea that African Americans were uncivilized and potentially a threat to the social order.

The pattern of alluding to the first lady as a Sapphire figure began during the Obamas' first presidential campaign. In the summer of 2008, a cover of the *New Yorker* magazine portrayed Michelle Obama with an Afro and a machinegun slung over her shoulder—reminiscent of 1960s-era Black Panther Party members. She stands in an Oval Office in which an American flag burns in the fireplace.[14] The image alluded to a time period in which vocal black radicals were asserting their rights and summer riots dramatically upset the status quo. Melissa Harris-Perry has observed that this infamous illustration "captured the growing characterization of Michelle Obama as an angry black woman."[15] In addition to the *New Yorker* cover, two other events contributed to the characterization of Mrs. Obama as a Sapphire figure during the 2008 campaign. Speaking at a campaign stop in Madison, Wisconsin, in February, Obama gave a frank assessment of the country's political climate. She noted that talking with people across the nation while on the campaign trail had made her "proud" of the country for the first time in her "adult lifetime" because it was clear that people were "hungry for change" and hope was "making a comeback."[16] Critics quickly pounced on this statement. Her patriotism was questioned and some called her a "vain pessimist," while Republican candidate John McCain's wife, Cindy, seized the opportunity to reassure Americans that she had always been proud of her country.[17] One editorialist observed of the media circus: "Suddenly" the Ivy graduate "was transformed into the female equivalent of [Black Panther] Eldridge Cleaver."[18] The Obama campaign quickly offered reporters a corrective, which said that Mrs. Obama was proud for the "first time in a long time" because of the "grassroots movement for change" that she had witnessed.[19]

That same month, Michelle Obama's senior thesis from Princeton University, "Princeton Educated Blacks and the Black Community," was dragged out and parsed incessantly.[20] In 1985 a young sociology student, Michelle LaVaughn Robinson, had surveyed black Princeton alumni about their perspectives on various racial issues. The personal observations included in her thesis about feeling marginalized as an African American at an overwhelmingly white institution were met with scrutiny in much of the press. Sean Hannity wondered if Obama "had a race problem" and bloggers referred to her "racial animosity."[21] During the fray, Barack Obama even met with Fox News executives in part to "insist" that his wife be treated more respectfully on their network.[22] When Princeton University's Mudd Library initially restricted public access to the document, reporters wondered what Michelle Obama was hiding. Such was the outcry that the Obama campaign released a copy of the thesis to Politico.com, which posted it online.[23] This strong backlash against Mrs. Obama led to a carefully crafted and well-received speech at the Democratic National Convention in August 2008 and a recasting of her public persona.

A former White House aide in the East Wing has pointed out that the recoil against Mrs. Obama in early 2008 was "a defining moment for her."[24] When she entered the White House in 2009, Obama took a cautious and deliberate approach, studiously shaping her agenda and stressing to her staff that anything they do must be done well.[25] Having learned from the 2008 media fracas, she worked to consciously manage her public persona, and it was at this time that food reform became central to her identity as first lady. Through her food advocacy, Michelle Obama has aimed to cultivate a public image that foils the stereotype of an angry black woman. Both the White House kitchen garden and Let's Move have provided multiple avenues for Obama to address food and nutrition issues in an educational and joyful manner—the antithesis of Sapphire.

Working in the garden has helped to establish a public persona for Obama that is genial and approachable. Her book *American Grown: The Story of the White House Kitchen Garden and Gardens across America* emphasizes that she is not an expert gardener but is learning about gardening because of her strong belief in the good nutrition that results from eating fresh fruits and vegetables.[26] The message of the book is that she is a student of gardening who is open to collaboration and wants to share what she has learned. For example, Michelle Obama joins forces with the gardening team to select plantings for each season and troubleshoots on issues like drainage for the vegetable beds. Urban school children come to the garden in groups to get their hands dirty with Obama and learn about how food is grown. They also munch on fresh cauliflower together and taste vegetable pizzas crafted by the White House team of chefs. Volunteers from the White House staff learn to help weed and harvest in the garden. Therefore, the collaborative spirit in the garden and its accessibility to children from the community as well as White House staff stress an openness grounded in education and the enjoyment of good, nutritious food. The glossy photos in *American Grown* of Mrs. Obama and Bo, the first dog, cuddling in the garden together speak to good nutrition (Bo likes broccoli!) and, importantly, present a warm and approachable vision of the first lady that tries to counter the Sapphire trope.

Let's Move has also been a vehicle for Michelle Obama to speak about exercise and nutrition while cultivating an active and fun-loving public image that is the opposite of the overly aggressive Sapphire. In the name of Let's Move, Mrs. Obama has, for instance, played tug of war in the White House, led a group of children to break the jumping-jack world record, introduced yoga at the annual White House Easter egg roll, and appeared in the music video for the hip-hop album *Songs for a Healthier America*. The following example is indicative of the public identity that Obama has developed for herself. Millions of viewers have watched the footage of the first lady's appearance on the program *Late Night* with comedian Jimmy Fallon in the sketch "The Evolution of Mom Dancing."[27] The skit features Mrs. Obama and a cross-dressing Fallon interpreting of a variety of dance moves before a loudly enthusiastic studio audience. The introduction to the piece notes that it was created in honor of Let's Move to encourage parents to get up and exercise with their children for good health. A *Washington Post* writer called the sketch "genius" and observed that Obama is also clearly "comfortable in her own skin."[28]

It is significant that these seemingly frivolous and carefree interactions on behalf of Let's Move are carefully planned and enable the first lady to exert control over her public image. A former White House assistant press secretary has observed that while her husband is known for his ability to improvise, "Mrs. Obama depends on structure to support her public warmth [including] the ease with which she'll pick up a hula hoop or, say, do the Dougie with school kids."[29] The media can summon Sapphire at any moment to potentially undermine her authority, so Obama proceeds in public cautiously. Through her work with the White House kitchen garden and Let's Move, the first lady has conscientiously molded a public image that encourages healthful eating and regular exercise in a manner that accentuates the delight of eating strawberries right off the plant or the exuberance of hula hooping with friends. This approach offers a counter to the overbearing, bossy Sapphire trope while still conveying a vital message about good nutrition and daily exercise. As Bill Yosses summarized of Obama's food advocacy, "She has done it with humor and good will" and "without preaching."[30]

Despite Michelle Obama's efforts, however, condemnations of her food reform persist in conjuring her as an angry black woman, as was done when Yosses resigned as White House pastry chef in 2014. For instance, in one online cartoon, Obama is depicted as a policewoman who grabs a child so hard that the burger and soda are thrust out of his hands. She is pointing in the cartoon presumably toward the penitentiary where she is taking him. The caption reads, "Why does Michelle Obama criticize us for eating junk food, but doesn't say 'jackschitt' [sic] about her husband?"[31] Another rendering includes an acerbic-looking Michelle shouting, "Eat What I Tell You to Eat!" under a protest about her school lunch ideas raising the cost of meals for students.[32] One more upset blogger asks, "Where in the Constitution is the federal government given authority to tell me or my children what we can or cannot eat?" This is posted next to a picture of Michelle Obama eating a dessert and chiding, "Do as I say, not as I do."[33] Under the provocative heading "Watergate 2013," Mrs. Obama is pictured urging Americans to drink more water and then laughing maniacally. This web page poses the question, "What sinister reason does Michelle Obama have for wanting Americans to drink more water?"[34] Revealing perhaps more about his own psychology than his views on food selection, radio host Jason Mattera cast Mrs. Obama as a "dietary dominatrix" on a Fox network program in 2011.[35]

While all of these denunciations of Obama allude to the long-held racial stereotype of a bossy, wrathful black woman, they also point to a host of other latent anxieties that surface in the backlash against the first lady. For example, class is highlighted in the fears about potentially higher costs for school lunches if new standards are legislated. Obama is seen as overstepping constitutional bounds by infringing on the crucial personal freedom of deciding what to serve for dinner. Furthermore, insecurities about a woman in a position of power seem to underpin Mattera's assessment of Michelle Obama's food advocacy. Plunging into the prism optics of the angry black woman and Obama's food advocacy illustrates a complex array of race, class, and gender tensions while also showing how Obama has aimed to shape her own public persona with varying degrees of success. The narrative of Obama as Sapphire, then, opens a broad dialogue not just on racial tensions but also on food choices as personal freedoms, apprehensions on female leadership, and class concerns about the cost of healthy food.

While Obama's food activism aims to refute the Sapphire trope, her work also repudiates another historical stereotype: Mammy. Yet, like the narrative of Obama and Sapphire, exploring associations between the first lady and Mammy uncover the prism optics of numerous overlapping issues. The stereotype of Mammy, the plump, submissive, domestic servant, has an even longer history than her sister Sapphire. Sharpless explains, "The figure of the African American woman as a cook has been a mainstay in white American popular culture."[36] The segregation system helped maintain a strict racial hierarchy beginning in the late nineteenth century. This racial order was a reflection of the slave system, and specific symbols, like Jim Crow and Mammy, reinforced the idea of white supremacy. Mammy is, thus, a cultural reminder of the ideology of the Old South and its "ideas about race and class and gender and order."[37]

Mammy depictions like Aunt Jemima have been "rooted deeply into the white American consciousness, representing a reassuring tie with the Old South in which cooks worked happily for whatever reward came their way."[38] Mammy, thus, represents a clear historical connection between black women and food that depicts them as preparers of meals. For centuries, generations of black women boiled and stewed suppers during enslavement, and domestic workers fried and sautéed dinners during segregation. This work made the kitchen a familiar locus for black women to be associated with food. Mammy was important in a household because she nourished the family for whom she labored, but as a servant she was not a threatening figure. In fact, she is often portrayed as perhaps a little sassy but ultimately obedient and loyal, as is the character in *Gone with the Wind* who is unnamed and only known as Mammy.

Michelle Obama, however, has broken away from the long-standing Mammy stereotype and is instigating a paradigm shift in the relationship between black women and food by severing herself from the stove. This is a move that she has made consciously even though some commentators have lamented that the act of cooking is missing from Obama's food activism and wished that she might become a cooking "role model" or "use her bully pulpit to promote home cooking."[39] It is true that Obama is rarely seen standing over a range, and when she is in a kitchen she is more likely to be serving a meal to the underprivileged than preparing it. Still, she has been quite clear about her decision to step away from the stove. The first lady has on more than one occasion stated, "Cooking isn't one of my huge things," and she is "just fine with" other people doing the cooking.[40]

The fact that Michelle Obama has taken on the issue of food advocacy but has done so largely from outside of the kitchen is one of the most powerful aspects of her work. She has declared "when and where" she will enter the discourse on food and she chooses not to do so from behind a stove.[41] Through these actions Obama is not only derailing the historical stereotype of Mammy. By declaring that food and nutrition are vital while letting other people cook the food, she is opening new spaces for interaction with food issues. If "feminine virtues are defined by task," then a message of Michelle Obama's activism is that black women do not have to be situated in a kitchen to care about food and nutrition.[42] In fact, this is a message not just for black women. Cooking food as a duty within the domestic sphere has helped define the relationship that just about all women in the United States have with food. The first lady's advocacy on food, which takes place in many venues, from a garden to a television studio to a jumping-jack competition, liberates all women from the drudgery of cooking by revealing many arenas in which to engage with food.

And yet, this new paradigm comes with a significant caveat. Michelle Obama has only been able to position herself outside of the kitchen because of her class status. Let's be clear: she does not cook because she does not have to cook. A team of chefs cooks for her and her family every day for each meal. While her advocacy offers exciting prospects for women, her position is, of course, exceptional on many levels. She is the first lady of the United States and she is part of the Ivy League–educated upper class; this affords opportunities that are clearly not available for working women and middle-class women who must quickly pick up dinner from a drive-through window for their families when returning home from a full-time job. (It is worth mentioning that Obama often invokes her years as a working mom before her husband entered politics, when she "was all about grab and go" food herself.)[43] Acknowledging her class status does not invalidate her food advocacy, but it does complicate it by raising important questions. For instance: Is Mrs. Obama still sufficiently in touch with the needs of working families and what they can afford to put on the table? Does she take into consideration the limited time that working families have to engage in exercise together or to start a garden to grow healthier food? What does it mean that some commentators would like to see her back in a kitchen? Therefore, looking through the prism optics of Obama's relationship to cooking and the Mammy legacy offers a vital break from past racial and gender identifications but necessitates that key questions about class are not ignored.

Lastly, Michelle Obama's food activism has been criticized by some feminists who seem to balk at the first lady's embrace of an issue that is closely connected to domesticity rather than focusing on educating young women or maintaining her own career during her husband's presidency. For instance, when Mrs. Obama declared in 2008 that her main priority would be caring for her children as "mom-in-chief," some feminists bristled that she was not continuing her career as a lawyer.[44] In 2012, after she worked as a food reformer for four years, some commentators wished that she would take on more substantial issues. In an editorial in the *Washington Post*, Courtland Milloy announced, "Enough with the broccoli and Brussels sprouts," and lamented, "We're more likely to hear her talk about stems in a White House vegetable garden than about [more] girls excelling in science and math."[45] Feminist writer Linda Hirshman has labeled the "first mom, gardener thing" as "silly."[46] In a controversial article that presented Michelle Obama as a "feminist nightmare," Michelle Cottle recalled the expectation that the first lady would tackle "tough issues" but rued that "it was not meant to be."[47] Columnist Keli Goff regrets that Mrs. Obama traded her "power suits" for "pastel cardigans" and yearns for Obama to disclose that she cares "about issues besides healthy eating, gardening and water."[48] Other analysts have rushed to Obama's defense by pointing out, for example, that because of its impact on women and families, proper nutrition "is indeed a feminist issue."[49]

Such discussions, while primarily emanating from the educated middle and upper classes, help illuminate the prism optics of Michelle Obama's complex relationship with the broad array of analysts who write from a feminist perspective. She is a woman in a position of authority, which is rare enough in the United States, but she is also the first African American first lady. This position carries weight but is also accompanied by a score of idiosyncratic expectations. That being the case, she fails to fulfill some feminists' vision of a feminist icon. These writers do not view food activism as being as important as, for example, channeling more girls from neighborhoods like Chicago's South Side, where Obama was raised, into STEM jobs or advocating for professional working moms. Such critics also object to the first lady engaging in activities like dancing on late-night television that are not sufficiently dignified for a women of her stature.[50] Whether Michelle Obama should be using her status to advocate for education rather than for food and exercise is a question that can be debated ad infinitum. However, this is a decision that only Mrs. Obama can make. What is exciting is that she is in a position to ponder these issues and determine her own agenda as first lady. She has resolved to pursue food reform and she has the opportunities to engage in this work at an almost unparalleled level because she has access to the resources and prestige of the White House. Surely, the power for women to make individual choices about their work must ultimately be at the heart of any feminist model. Still, Obama as a feminist icon is complicated by the range of opinions from various analysts who seek a president's wife who will animate their personal feminist ideologies. This ongoing discourse necessarily raises multilayered questions, including whether food activism is a feminist issue and the extent to which personal agency figures in Obama's relationship with food reform.

In conclusion, the prism optics of Michelle Obama's food reform reveal complexities inherent in parsing the import of her work. For example, she does not seem to be able to completely shed the Sapphire trope despite recasting her public persona. The backlash against her food advocacy, which invokes Sapphire, also reveals class anxieties. While some writers wish to see her carrying out her food activism from the kitchen, she has purposefully steered away from the stove. This shatters the idea exemplified by Mammy that cooking forms the basis of the relationship between black women and food. However, she has been able to abstain from cooking only because of her class status. As a result of her food work, Mrs. Obama has failed to embody the feminist model that some envisioned when she entered the White

House. These critics wish to see Obama invoking her professional background to speak to educational issues.

The categories Sapphire, Mammy, and feminist icon are all complicated by class considerations; and none of them, or the reactions to them, are thoroughly adequate to conceptualize the first lady's activism and all of the questions it raises. Racial tropes do not do justice to the multifaceted class and gender issues that also emerge from her work, and feminist analysis often places her at the center of subjective models based on that specific writer's expectations. Moreover, any analysis of Michelle Obama is complicated by the cascade of information available on her endeavors and the myriad of responses to her activities. Despite the breadth of data about Obama that is accessible on the web, there is a comparative dearth of substantive cultural analysis on her food activism. Therefore, innovative methods of analysis and more dynamic theoretical constructs are needed to conceptualize Obama's advocacy, its significance in determining new directions in the relationship between women and food, and what it reveals about American culture in the twenty-first century.

PART III ▪ Politics

CHAPTER 11

Theft, Food Labor, and Culinary Insurrection in the Virginia Plantation Yard

CHRISTOPHER FARRISH

In her 1824 cookbook, *The Virginia Housewife*, Mary Randolph wrote, "When the kitchen breakfast is over, and the cook has put all things in their proper places, the mistress should go in to give her orders."[1] A contemporary reader may pass over the spatial implications of this passage, moving quickly to the recipes contained in the text. However, a plantation mistress would have understood clearly Randolph's intent. On the antebellum plantation, meals emerged through recipes, relation of power, and domestic space itself.

The plantation domestic space and the kitchen yard, in particular, were sites of culinary conflict. On the one side were the mechanisms of control: the outbuildings of the plantation yard, the keys to the items contained therein, and the form of plantation rationing. These mechanisms were designed to accomplish several things: they worked to alienate the enslaved from the products of their labor, they imbricated the mistress and the enslaved within the patriarchal order, and they regulated the dense cultural import of cooking and eating for the enslaved. On the other side were the spaces and practices of black resistance: acts of theft, the subversive space of the kitchen, and unacknowledged black culinary power. This brief essay cannot take on all of the conflicts and contradictions of the plantation domestic space. Instead, it will focus on two power dynamics from which black and southern food culture emerged: rationing (with its subversive counterpart, theft) and the tools that empowered white mistresses and enslaved cooks—plantation keys and kitchens, respectively. The culinary practices of the enslaved both undermined and underwrote the mechanisms of plantation power. Theft was furtive: it produced food culture in a space of life outside the plantation order and its reflexive archival record. While cooking was a mode of power in plain view, it produced food for both black folks and white folks alike, and its products were well documented, if misattributed.

Any study of black food culture in the antebellum Southeast should avoid what literary scholar Kyla Tompkins has called the "object-based fetishism of foodie culture," an analytical frame that sacrifices critical inquiry or historicism in favor of culinary celebration.[2] Too easily, the traces that endure in a dish obscure the precarious and contingent nature of their emergence. Dishes and meals—the culinary objects of consumption and critique—should be celebrated less for their existence and more for the improbability of their becoming.

Geographer Judith Carney demonstrates the delicate balance between celebration and contingent historicism in her research on eighteenth-century rice cultivation. Carney argues that West African agricultural techniques enabled rice cultivation in the southeast and constituted a major contribution to the region's agricultural history.[3] Those enslaved in the coastal Carolinas and Georgia reinforced various African identities through putting their agricultural knowledge into practice. Planters were largely beholden to the skills and practices of the enslaved, and this expertise afforded black workers latitude in "negotiating the terms of their bondage."[4] Carney does not see the movement of African agricultural methods into the plantation system as a contribution or an ahistorical *fait accompli*. Instead, she emphasizes "the depth, uncertainty, and complexity of power relations that shaped the transfer of rice culture during the charter generations of slavery."[5]

Carney moves us away from an object-based fetishism and toward a historically situated analysis of culinary "exchange" under relations of unequal power. She sees in the coastal rice plantation a "diffusion of an indigenous knowledge system."[6] Rice cultivation emerged within a specific historical moment, an atmosphere of contingency within which the enslaved adapted to and influenced their surroundings. This organic diffusion of knowledge occurred both with and without the sanction of the planter: it reinforced and undercut systems of power, and it created life within the structures of social death. And while Carney focuses on the coastal rice plantations of the charter generation, the delicate and contingent nature of cultural diffusion resonates with a larger culinary evolution.

The Structures of Power
and the Keys to Their Contents

The domestic space of the Virginia home also evolved within the context of historical contingency in which the plantation yard developed highly specialized spaces of food production and storage. Food production was similar to what contemporary eaters may call farm-to-table: hogs were butchered and their meat cured and stored; cows were milked; dairy products were made; chickens laid eggs; meals were cooked and sent to both the plantation home and the slave quarters or field. All of this activity moved through the plantation yard, a utilitarian space in which the white mistress oversaw enslaved labor. However, products and people were not the only actors within the yard. Space itself regulated the culinary process. Meats were cured in smokehouses, milk was kept cool in dairies, dovecotes attracted game, vegetables were grown in gardens, food was stored in tightly locked larders, and elegant meals were made in sweltering kitchens.[7] On the antebellum Virginia plantation, these spaces produced food, policed the enslaved, regulated work, and guarded against theft. Orders were given and disobeyed; food was rationed out, measured, stolen, or poisoned. This space of control would also set the scene for both the emergence of black food culture and its transfer to the big-house table.

Eighteenth-century planters built larger homes and transformed their old dwellings into kitchens once they accumulated enough capital.[8] Removing the kitchen from the home separated labor from leisure and black from white. By the nineteenth century, the spatial and racial divisions of the yard were a hallmark of Virginia plantations.[9] The yard regulated the movements of the enslaved and insulated the planter from the crude machinations of food labor. Outbuildings enabled food production as well as storage, while their measured contents facilitated rationing and their locked doors prevented theft. The yard and its outbuildings instituted a unidirectional form of power, which harnessed the work of the enslaved while estranging them from their labor.

The dictates of plantation patriarchy and racial supremacy placed the mistress at the center of domestic space, where she marshaled enslaved labor for the various chores associated with food preservation, preparation, and presentation.[10] The mistresses evoked power over space and labor through punishment, coercion, and strategic consent. She controlled the material of the yard, policed its buildings, and oversaw the agricultural products of enslaved labor. Perhaps most powerfully, she held the keys. If she could not command enslaved labor, her control of comestibles would demand their attention. Plantation keys and the key baskets that often held them reflected a woman's power—both real and symbolic—in the domestic sphere. A woman's ownership of the keys represented her central place in protecting and providing for the white family while also monitoring and regulating the lives of enslaved domestic laborers.

The yard's constellation of outbuildings was held under literal lock and key, what Virginians called a "turnkey system."[11] Anywhere from once a week to once every several months, food and supplies were meted out to the enslaved; otherwise, the mistress made sure the yard's outbuildings were tightly locked and guarded by the mistress. Power over the culinary "treasury" was guarded in elaborately designed key baskets, which mistresses carried with them as they oversaw plantation space.[12] Although these decorative forms may have been used as far north as Pennsylvania, extant examples suggest that they were most common in North Carolina and Virginia—the Richmond area in particular.[13] The keys ensured a mistress's control of the yard and its products, and the beautifully imprinted baskets showcased a new bride's place within the racial and gender order of the plantation home.

Elite Virginians were well aware of the material and symbolic power of the plantation keys. In an 1845 letter to her brother discussing the courting of Elizabeth Morris by widower Dr. John Minor, Huldah Lewis (Holladay) wrote,

> I went to see Lizzy Morris a few days ago at Dr. Minor's and for the first time saw her take the keys; she even went to the kitchen to give directions about making beefsteak for dinner

and took me along with her; don't you think it looks suspicious? Perhaps she sees how necessary it is for young ladies to learn the art of cooking in case she should go for housekeeping. I suspect [plantation overseer] Mr. Collins thought, from our going to the smokehouse and kitchen[,] we were looking over his provisions. You may be sure we had some fun of it.[14]

Lewis's reflection made clear the embedded power of both plantation keys and access to domestic outbuildings. Lizzy Morris had yet to wed John Minor, but by taking up the keys and going into the plantation kitchen, she tapped a power and position that were no less real for her lack of wifely status. The suggestion that Morris and Lewis were conscious of playing a role—having "some fun of it"—testifies to the assumed nature of a mistress's power in plantation space and over enslaved labor. Morris "tried on" the power of moving through the space between white dwelling house and kitchen. By giving culinary orders to an enslaved woman, Morris evoked her soon-to-be power over both space and the occupant-laborers who lived and worked in that space. Young Morris knew that by holding the keys she would hold a great deal of power, and she appeared to delight in the prospect. She understood that mistresses directed the labor of others and oversaw the larder and kitchen that sent meals to the big house, but they also controlled the foods that went to the tables of enslaved workers.

The Mutual Production of Rationing and Theft

In antebellum Virginia, black food culture emerged within a system designed to eliminate power and flatten culinary expression. Rationing transformed cooking, eating, and the pleasures associated with food into a metric of accounting, a system of inputs and outputs. Rationing was the central element in controlling alimentation and alienating worker from works. The various foods rationed out to the enslaved were coarse and contained little variety. Bacon, flour, and molasses were central elements. Frederick Law Olmstead observed in 1853, "The general allowance of food was thought to be a peck and a half of meal, and three pounds of bacon a week."[15] Other accounts bear similar findings. Historian Peter Kolchin estimates that a "peck (eight quarts) of cornmeal and two and a half to four pounds of pork or bacon per week ... became the widely accepted standard ration for healthy adult field hands."[16] The monotonous diet of the enslaved may have filled one's stomach, but it did not stave off pellagra and other diseases associated with a nutrient-poor diet.[17]

The claims made in Robert Fogel and Stanley Engerman's controversial text *Time on the Cross* (1974) instigated a debate over the conditions under which the enslaved worked and lived. The authors argued that the conditions of slavery were not as severe as previously thought. Slavery was profitable and efficient, and the enslaved enjoyed an adequate diet.[18] Historians were quick to criticize the claims laid out in *Time on the Cross,* and subsequent scholarship has continued to trend away from the text.[19] Recent work on the mechanisms of slavery and plantation rationing has focused on both the content of a bondsperson's diet and the form of rationing itself. Walter Johnson has argued that planters in the Mississippi Valley used rations to maximize production and minimize cost.[20] Narratives provided by the formerly enslaved, which suggest that food was adequate, if not entirely abundant, complicate the picture.[21] Archeological studies simultaneously demonstrate the inadequacy of the rations provided and the related adaptations made by those living in bondage: many dig sites have uncovered evidence of game hunted and other items foraged or fished in the area surrounding plantations. These faunal remains expose a variety of plants and proteins in the bondsperson's diet, but it was a variety born of necessity.[22]

Rather than focusing merely on the quantity or quality of the rations provided for the enslaved, regional variations, or furtive additions, I suggest that the form of rationing itself is what warrants our attention. Studying dietary adequacy in terms of caloric intake or regional or seasonal variation misses a central component of rationing. While it is true that meager rations were quantitatively and qualitatively inferior to more generous supplies, and that the enslaved adapted and enriched their diets in profound and culturally significant ways, neither of these issues addresses the larger systemic problem. The violence that underwrote the system of rationing cannot be measured in quantity or quality. The violence of rationing was the system itself. Regulating and rationing reduced the act of eating to a metric of inputs and outputs, and shifted power away from the enslaved.

Rationing acted as the sanctioned culinary flow of the antebellum plantation home, and it defined the conditions of culinary production for the enslaved. This was the system within which black food culture emerged.

If rationing was a form of violence, then theft was a form of resistance imbricated with the regulation of comestibles. Woven into the material practices of white supremacy were the modes of resistance enacted by the enslaved. As the locked larder and the closely guarded keys suggested, the system of rationing was inextricable from the practice of theft. Narratives of the formerly enslaved frequently blend their discussion of rations with reflections on theft. Williams Brooks (b. 1860) recalled that the enslaved received six pounds of meat and five pounds of flour each week, which was not enough to "last a 'dog a day." Brooks recounted the brutal chain of rationing and theft, stating, "So dem niggers steal an' cose when dey steal dey git caught, an' when you get caught you git beat."[23] Brooks saw rationing as a death-dealing institution linked to theft and the covert practice of life. In his account, provisions and punishment intertwined; food and freedom moved between spaces of control and resistance. If this furtive movement was discovered, a beating reinstated and redoubled racial dominance.

Theft was also used to resist a planter's will. Beverly Jones (b. ca. 1848), whose mother was a cook, claimed that there was "plenty to eat" and no theft on the farm where he was enslaved. However, he thought that where plantation masters were "mean an' ornery" the enslaved would "git to stealin' an' lyin' 'bout it."[24] For Jones, theft was not so much an act of necessity as it was a mode of resistance and retribution built into a cruel system, or the cruelty of a master. He thought that where the enslaved stole, a "bad master . . . made 'em that way." Whereas Brooks's account folded theft back into the methods of control and punishment, Jones emphasized the subtle weave of power and resistance in stealing *and* lying. For both men, rationing and theft were intertwined.

Theft was a mundane and frequent mode of resistance, and its everydayness underwrote its power. Court records indicate that theft was the most common "crime" committed on Virginia plantations through the eighteenth and nineteenth centuries. In fact, court records only reveal a fraction of thefts tried in court. These statistics say nothing of those thefts that were *not* discovered or those that planters dealt with themselves.[25]

The enslaved often saw theft less as stealing and more as covert access to the items produced by their labor. Following the work of James Scott and E. P. Thompson, historian Alex Lichtenstein has argued that in the antebellum South theft was part of a "sustained struggle" between enslaved and enslaver to define "the parameters of power" and the rightful claim to agricultural production.[26] In the mid-nineteenth century, polymath Frederick Law Olmsted even suggested an estrangement of labor when he observed that theft was a "fixed point" within the ethics of bondage: the enslaved believed that "the result of labor belongs of right to the laborer," so the unity of worker and agricultural works justified what would otherwise be considered theft.[27] And as Frederick Douglass famously remarked, to the enslaved, stealing was simply "taking meat out of one tub and putting it in another."[28]

To the planter class, theft—and the more threatening, if less common, act of poisoning—undermined racial order and control of food production.[29] Theft removed food from a system of rationing and restored it to a space of life, of individual and communal pleasure rather than the profit of another. Thus, while the contributions of black food culture to southern cooking endure into our own historical moment, the richness of a bondsperson's diet was defined not by what was added to a larger culinary scene but by what was taken from that system. In this sense, records of theft tell us as much about black food culture in the antebellum South as do the legacies of culinary contribution. Theft moved food, cooking, and eating to the margins of the historical record. The meals, memories, and conversations that emerged over stolen food, like so much culture of those enslaved, cannot be reproduced; they are defined by their absence. Nonetheless, these foodways played a central role in the lives of those held in bondage.

Labor and Power in the Plantation Kitchen

The labor of cooking was also fraught with the contradictory forces of control and resistance. Theft and cooking were both forms of black power. In fact, the only time the enslaved *did not* have direct contact with food products was when goods were locked away in the plantation larder—hence the power of the keys. Theft was secret and subversive, but the power of cooking and black culinary labor frequently circulated in plain view. The plantation kitchen stood as the space in which cooking could work to support the plantation order or undermine its structures of power. Subsequently, the kitchen stood as a forceful agent at the ideological center of the plantation domestic sphere.

The kitchen may have been central to the alimentation of the plantation home, but it was marginalized within domestic space. Kitchens were located anywhere from 20 to 220 feet away from the main dwelling and frequently housed an enslaved cook and her family.[30] The distance separating the enslaved cook from the white family protected the latter from the dangers associated with hearth cooking. The kitchen was hot, noisy, and prone to fire; separating this space made the white dwelling home safer and more pleasant for its inhabitants.[31] This separation also marked the kitchen as a black space, a building in which interactions between black and white undercut racial supremacy and relations of power. The white mistresses had to traverse the yard; she had to go into another woman's space to give her culinary directives.

Remarking on the power of enslaved cooks in plantation kitchens has become a commonplace in studies of the antebellum South. The white mistress may have held the plantation keys, but it was the black cook who controlled the kitchen. Historians have detailed the complex relations of power that linked black and white women in the plantation domestic sphere. The plantation kitchen was marked by an inversion of plantation power, which was central to the relationship between white and black women in the plantation home.[32] Cooks were frequently older and more experienced than young mistresses, and they frequently lived with their family in the plantation kitchen, which amplified their connection to this space.[33] A detached kitchen may have helped to remove noise and vermin from the plantation household, but it introduced new dangers that threatened the power of the mistress and her control of the domestic sphere.

Writing in her *Lady's Annual Register and Housewife's Memorandum-Book* in 1838, Caroline Gilman told readers to "let the first walk of the housewife after breakfast be—not to her boudoir or to her library, but—to the kitchen." The author claimed that visiting the kitchen early and often would "stimulate" the cook to perform more efficiently.[34] Enslaved cooks, meanwhile, had to wake well before dawn to rekindle fires, haul wood, and begin preparing breakfast.[35] In this hierarchy of feminine virtue—or the author's prioritizing of virtue—power in the kitchen came before appearance and knowledge. Gilman's advice belies its own stakes: on the antebellum plantation, the first order of the day, and the highest feminine virtue, was to control the life of another woman. These recommendations exposed the brutal core of the chattel system, but they also gestured toward the power of enslaved cooks.

Historian Elizabeth Fox-Genovese notes, "The assertiveness of cooks and so many other skilled slaves suggests that, in their own scale of values, competence had its own hierarchy, as even the master himself could appreciate."[36] Though the competence of enslaved cooks is rarely recorded as such, plantation tables groaned under the weight of black culinary power and skill. This knowledge was evinced by the inclusion of ingredients of African heritage—benne, okra, and other foods of the enslaved—but most of the culinary skill and influence of a cook was demonstrated less through what ingredients she used and more in the practice of her labor.

In 1853, while visiting a plantation outside of Petersburg, Virginia, Frederick Law Olmsted was treated to a meal that showcased the skill and far-reaching power of an enslaved cook. During the course of dinner, Olmsted may have even observed the unnamed cook, "an old negro woman [who] frequently came in from the kitchen, with hot biscuits and corn-cake." The meal showcased the abundance of the region:

> fried-fowl, and fried bacon and eggs, and cold ham; there were preserved peaches, and preserved quinces and grapes; there was hot wheaten biscuit and hot short-cake, and hot corn-cake, and hot griddle cakes, soaked in butter; there was coffee, and there was milk, sour or sweet, whichever I preferred to drink.[37]

This elaborate meal spoke to a tremendous amount of culinary knowledge and, indeed, influence. The power of a cook's labor was shown in a profusion of dishes; the meal itself testified to the skilled labor of the enslaved cook.

Culinary productions like those Olmstead recounted may have been celebrated, but black cooks were not expected—or even considered able—to apply their intellect to the labor of cooking. In other words, the products of their labor were recognized while their labor was not. Given these historical realities, I suggest that the historical record does not pay full tribute to the movement of "black foods" into white plantation homes. Psyche Williams-Forson makes a similar point in her discussion of what she terms "gender malpractice." She suggests that the "influence" of enslaved cooks expanded well beyond either the historical record or the circulation of African ingredients. English recipes were frequently "modified by African and African American female cooks to include their own creative twists," and these hybrid dishes gradually evolved into what we know as southern cooking. But while okra or other African plants attest to a culinary "contribution," mundane adaptations or alterations of recipes are "susceptible to cultural, social, and physical appropriation by white women (and men)."[38] Williams-Forson provokes us to reckon with a legacy of black culinary power located not in a remainder but at the very core of southern cooking. In other words, benne seeds or chili may have given a dish an African signature, but they were not the only marks left by black cooks. Enslaved women cooked, but they did not "write the book" on southern cooking. White mistresses granted themselves that privilege.[39] Thus the black influence on southern cooking was obscured through the very act of its recording.

Both theft and cooking were *modes of production* that affected the food culture of the antebellum plantation, if in divergent ways. As I have suggested, through pilfering, theft created a food culture outside of the metrics of the slave system. Cooking sent food in one direction, toward the elegant tables of the big house; theft reversed that flow. However, while the products of this movement are often seen as having African, European, or mixed provenance, the labor power that produced them was that of the black cook.

Historian Stephanie Camp emphasizes the "hidden, everyday acts that help[ed] to form overt resistance" to the slave system.[40] Kitchen labor was difficult and dangerous; cooks improvised where they could, saving time and strategizing how to best create downtime. These choices enacted power—if not over what was produced, at least over how it was made. The tricks and techniques of this culinary labor are largely lost to the contemporary audience. However, the volume of discourse on controlling the kitchen and its laborers and policing culinary products surely speaks to a firm intransigence on the part of enslaved cooks. The power of this labor, rather than the misrecognition of its products, is what demands our attention.

Insurgent modes of black food production—both hidden from and sanctioned by slavery—resisted mechanisms of control. Theft defied a system that reduced the meaning of life to the columns in an account book. But this culinary insurgence was not limited to stealing life away from social death: it also infiltrated the food culture of elite white southerners and, eventually, the foodways of the entire region. In hidden, hybrid, or whitewashed ways, the culinary products of enslaved labor were both pulled from and pushed toward the elegant tables of the big house.

The African, Caribbean, and black American culinary presence in southern foodways is frequently referred to as a *contribution* or *influence* celebrated alongside English, French, Spanish, and Native American traditions. Southern food is seen as a kind of living archive, a mixture of cultures and a testament to the power of food to outlast the brutality of slavery and the slow-motion genocide of native peoples.[41] Culinary historians see the influence of enslaved cooks in Mary Randolph's 1824 cookbook *The Virginia Housewife*, which included recipes for okra and tomatoes, benne, yams, and the lowly field pea.[42] These meals are flavored with history, but their rich palate obscures their own provenance and ignores the historical realities within which these foods were created. Far from a contribution or influence, this movement was a radical act, a culinary insurrection. A tight focus on the dish itself elides the quotidian brutality of slavery and the subtle techniques of resistance employed by the enslaved. A dish only says so much about *antebellum* black food culture and those who produced it.

I would like to suggest another way to look at this culinary history, an approach derived less from the foods that would come to be and more in the historical conditions that were bent on preventing their emergence. The culinary evolution, cultural import, and eventual migration of black food culture onto white tables should be seen from the perspective of where and when it emerged. Southern and black food cultures are rooted in the antebellum plantation yard: a space of culinary production, conflict, hierarchy, and policing. Meals were made through cooking and acts of insubordination, work slowdowns, theft, and resistance. Antebellum black food culture emerged from within this space of conflict, but it was by no means guaranteed. The food culture of the enslaved flourished in spite of every effort to extinguish it and to deny the humanity it sustained. Instead of placing the emergence of antebellum black food culture in conversation with what it would become—southern foodways and soul food—I would suggest locating it within its historical moment and the space in which it was produced. Southern food does not always testify to these material conditions, yet without them it can never be fully understood.

CHAPTER 12

Dethroning the Deceitful Pork Chop

Food Reform at the Tuskegee Institute

JENNIFER JENSEN WALLACH

On April 25, 1901, the students at the Tuskegee Normal and Industrial Institute, located in eastern Alabama, ate soup, roast beef and gravy, asparagus tips on toast, stewed corn, and blackberry pie for their mid-day dinner.[1] This spread was more abundant and varied than the meals that most of the black, working-class students were accustomed to eating. This repast also featured an ingredient that was in particularly short supply in the southern larder: beef. Significantly, beef, which was rarely eaten by other rural Alabamans, was frequently served for one or more of the three daily meals at the Tuskegee Institute. Its recurrent appearance on the table was at the personal insistence of the principal, Booker T. Washington, whose unorthodox dining choices were an outgrowth of his sometimes-contradictory vision for racial uplift. Washington and his administrative staff went to great lengths to micromanage the campus diet. They did so believing not only that food was a source of physical nourishment but that it came to the table embedded with messages about culture, status, politics, and economics. In the Tuskegee mindset, the method with which food was prepared and consumed was of equal importance to what items appeared at mealtime. By decoding Tuskegee foodways, we can gain insights into a yet still unexamined aspect of Washington's tactics for achieving racial progress: a dietary program that reflected both assimilationist and nationalist beliefs.

Tuskegee Institute food habits were an outgrowth of contemporary ideas about racial uplift. During the period of Jim Crow's most brutal tyranny, African Americans, especially but not exclusively those living in the South, had few viable ways to combat state-sanctioned racism and unchecked racial violence. Direct protest was dangerous and could lead to economic sanctions in the best-case scenario or death by lynching in the worst. Faced with this conundrum, many African Americans chose to fight the battle for human dignity within the realm of culture and embarked on the uphill challenge of trying to convince white racists of their shared humanity. They strove to "uplift" their race by adhering to strict standards of public decorum.[2] The dinner table is an under-examined space where African Americans could act out the politics of respectability by rejecting food habits associated closely with slavery, a southern regional diet, and poverty as well as by insisting upon a rigid system of dining and cooking etiquette.[3]

Washington's ideas about proper eating habits were, in part, also the outgrowth of an intellectual debt to the white, progressive food reformers of the era who believed food could serve as a vehicle for social change and assimilation. Although Washington was intrigued by their ideas, he never completely subsumed local, African American food traditions to the dictates of outside specialists. He continually advocated for a food system managed by and for black people. He believed that food practices were an important means of preparing the black population for first-class citizenship, if racism could be ameliorated, or for independent racial sustenance if it could not. During Washington's tenure at Tuskegee Institute, which began in 1881, he helped create a food culture that simultaneously paid homage to the high moral tone of progressive food reformers and to an African American culinary heritage rooted in slave culture.

Throughout his life, Washington demonstrated a sustained interested in familiarizing himself with the latest scientific information about nutrition. He was influenced by Progressivism's faith in science and by the belief that giving students "technical and scientific knowledge" would enable them to, first, "supply the immediate wants of the body" but, eventually, would lead them to "that higher atmosphere of truth, virtue, love and unselfishness."[4] He corresponded, at least briefly, with white food reformers who shared his belief that scientific

POLITICS

knowledge could be used for the betterment of individuals and of society at large. Fannie Farmer, the "mother of level measurements"; John Harvey Kellogg, director of the famed Battle Creek Sanitarium; Edward Atkinson, the inventor of the slow-cooking Aladdin oven; and the chemists Ellen Swallow Richards and Wilbur Atwater were among the individuals he wrote to who shared his belief that proper eating habits were a reflection of one's moral virtue.[5] His interest in making connections between his work at Tuskegee and the larger national conversation about domestic reform was prompted, in part, by his affinity for progressive reform efforts but was also encouraged by advice he received from J.L.M. Curry, agent for the Peabody and Slater Funds, organizations that provided financial support for the institute. In 1894, Curry supplied Washington with a grant to hire "some competent and trained woman to give her attention to household improvement."[6]

Although Booker T. Washington had a strict policy against hiring white faculty for fear that whites would be given credit for the success of Tuskegee Institute, he bent those rules to hire Alice J. Kaine, a white home economist from Wisconsin, who made several extended trips to Alabama with the mission of improving domestic life on campus.[7] Her racial status and the significance of her work to the mission of Tuskegee were reflected in her salary. She was paid eighty dollars a month in addition to room and board, a figure that was twice the remuneration an average woman teacher received.[8] She was charged with a variety of tasks, including giving advice on how "the cheapest food consistent with health [could be served] at the smallest possible costs," and was given broad authority to implement her program, a situation that led to interpersonal difficulties with some permanent members of the faculty.[9] She wrote to Washington accepting the position with the caveat that she had never worked with "the colored people." She had, on occasion, attended their "Schools and Churches." However, visiting black community spaces was an activity that she regarded as "one of my hobbies—that is all."[10]

Washington had pragmatic reasons for cooperating with Kaine and for inviting her to practice her "hobby" of taking an interest in the disadvantaged at Tuskegee Institute. Her presence pleased white donors and built a bridge between the work at Tuskegee and advancements in domestic science elsewhere.[11] It seems likely that his connection with Kaine and other white food reformers encouraged Washington to value beef not only as a nutritious food but also as an instrument of civilization. Contemporary white food reformers, working through the auspices of programs like the "New England Kitchen," used cheap cuts of beef and other bland New England foods as tools of Americanization, asking immigrants to shed their native cuisines, which were a manifestation of their otherness.[12] Self-trained domestic scientist Mary Hinman Abel perfected the organization's low-cost recipes for beef broth and beef stew, meals that the staff saw as tools of assimilation and symbols of citizenship.[13] Anita J. Atkinson, a white domestic scientist who taught at the black liberal arts college Atlanta University in the 1890s, helped spread these ideas southward, promoting "soups and stews, a la New England Kitchen, roast beef, rare steak, Boston baked beans, Boston brown bread, codfish balls, creamed codfish, Johnny cake, Graham gems and hash" to her African American students. She, like Washington, felt that displacing "the principal diet of fat pork, hoe cake, pone, hominy and molasses" was a prominent part of what she regarded as her mission to spread civilization.[14]

The foods these reformers promoted had obvious English culinary antecedents. The partiality for beef was certainly rooted in traditional English preferences, making the meat a convenient symbol for proponents of an Anglo-accented American culture.[15] In this context, this form of animal protein soon became associated with civilization and whiteness. Prominent nineteenth-century neurologist George M. Beard proclaimed, "Savages who feed on poor food are . . . intellectually far inferior to the beef-eaters of any race."[16] Beef consumption, it follows, could transform the eater from the inside, priming him or her for full incorporation into the US nation-state. Thus Tuskegee Institute's beef eaters were making a case for national belonging.

The beef that appeared on the Tuskegee Institute table in the form of roast beef, veal cutlets, beef gravy, soup, and liver and onions may also have been a reflection of the fact that Washington and other members of the Tuskegee staff shared some of the culinary prejudices of self-consciously refined African American eaters who wished to disassociate themselves from foods like pork that were evocative of slavery or of southern regionalism. The prominent intellectual W.E.B. Du Bois was such an eater. Du Bois declared in the pages of the National

Association for the Advancement of Colored People's organ, the *Crisis*, "The deceitful Pork chops must be dethroned in the South and yield a part of its sway to vegetables, fruits, and fish."[17] Agreeing with Du Bois about the problem of pork consumption, Washington criticized those who subsisted primarily on "grits, meat [pork], corn bread" and urged black southerners to "throw off the old habit and not grow into the slavery of using a certain thing on the table because it has been used that way generation after generation."[18] He attributed the high mortality rate of urban African Americans to poor diets consisting not only of fatty pork but also of what he called "knickknacks," cheese, crackers, cake, and pie. He told his students they were fortunate to have avoided those pitfalls, claiming, "You are five times more healthy and stronger by eating [the] clean, fresh beef" served at the institute.[19]

Washington traveled as much as six months of the year raising funds to support Tuskegee Institute, but he kept close tabs on the daily operations of the institute and encouraged beef consumption even from afar. In 1899 he wrote to an administrator from New York complaining that the students were "having too much fat meat; you will notice that they had bacon and gravy for two meals."[20] Beef appeared with regularity on the Tuskegee menus despite the fact that the institute had difficulty in maintaining a profitable herd of cattle. In 1906, the farm superintendent reported that the school was losing $300 a month attempting to raise beef. Rather than turning to another form of animal protein, E. T. Atwell, the institute's business agent, resorted to purchasing beef from large meatpacking companies. This decision was made despite the fact that they hoped to raise locally most of the food the community consumed.[21] The consistent inclusion of beef on both student and faculty menus was clearly a calculated decision and an unusual one, not only given the difficulty the institute had in raising cattle, but also given beef's status as a luxury item in a region where pork was the least expensive and most widely consumed protein.[22]

The mystique of beef-eating at Tuskegee Institute was likely also enhanced by the meat's relative scarcity in the South. Beef was a product harder to preserve in a form nineteenth-century Americans found palatable than pork and was perceived by many as a luxury item well into the twentieth century. As late at the mid-1930s, only 12 to 14 percent of the meat consumed by rural southerners was beef.[23] Thus, the

beef that was served at Tuskegee was a luxury item for rural southerners of both races. The Tuskegee students who dined on beef were
actually subverting the racial order by eating a product most local
whites could not afford.

Outside of the Tuskegee Institute, most African Americans likely
never tasted beef. The federal Department of Agriculture sponsored
a study of the foods eaten by African Americans in Alabama in 1895
and 1896 and determined that rural African Americans consumed
salt pork almost exclusively as their only form of animal protein.[24]
Although the researchers who conducted the study regarded black
residents of Alabama as almost universally "improvident . . . [having]
very little ambition," they believed that those who lived the closest to
the Tuskegee Institute showed some degree of moral improvement.[25]
Beef consumption was one implied measure of civilization and refinement in the report. Only one respondent consumed beef during the
period of the study, and he was a carpenter who worked at Tuskegee.[26]

Although the beef served at Tuskegee Institute reflected an
understanding of the dietary preferences of white domestic scientists,
Tuskegee food practices were not created purely for the benefit of a
white audience. In compiling publicity for the institute, Washington
published some Tuskegee menus, surely with the knowledge that
his efforts at food uplift would meet the standards of white food
reformers. However, identical meals were also served at the institute
daily with no fanfare.[27] Washington and his staff at Tuskegee clearly
believed that the dietaries he recommended were of intrinsic value to
those who consumed them in the proper fashion, regardless of who
was watching.

At the Tuskegee Institute, specific ingredients like beef were significant, but proper presentation and etiquette were also indispens-
able elements of the local food culture. When young Washington,
who had been born into slavery, arrived at the Hampton Normal and
Agricultural Institute in Virginia in 1872 to receive the education he
craved, he recalled being struck by revelations about a more gracious
way of living that transported him into a "new world." He claimed
that he was introduced to the practices of "eating meals at regular
hours, of eating on a tablecloth, using a napkin."[28] Given the fact that
his mother was an enslaved cook, these practices must not have been

completely new concepts. Nonetheless, in his narration of his own life, Washington recalled that being introduced to these seemingly unremarkable rituals was life changing. He made sure that his own students would learn similar lessons about proper food etiquette. For Washington and his staff, proper food behavior consisted not only of eating healthful, "civilized" ingredients but also of practicing good table manners. Students who were late to meals at Tuskegee were not permitted to eat, and proper table manners were to be observed at all times.[29] Margaret Murray Washington noted that one of the ways that Tuskegee students judged each other was on "the niceties of table-training." She encouraged students to criticize one another for lack of refinement, noting that these critiques "play no small part in the development of students."[30]

In what was partially an attempt to construct an unthreatening vision of African American advancement for the benefit of white donors, Washington frequently focused his attention on the private rather than the public sphere. He proclaimed: "The Negro has had to learn the meaning of home since he learned the meaning of freedom. All work which has to do with his uplifting must begin with his home and its surroundings."[31] His timeframe for the racial uplift that was to begin at home was, however, more rapid than he implied in his carefully worded public statements on the subject, including his famous declaration, "It is at the bottom of life we must begin, and not at the top."[32] In order to demonstrate his humility, Washington told the white readers of his autobiography, *Up from Slavery*, about the first makeshift kitchen and dining room at Tuskegee, which was a basement that students dug themselves. He described carpenters' benches used for tables, cooking done outdoors over a fire, burned food served at erratic hours, and squabbles among students over the scant supply of dishes.[33] In retrospect he somewhat preposterously claimed, "I am glad that our first boarding-place was in that dismal, ill-lighted, and damp basement," speculating that better accommodations would have made them "stuck up."[34] However, Washington does not reveal how quickly the less-than-adequate conditions were remedied. He implies a slow evolution when, in actuality, a modern facility was erected in less than a year.[35] He did not intend for the faculty or student body to eat in that makeshift facility for long.[36] Behind his public, humble demeanor,

Tuskegee Students Exhibiting Good Dining Room Etiquette, circa 1902.
Photograph by Frances Benjamin Johnston. Courtesy of the Library of Congress,
Prints and Photographs Division, reproduction #LC-DIG-ppmscd-00085.

Tuskegee men are serving a meal outside in a more elegant fashion than the one
Booker T. Washington described in his *Up from Slavery,* sometime between 1890
and 1910. Courtesy of the Library of Congress, Prints and Photograph Division,
reproduction #LC-USZ62-137808.

which bore the desired fruits of much-needed white philanthropic dollars, was a hidden, more radical domestic reform agenda.

Booker T. Washington wanted to be judged on his domestic accomplishments, both in creating impressive dining and living spaces for his students and in maintaining his own home, The Oaks, which was situated next to the campus. Completed in 1900, Washington's fourteen-room, five-bath Queen Anne–style home was handsomely decorated and furnished to convey a public face of African American refinement for local whites and visiting philanthropists as well as for Tuskegee students who were charged with emulating the Washingtons' domestic sensibilities.[37] Students assigned to work at The Oaks lived on the third floor, gaining firsthand impressions of Washington's personal desire to create living spaces that conveyed "from kitchen to parlor a delicacy, a sweetness and refinement that made one feel that life was worth living."[38]

The students who were responsible for making life at The Oaks adhere to Washington's standards learned, as all Tuskegee students did, according to Carla Willard, "*to be* served, as well as to serve."[39] Although the vocational training that Washington advocated for would seemingly have trained his students to be merely cooks or waiters and not the employers nor customers who were waited upon, their education actually prepared students to fulfill both roles. The Tuskegee pupils who were taught the art of cooking and serving not only doled out simple, cafeteria-appropriate meals to their fellow students in the dining halls on campus, but also had the opportunity to prepare and serve more elaborate cuisine to distinguished members of their own race at The Oaks. This performance prepared students for roles beyond that of becoming domestic servants to white people. While serving fellow African American diners, students could more easily imagine themselves in the future role of dinner party guest and not just as perpetual cook or waiter.

In 1910, to celebrate Washington's return to Alabama after a European tour, students served the institution's executive council an elegant meal in the president's home, with a menu consisting of the following:

Blue Points
Sauce

Brown Bread Sandwiches
Consomme Cheese Straws
Olives Cheese Radishes
Swedish Timbales Mushrooms
Broiled Halibut Tartar Sauce
Bread Sticks Cole Slaw
Brown Hashed Potatoes
Orange Sherbet
Birds on Toast Jelly
Green Peas Rolls Candied Potatoes
Tomato Salad
Ice Cream Lady Fingers Bon Bons
Wafers Cheese
Black Coffee[40]

The menu choices demonstrated, once again, an insistence that high-status food items were not out of place on African American tables. Luxurious Blue Point oysters, imported from New York, also demonstrated that Tuskegee was connected to the national market economy. Their appearance at the feast indicated that Tuskegee students had been well trained in current dining and cooking conventions and were thus demonstrating their possession of cultural capital befitting first-class citizens. Paul Pierce, superintendent of the food exhibitions at the St. Louis World's Fair and author of *Dinners and Luncheons: Novel Suggestions for Social Occasions* (1907), would have concurred with the decision of the Tuskegee students to serve Blue Point oysters, "a favorite first course in season," followed shortly after by consommé, believing as he did that "a heavy soup will so far cloy the appetite as to render one indifferent to the rest of the dinner, while a clear soup refreshes, and prepares one for the enjoyment of the succeeding solids."[41] Their recipe for birds on toast may have been adapted from the recipe "Reed Birds on Toast" that appeared in the influential 1887 *The White House Cookbook*.[42] They may also have culled the recipes for Swedish timbales, cheese straws, coleslaw, and other items from Fannie Farmer. The second edition of her *Boston Cooking School Cook Book* had appeared in 1906, four years before this Tuskegee meal.[43]

The care with which the feast was planned represents the Tuskegee Institute's belief that the stakes at the dinner table were high.

The Dining Room at the Oaks, Booker T. Washington and Margaret Murray Washington's Home. Photo by Carol M. Highsmith. Courtesy of the Library of Congress, Prints and Photographs Division, reproduction #LC-DIG-highsm-08248.

Culinary missteps could reflect badly on the race and thus impede racial progress. In 1906, Washington wrote to his wife, Mary Margaret Washington, who was the lady principal at Tuskegee, and complained about aspects of a formal dinner service that were not up to his high standards. He noted:

The tomatoes were served in soup plates. There were no fresh flowers on the table. The girls did not wear caps. The menu card was cheaply gotten up, it was cheap paper poorly cut, and the writing was not in attractive form.[44]

Two days later he again chided his wife for the lack of cleanliness and organization in the school's cooking facilities, noting, "I have very seldom been more disgusted than when I visited the small model kitchen.... The whole thing needs serious attention."[45] In Washington's mind, food practices were about more than obtaining adequate nourishment.[46] Mistakes at the table, such as using the wrong plate or creating an unattractive menu card, provided evidence of poor character and could not be overlooked. Students were charged with paying careful attention to the practices of cooking, eating, and serving because proper food habits would prepare them to assume the rights of first-class citizenship should they be proffered. However, equally significantly, Washington wanted black people to take seriously the challenge of achieving food self-sufficiency as a means of becoming less dependent upon white goodwill, should it fail to materialize.

Although Washington attempted to intervene in the traditional southern pattern of consuming pork as a primary source of animal protein, his vision for dietary reform did not eschew all traditional southern food items, nor was it inflexible. In the food front as in all aspects of his uplift philosophy, Washington combined assimilationist and nationalist sensibilities. He believed that food could be used as a tool to demonstrate black worthiness for full incorporation as citizens, but he ultimately valued self-sufficiency far more than adherence to contemporary ideas about proper food habits. Furthermore, Washington publically indulged in items that would never have been served in a New England kitchen.

Washington maintained a lifelong fondness for opossum, a low-status, regional food. In 1914, he invited the teachers of Tuskegee Institute to a "'Possum & 'tater Supper and Candy Pulling," an old-fashioned meal that certainly had antecedents in slavery, when small game was used to subsidize monotonous, minimal diets.[47] Occasionally, he sent friends or associates shipments of opossum, giving, for example, a gift of the animal to Jeannette Tod Ewing Bertram, whose husband was employed as Andrew Carnegie's secretary.[48] The animal was accompanied by a note that suggested pride in the culinary heritage of African Americans, with Washington's declaration that "a Southern colored woman knows how to cook the opossum better than anyone else."[49] Thus Washington's vision for dietary reform was moderated by a persistent regard and affection for some aspects of traditional southern African American foodways.

Washington advocated for the maintenance of southern food practices for reasons of practicality and not just for pride and affection. For example, he urged African Americans to eat more cowpeas, an inexpensive, local food, which he deemed "one of the most nutritious foods, when properly cooked." In his advocacy for what was commonly known as the black-eyed pea, he directly invoked a favorable comparison between southern food and that promoted by white, northern, domestic scientists with his argument that cowpeas were just as nutritious as the "far-famed Boston bean," an item, like beef, that figured heavily into white food reform efforts.[50] Ultimately, Washington proved willing even to challenge beef's supremacy. In 1912, he asked members of the Boarding Department to economize on meal planning and to investigate the possibility of serving "pig feet, ears and so on," which "can be gotten cheap."[51] To Washington, the symbolic significance of beef was ultimately far less important than the frequently struggling institution's financial solvency.[52]

Washington accused the southern black community of not making the "vital connection between vegetable life and the life that sustains the body," and he advised African Americans to exploit their natural environment in search of food.[53] Fresh, local produce, including tomatoes, sweet potatoes, snap peas, blackberries, and greens, were served regularly at Tuskegee Institute. A sample 1902 student menu of beef and gravy, greens, and cornbread epitomizes Tuskegee's hybrid culinary sensibilities. Pork was removed from the classic southern plantation menu while other southern staples were maintained in a nod to both the past and the future, a divide Tuskegee students were obligated to travel in their journey toward racial uplift.[54]

Although Tuskegee Institute's survival depended upon the largesse of northern, white philanthropists, Washington and the Tuskegee staff balanced this reality with an emphasis on black culinary self-reliance. Washington's endless fundraising schedule demonstrates how dependent the institute was on aid from the outside, but Washington strove to create a daily environment for his students that shielded them from this reality and emphasized black agency. Food at Tuskegee was to be raised, prepared, and served by and for black people. In 1910, Washington boasted to the readers of *Good Housekeeping Magazine* that the young women who learned to practice domestic science by living together in a "Practice Cottage" on campus prepared meals for themselves with food supplies raised on the school farm, including milk, butter, cheese, vegetables, and beef.[55]Achieving such self-sufficiency was a matter of ongoing concern for the staff, which strove to limit dependency on canned goods and to revise menus to utilize foods produced on the school grounds rather than those imported from the outside.[56]

Washington repeatedly ordered the staff to strive for food self-sufficiency. In 1902 he instructed the institute's treasurer, Warren Logan, "to purchase as little in way of provisions from the store as possible." He acknowledged, "It is so much more convenient to open a can of salmon or a barrel of grits than to prepare our own vegetables for the table." For this reason, Washington advocated vigilance on the issue of provisioning, warning, "You cannot prevent the use of store bought goods without constant attention."[57] To help reach these goals, the staff and students of Tuskegee not only grew their own produce, but preserved it as well. Workers in the campus cannery put up five thousand gallons of fruit and vegetables each year.[58]

Washington's vision of black food autonomy was not limited to the education of his students, and the staff at Tuskegee promoted the message of food self-sufficiency beyond the grounds of the institute through a series of outreach programs designed to educate local farm families. Both female students and local women were encouraged to learn to raise poultry as a potential means of achieving economic independence. An 1899 article in the *Tuskegee Student* declared, "Any woman of ordinary intelligence can make a good living by raising poultry scientifically. . . . The more independent life a woman can lead, the better it is for her."[59] For similar reasons, Washington urged black farmers to diversify their production, to grow their own food and not just the cash crop of cotton, in order to reduce their dependency on food purchased at plantation commissaries for high rates of interest.[60]

He proclaimed, "The Farmer who wants to get out of debt will have large patches of greens, his garden will have something growing in it the year round. His table will be loaded with wild fruits. . . . His potatoes will keep him from buying so much corn meal and flour on credit."[61] Given the restrictions sharecroppers had to contend with regarding land usage, Washington's advice may not have always been practical, but the theory behind his recommendations was significant. Food was a tool of economic independence and could ameliorate the impact of racism if African Americans became less dependent on white employers and creditors to fill their stomachs. The ability to assert black national culinary independence could indeed have softened the blows of dependency and oppression.

For Washington, the manner in which food was produced and by whom was just as important as what particular items were consumed. Domestic science–endorsed food habits, such as those frequently practiced at Tuskegee Institute, were designed to prepare graduates for full incorporation into mainstream American culture should the strategies of racial uplift ever achieve their desired result. But Washington's culinary flexibility and interest in utilizing local goods reveal that the goal of black food autonomy was ultimately even more important. Food production was one of the pillars of Washington's vision for economic nationalism. In choosing beef over pork or in insisting upon strict standards of dining decorum, Washington was refuting white racist ideals about uncivilized black behavior and subversively insisting on the right of his students and staff to nutritious, even luxurious, meals. In encouraging food independence he was—in his typically covert fashion—reaching for an even more profound goal, a self-reliant black community that could function with or without the approval of either white racists or paternalistic white supporters. If racial uplift at the table could have indeed helped convince white society to bestow full citizenship rights on the African American community, that development would have been welcomed, but if Washington's radical vision of self-sufficiency had been realized, the issue of white attitudes about black food behavior would ultimately have become far less significant.

CHAPTER 13

Domestic Restaurants, Foreign Tongues

Performing African and Eating American in the US Civil Rights Era

AUDREY RUSSEK

Around seven o'clock on the partly cloudy, chilly evening of March 9, 1961, Dr. William Fitzjohn, chargé d'affaires of Sierra Leone, and his African American driver, Stewart Robinson, pulled up to a Howard Johnson's restaurant in Hagerstown, Maryland, along Route 40 about seventy miles northwest of Washington, D.C. En route to deliver a lecture in Pittsburgh, Pennsylvania, that evening, Fitzjohn—who earned his PhD from Columbia University—intentionally selected the ubiquitous orange-roofed chain restaurant because of its reputation for serving black customers.[1] Much to his chagrin, though, a "hostile and unfriendly" white waitress denied them service, even after Fitzjohn displayed his diplomatic credentials. The pair waited for fifteen minutes to see if circumstances changed before departing.[2]

When they learned about the incident, President John F. Kennedy and officials at the State Department cringed at yet another highly visible blot on the United States' civil rights record, one with a direct impact on foreign relations and the perception of the United States among newly independent African nations. This latest snub against Fitzjohn only added to the long list of reported instances of discrimination against visiting dignitaries from Africa and Asia, episodes of domestic racism that posed a liability for the United States as it fought the Cold War. Heightened concern over the damage to America's image on the world stage led President Kennedy and Secretary of State

Dean Rusk to approve formation of the Special Project Service Section (SPSS) division in the Protocol Office of the US State Department. Charged with reducing discrimination against foreign delegates, which included educating restaurant workers in methods of racial and national profiling, the SPSS deliberately sidestepped the domestic debate over integration and civil rights, citing its jurisdiction as limited to international affairs. President Kennedy also issued a strong statement to restaurant operators along Route 40, implicating their refusal of service to foreign dignitaries in fueling anti-American propaganda around the world. In late August 1961, the publisher of the *Baltimore Afro-American* newspaper decided to test the success of Kennedy's warning.

On August 22, 1961, three reporters from the *Baltimore Afro-American* rented a limousine along with elaborate, decorative costumes and styled themselves as African dignitaries to test the color line in restaurants along a 125-mile stretch of Route 40 between Washington and New York. Although posing as an elite foreigner to gain access to segregated restaurants in the United States was a time-honored (if infrequent) tradition among African Americans from the earliest days of Jim Crow, the widely publicized hoax followed on the heels of the Fitzjohn fiasco and highlighted the hypocrisy of American freedom and democracy in the midst of the Cold War.

A handful of previous studies document the discrimination against African dignitaries in American restaurants and the *Baltimore Afro-American* journalists' performative hoax. However, this body of scholarship locates these historical narratives solely within the framework of US civil rights and Cold War foreign policy and treats the journalists' ruse as an isolated event, folding the cultural activity of restaurants into larger discussions about foreign relations, global decolonization, and domestic desegregation.[3] Instead, in this essay, I resituate these events by casting restaurants as both the site and subject of political and social debates in their own right. I argue that to neglect the spatial and material importance of restaurants and the cultural positioning of the restaurant industry at large during this time period overlooks the symbolic significance of restaurants as sites of cultural work and as representations of American democratic values for national and global audiences alike. As this essay demonstrates, the simple fact that the US State Department worked tirelessly to negotiate with individual restaurant owners and state restaurant associations indicates the cultural power and social relevance of restaurants beyond places to grab food away from home. Thus, the State Department's solutions for alleviating discrimination against foreign dignitaries, modeled after nationally recognizable restaurant mainstays, including popular dining guides and restaurant rating systems, shows the simple yet profound influence of restaurants on national policy-making and American culture writ large.

This essay also points to multiple types of performances and ways of racial seeing that emerge out of these historical episodes. For instance, I locate the *Baltimore Afro-American* journalists' ruse within a more extensive history of foreign posturing in order to break the color line (what I refer to as "ethno-national impersonation") and argue that African Americans' hoax performances as African dignitaries should be understood as performances of perceived whiteness.[4] After all, as Tavia Nyong'o asserts, "race is a theory of history," and the "performative effects of history" include recognizing "performance as ambivalent actualization of a troubling potential."[5] In the case of ethno-national impersonation, the "troubling potential" was the exposure of "black" as an unstable racial construction and the demarcation of "white" as an unsustainable category of American identity, where whiteness is a metonym for privilege. Martin A. Berger's compelling work on the relationship between racial identification and visual texts affirms that "despite the human propensity to privilege sight, and the long-standing Western tendency to root racial designations in observable traits, images do not persuade us to internalize racial values embedded within them, so much as they confirm meanings for which the discourses and structures of our society have predisposed us. Instead of selling us on racial systems we do not already own, the visual field powerfully confirms previously internalized beliefs."[6] Spectacular performances of racialized foreignness in American restaurants did *not* visually confirm the elite status of the customer. Instead, these examples of ethno-national impersonation exposed white restaurant employees' predisposition to understand their own whiteness as a type of privilege that could be achieved through symbolic visual, aural, and material signifiers as a substitute for "white" skin. Thus, cues such as "native" costumes, accented speech, "foreign" names, diplomatic credentials, and material objects including guide-books, limousines, and menus all functioned as tools to claim a white, privileged experience in the United States.

Eating, too, is a "racially performative act."[7] Therefore, in a volume on African American food and foodways, this essay focuses on the materiality and politics of public eating spaces rather than on food objects, extending Kyla Wazana Tompkins's assertion that the cultural and social practice of eating plays "a significant part in the privileg-ing of whiteness."[8] Pedro Sanjuan, assistant chief of protocol at the State Department and director of the SPSS, affirmed as much when he addressed the Maryland National Assembly in 1961 on the topic of curbing discrimination against African delegates: "How can we expect the respect and friendship of new non-white nations when we humili-ate the representatives of these nations by denying them the right to be served in a highway restaurant or city café?" Sanjuan asked, "How can we expect these diplomats not to notice when the proprietor of a road-side café on Route 40 or a waitress in a Howard Johnson's restaurant informs them that they cannot be served because they are automati-cally presumed to be inferior to the average white American citizen?"[9] While classifying the visitors as "non-white," Sanjuan then expressed frustration that African delegates were presumed inferior to *white*, not *all*, American citizens. In other words, in the name of positive foreign relations, Sanjuan wanted state leaders to pressure restaurant owners to recognize dark-skinned diplomats as *white* by granting them the respect afforded white American citizens.

Because this essay positions restaurants as central to construc-tions of race and the framing of privilege as whiteness, and because restaurants are public spaces of food production and consumption, discrimination against visiting African dignitaries and public perfor-mances of "African" must be situated within African American food culture. I suggest that we expand African American foodways to con-sider Africans in the United States and these visitors' encounters with American food culture. For African diplomats, who positioned them-selves as privileged foreign elites and expected to be treated in kind, their interactions with American restaurants converged with those of African Americans. Despite the State Department's efforts to offer visiting dignitaries the privileges of whiteness, the federal government was unable to guarantee that experience to all international leaders.

I have organized this discussion into four main parts: The first section historicizes the *Baltimore Afro-American* journalists' charade by situating their form of activism within a longer trajectory of ethno-national impersonation. The second section analyzes the journalists' performative hoax in greater detail, showing the importance of visual and aural symbols as tools of profiling for restaurant employees. The third part highlights the concrete ways in which the SPSS looked to restaurants' material culture as a model for helping foreign diplomats avoid encounters with American racism. The fourth and final section examines suggested methods for teaching white American restaurant workers how to distinguish between dark-skinned Americans and elite Africans, an education in profiling racial and national identity intended to code privilege as whiteness.

Negroes in Turbans Only

A survey conducted in 1960 on behalf of the Commission on Intergroup Relations of the City of New York revealed that in contrast to non-white foreign nationals working as United Nations representatives, who tended to practice "self-imposed isolation" in response to acts of discrimination, "[middle- or upper-middle-class] American Negroes were less likely to accept a passive response of avoidance to the discrimination. Instead, they seemed more prone to taking action."[10] One form of activism was posing as foreign. While this practice was not common in the early to mid twentieth century, neither was it obscure. Decades before the Black Arts Movement of the 1970s and the popularization of kente cloth, dashikis, and kufis, the turban as headpiece signified as foreign to American audiences. African Americans recognized the turban's symbolic power both as a performative prop for crossing the color line and as an object for exposing the hypocrisies of segregation. When African Americans posed as African dignitaries to test the illogical structures of segregation, they implicitly mocked white employees who projected their internalized beliefs of white privilege onto visual symbols of elite status such as turbans.

Ethno-national impersonation as a guise for accessing segregated restaurants dates back to at least the early twentieth century. In 1917, the African American author Charles Chestnutt stopped at a restaurant in Pennsylvania to eat with his family. Although they were seated without incident, Chestnutt noticed the manager scrutinizing them. Promptly, Chestnutt began conversing with his daughters in French, and the manager, who assumed they were foreigners, backed off.[11] In the 1920s, a restaurant in Chicago refused to serve Ed Gordon, an African American track star. Gordon bet his friend he could wrap a towel around his head and gain entry. According to one journalist, "he did return with the towel-turban plus a heavy French accent—and was waited on with a flourish."[12]

In 1947, a black clergyman from Queens, New York, Rev. Jesse Wyman Routté, proudly shared how he had impersonated a foreign dignitary in Alabama. Outfitted in a colorful, bejeweled purple turban, Routté affected a Swedish accent (he was ordained in the Swedish Lutheran church) and used the turban and accent as a "passport across 'Jim Crow' lines," opening doors to the popular, segregated restaurants.[13] His account led one newspaper to conclude, "In the United States the wearing of a turban makes a man with black skin a first class citizen, whereas the absence of a turban exposes the same man to insult and ridicule. . . . It gives the lie to those who proclaim that there is something personally objectionable about a colored man, and it makes it clear that the objections are all to be found in the conscious or unconscious mind of the objector."[14]

Tales of similar episodes followed in Routté's wake. A national report, "Segregation in Washington," suggested that "wrap[ping] a turban around one's head" was the most successful method for black Americans "who wanted to test the advantages of being a foreigner."[15] In November 1957, the editor of the St. Louis Argus newspaper sent two African American men on assignment to a local Howard Johnson's restaurant bedecked in "turbans, berets, goatees, foreign accents, and a chauffeured Cadillac limousine" to gain admittance to the restaurant. Claiming to be representatives of Liberia, the duo seated themselves only to have the embarrassed hostess haltingly explain she would not serve them. When the men asked her to clarify why not, she added, "I can't make any exceptions. You might be better than they [black Americans] are, but you all look alike."[16] These activist performances set precedent for the journalists who tested restaurant integration along Route 40 in August 1961.

All of these experiments in ethno-national impersonation, whether successful or not, highlighted the fundamental injustice of race-based segregation and the precarious terms in which coded national identity factored into racial profiling. And with every example of this hypocrisy that found its way into the mainstream press and anecdotal folklore, African Americans vehemently protested the privileging of foreigners: "If the bars come down, they come down for everybody," declared Clarence Mitchell, the Washington director of the NAACP. "No restaurant would put up a sign that said, 'Negroes in turbans only.'"[17]

His Highness Is Given Soup

By August 1961, Carl J. Murphy, chief editor of the *Baltimore Afro-American*, long frustrated at witnessing restaurants around Baltimore seat African nationals while closing their doors to African Americans, helped devise a "trap-hoax" to test whether restaurants along Route 40 were willing to serve foreigners of color. Instructing his secretary to find a costume store that rented elaborate "African" robes and a funeral home willing to lease a limousine, Murphy then pointed to three of his reporters: "You are officials of the finance ministry of the newly independent 'Goban.' And that's exactly what we're going to do— 'go ban' racial discrimination."[18]

The three journalists—Herb Mangrum, Rufus Wells, and George Collins—detailed the hoax two weeks later in an extensive newspaper spread. Collins described how the trio posed as "non-existent African diplomats, from a non-existent African country," choosing an apt phrase to pinch at the hypocrisy of restaurant operators: as American Negroes, the journalists did not exist as customers, either. Mangrum assumed the identity of Orfa (Afro spelled backwards) Adwiba, finance minister of Goban, an imaginary country on the east coast of Africa. Wells personified Dula Okoro, Adwiba's aide-de-camp, and Collins adopted the persona of Loua Aklulu, the attaché and spokesman for the delegation, who "spoke mangled English, with drippings of an Oxford accent." Rounding out the delegation was the official photographer (played by the *Afro-American's* own photographer, I. Henry Phillips) and a hired chauffer whose family operated the funeral home that provided the sparkling, brand-new 1961 Cadillac limousine. Mangrum wrapped himself in a luxurious, deep maroon robe accented with gold and blue trim and donned a turban decorated with a leopard-skin crown and bejeweled with bright, colorful stones. To signal their supporting roles, Collins and Wells dressed in coattails and striped pants with the added touch of ties and top hats. Of the five restaurants tested that day, three accommodated the entourage and two denied service, although one claimed it was closed for dinner preparations.[19]

At the first stop, the Madison House, restaurant staff seated the men and repeatedly inquired if they needed help interpreting the menu. Although the group declined, the menu operated as another material testing device: not to test the trio's "authenticity" as African nationals but for restaurant employees to gauge their own barometers of privilege. The offers to interpret the menu can be read as gestures of hospitality that authorized the status of the recipient. Collins and his comrades deemed the first stage of their hoax a success when the waitress "got the message that Mangrum was top dog, without being told," and served him first. Then, much to the group's surprise, the waitress produced a picture postcard and requested Mangrum's autograph. The autographed card, costumes, mangled English, and other visible and audible cues completed the white waitress's internal script of expectations for the appearance of African dignitaries. She believed the hoax because *she* was inclined to "see" (and "hear") privilege through these objects.

At the Redwood Inn in Aberdeen, Maryland, the contradictory power of visual evidence emerged in two ways. First, the host questioned the group's African origins before seating them apart from white diners. After eating with "the best of table manners," Collins handed the check to the same worker, who repeated the name "Goban" with an edge of disbelief and a "stony stare," murmuring acknowledgment "in a voice that could have easily said 'you are lying to [*sic*] your teeth.'" The man's position as white, working in an openly segregated restaurant, conditioned him to see the trio as racially inferior despite their formal clothing and refined table manners, symbolic representations of high-class status. In this case, the power of visual texts *failed* to fully persuade the restaurant host of the group's privileged rank. However, the managers also refused to allow the group's photographer to take pictures of the trio dining inside. They feared the images would *succeed* as visual evidence of the restaurant's willingness to serve African American customers. Through the medium of the printed photograph, other cues used to profile "foreignness" dissolved, such as accented speech and printed credentials, transferring the power of profiling from the restaurant employee and into the hands of potential customers. How could a reader, gazing at a photograph, know if the dark-skinned customer was African or American? "You are not going to make an example of my place," one of the restaurant managers growled at Phillips. As this comment revealed, photographs, like other forms of visual evidence, could belie what they "really" represented.

At their final three destinations, the journalists encountered more obstacles. The manager at the Double T Diner (a site of student sit-ins the previous day) refused to seat the entourage without first seeing diplomatic credentials, which he falsely claimed was state law. The Hi-Way Diner claimed to be closed until the dinner hour. The host at Miller's Restaurant (also a site of sit-ins) first denied the group, but the manager backtracked out of fear the State Department would close the establishment.[20] Although in 1961 the federal government could not legally force restaurants to desegregate, it could strong-arm restaurants caught denying service to foreign diplomats. As the Redwood Inn manager clarified, "We don't serve Negroes. Africans, yes, because President Kennedy told us so."[21] This pressure forced white restaurant operators, as gatekeepers of privilege, to distinguish between diplomats of color and Americans of color. The wrong turn in the direction of the former risked the wrath of the State Department; on the other hand, to "mistakenly" seat dark-skinned *Americans* risked the exposure of the absurd rationale on which the illogic of segregation was based.

Guides to Discriminating Dining

The State Department was heavily invested in steering diplomats of color out of the path of American racism, and to do so, the SPSS brainstormed ways to mediate visiting delegates' travel within the United States. Importantly, much of the discussion centered on the cultural and material economy of restaurants and the industry's methods for helping Americans find reliable dining options away from home. The impulse to look at recognizable promotional staples of the restaurant industry, such as guidebooks and certificates of approval, points toward the relevant positioning of restaurants as both quotidian and culturally influential. Inspired by dining guides that highlighted popular destinations, state representatives floated the idea of creating a guidebook for UN delegates complete with entries for "the most accessible and the more favorable places," coded language for describing integrated restaurants.[22] Two restaurant guidebooks emerged as concrete models for this proposal: Duncan Hines's *Adventures in Good Eating* and Victor Green's *Negro Motorist Green Book*.

Adventures in Good Eating was the brainchild of Duncan Hines, an advertising salesman who spent numerous hours on the road for work and leisure in the 1920s.[23] The oft-repeated story of the book's origins assumed its own mythology: during his travels, Hines jotted down the names of good restaurants he encountered around the country. Hines gave copies to friends, whose rave word-of-mouth reviews generated more requests. Hines published the first *Adventures in Good Eating* in 1936. The guide, updated and published annually through 1962, became a restaurant patron's manifesto. *Adventures in Good Eating* claimed to be a guidebook "compiled from the viewpoint and in the interest of its users—the patrons of America's restaurants"—assuming America's restaurant patrons were white. For instance, two of the restaurants visited during the "'Go-ban' discrimination" hoax of 1961 appeared in the directory: Miller's and the Redwood Inn. Both the 1960 and 1962 editions (published in 1959 and 1961, respectively) described Miller's as "one of Baltimore's very finest restaurants."[24] Likewise, the 1962 edition praised the Redwood Inn as "modern and attractive."[25] This inclusion of restaurants actively known to refuse service to black customers highlighted African Americans' difficulty finding accommodations while traveling: most times when they stepped into a new or unfamiliar restaurant, mainstream dining guides failed them.

The *Negro Motorist Green Book* helped to even the field. In 1932, Victor H. Green, an African American mail carrier for the US Postal Service, traveled around the country only to encounter humiliating situations where hotels, gas stations, and restaurants refused to serve him. After hearing similar tales from black friends and colleagues, and acutely aware that white motorists had travel guides at their disposable, Green conceived of the *Negro Motorist Green Book*.[26] The first edition of the *Green Book* appeared in bookstores around New York in 1936; Green printed the last edition in 1964. The early editions concentrated only on sites around New York, but by 1940, the guide included information on forty-four states as well as the District of Columbia.[27]

With these two popular guidebooks firmly located in the public dining imagination, participants in SPSS brainstorming meetings turned to these restaurant mainstays as model solutions for guiding diplomats to welcoming restaurants. William C. Rogers, representing the Maryland Commission on Interracial Problems and Relations, asked the chief of protocol, Angier Biddle Duke, if he could assist the State Department by providing a list of restaurants in Maryland willing to serve black customers. Duke expressed both interest and skepticism. Frank Reeves, the first African American member of the Democratic National Committee and special assistant to President Kennedy, voiced concern that the list would mostly (or only) include black owned-and-operated restaurants, which would signal to diplomats their exclusion from mainstream dining spots. However, if carefully compiled, the collection could function as "sort of a 'Duncan Hines approved list."[28] William E. Murnighan, legal adviser for the Bureau of Near East, South Asia, and African Affairs, agreed: "If this came from a non-governmental source, if you took a regular commercial guide to a state, listing the good places to eat commercially, and then try to see if you can work something out with these and if somebody asked us to give this guide to them, instead of the Ford guide or the Duncan Hines guide . . . would this be the way to do it?"[29] Reeves acknowledged that a similar guide already existed—the *Negro Motorist Green Book*—but Murnighan clarified that the one for diplomats needed to be a synthesis of the *Green Book* and *Adventures in Good Eating*: a listing of restaurants welcoming to black customers but "not necessarily just for Negroes."[30] To keep up the appearance that the SPSS was concerned with *all* diplomats, the group emphasized its materials would assist all visiting delegates, not only those from Africa and South Asia.

Several potential problems emerged from this proposal, though. First, how reliable were the selected restaurants and their assurances to seat delegates? After all, Howard E. Johnson insisted his chain served all, and yet frequent reports emerged of numerous Howard Johnson's restaurants discriminating against diplomats. Second, one of the reasons why the State Department decided not to distribute the *Negro Motorist Green Book* to African diplomats was to refrain from steering them only to black-friendly restaurants. The US government wanted African diplomats to have all of the privileges of whiteness— to be able to eat anywhere, to sleep anywhere, to use the facilities in any public restroom. To give them the *Green Book* would be a concession that regardless of their diplomatic status, the United States (and white American citizens, in particular) would not grant them these white privileges. Would the State Department's guidebook concede the same? Although by August 1961, the SPSS officially included as part of its program "compiling lists of acceptable places," ultimately, Sanjuan rejected the idea: "Some people keep suggesting a kind of 'Duncan Hines' list of restaurant for foreign diplomats," he remarked, "but we wouldn't be fooling anybody that way. A law here [to prevent discrimination] is the only answer."[31]

In addition to guidebooks, the SPSS turned toward another nationally recognized restaurant symbol as visual proxy for privilege: the Duncan Hines "sign of approval." Hines leased official "Recommended by Duncan Hines" signs to businesses listed in the current edition of his guidebook; restaurants could also purchase "small gummed labels," official Duncan Hines identification stickers, directly from Hines's office and affix them to table tents, menus, and other restaurant paraphernalia.[32] Caroline Ramsay, who served on Maryland's State Commission on Interracial Problems and Relations, floated the idea of signage endorsing restaurants willing to serve diplomats of color. Why not, Ramsay mused, "have a State Department seal of approval that you, like a Duncan Hines sign, would put on restaurants and places that would give them, as you say, the positive approach, the distinction of being approved by the State Department as a good facility?" Along with signs for restaurant windows, the committee imagined all diplomatic personnel receiving Duncan Hines–esque stickers for their cars and luggage to "indicate visibly their diplomatic status." D.C. commissioner Walter Tobriner acknowledged that "it wouldn't completely take care of the problem," but at least the stickers would offer "something *visible* to the public." Chief of protocol, Angier Biddle Duke, countered that all diplomats and members of their staff received identity cards authorizing their official status. According to Tobriner, though, the paper credentials inadequately protected diplomats, pointing out, "[they're] not *visible*."[33] Only a sticker on a windshield or diplomatic license plate—visual spectacles—signaled that the diplomat was coded "white" by the US government and should receive the "privilege" of service. Importantly, these visual labels were not really for the benefit of foreign nationals; instead, they assisted American service workers in deciding who should receive the full treatment accorded white citizens.

When Africa Was White

How did restaurant operators, intent on enforcing Jim Crow segregation, determine who was "white"? How did State Department officials, intent on curbing discrimination against diplomats, authorize white privilege to elite foreigners?[34] Much has been written about the challenge of authenticating race to justify and maintain segregation and the precarious, shifting definitions of racial categories. In 1959, author Stetson Kennedy published a scathing tongue-in-cheek critique of American racism, *Jim Crow Guide to the U.S.A.* In the book, Kennedy astutely observed that American legal definitions of race varied according to state and declared that "physical appearance is regarded as among the best evidence of race" and "more important ... than citizenship." In the section "Evidence of Whiteness," Kennedy listed types of court-admissible testimony that confirmed an individual's "whiteness," including that a person "is reputed to be white," "enjoys high social status," and "exercises the rights of whites."[35] These examples affirm Berger's observation that "the legal designation 'white' has never guaranteed equal treatment under the law, never mind social or economic equality, for those whose whiteness is less culturally secure."[36] One of the few explicit examples demonstrating the precarious designation of "white," and supporting the argument that privilege coded as whiteness, appears in an anecdote relayed by Carl Rowan, a decorated African American journalist and Kennedy's deputy assistant secretary of state, during an SPSS meeting. Rowan cautioned against using labels, badges, or other tangible gestures that promised special treatment to diplomats, citing this narrative:

> There was a little cruise on the Potomac the other night, and a diplomat from Ceylon was telling a little story which I think is indicative of the attitudes of a great many of these colored diplomats. He said that he got his driver's license, and he noted that on it he was listed as "white." So he called the driver's license office and got a young lady and said, "What does this listing on my driver's license mean?" And she said, "Well, *it means that we class you as 'white.'*" And he said, "I said to her, 'Young lady, have you looked at me? I am as black as the ace of spades.'" And he mailed his driver's license back because he thought that this was a special little categorization and a bit of special treatment that rather than appreciating he considered quite offensive. And that is why I think that we ought to be extremely careful in the adoption of any identification tags, and so forth.[37]

This example highlights how physical appearance alone was an unstable determinant of racial identity, a problem faced by restaurant workers charged with the task of assigning white privilege to potential customers.

How else to verify, to identify "whites" who were not white, if ways of seeing, of looking, didn't work? The SPSS began to organize meetings with restaurant associations and independent businesses to teach Americans how to ascertain a customer's privileged status regardless of the restaurant's standing policy of racial discrimination. "[We] somehow [need to] make them aware that when a Negro comes into the restaurant at least . . . be sure first he is not an Ambassador," pleaded Florida's representative, Scotty Fraser.[38] One solution to help restaurant workers learn to profile entailed increased exposure to "real" foreigners of color. Frank Reeves suggested, "It would be very educational . . . to a lot of people at our grassroots level in some of our states to have occasion *to see or to hear* some of these foreign visitors on local television or radio stations. It will, I'm sure, dispel a lot of misconceptions and false notions that some of the people at the grassroots level have about these people."[39] The goal of this familiarization, though, was not a greater understanding of foreign cultures and peoples. Instead, the person-to-person exposure could increase

American citizens' proximity to "real" Africans and provide cues and clues for seeing (or hearing) the supposed differences between foreign nationals and black Americans.

Other proposals included devising some symbolic form of identification for diplomats to verify their privileged status as foreign guests. These suggestions met with outright skepticism or dismissal by dignitaries as well as several government officials, including Secretary of State Dean Rusk. "Let me say with a Georgian accent," he emphasized, "that we cannot solve this problem if it requires a diplomatic passport to claim the normal rights of American citizens."[40] Rusk's comment, however, cracked open the window on second-class citizenship in the United States, where no passport, neither domestic nor foreign, permitted the nation's black citizens to "claim their normal rights." Ironically, African Americans often could only eat in segregated restaurants if accompanying a foreign diplomat. As Frank Reeves noted, "the problem if [sic] we are asking him [the restaurant operator] to make a distinction between an American Negro, who is present with someone from a foreign country, and an American Negro who many come in there by himself."[41] The diplomat functioned as a living "passport" for the black American citizen trying to access the basic right of eating in public dining rooms.

Conclusion

No seal of approval, no standard badge of identification provided white restaurant employees with an accurate tool for profiling customers based on race and nationality, despite some government officials' insistence that "clear identification" would help proprietors.[42] The failure of these directives to finesse the differences between black Americans and African dignitaries exposes the ways in which individual restaurant workers projected their own scripts of race, social status, and privilege onto potential customers. The mainstream black press took the opportunity to mock this trust in identification markers. "The impact of these hundreds of men and women who look like American Negroes but must be treated as foreign guests, has raised merry havoc with certain Caucasian customs," *Ebony* magazine observed, joking about the new dangers of the restaurant workplace. "Their presence has added new hazards to the occupation of waitress and sent café managers to ulcerous graves."[43] Additionally, the *Chicago Defender* reported how several exclusive restaurants in New York opened up their reservation lists to black customers "mainly because they did not know the racial identity of the guests seeking entrance": black foreigner or black citizen.[44]

Political cartoonist Herb Block brilliantly captured the complexity of profiling customers of color as either African or American in a cartoon captioned, "It's all right to seat them. They're not Americans" (see fig. 13.1). In the cartoon, the maître d' hustles toward a bewildered white hostess standing before an elegant, dark-skinned couple. The man, wearing a respectable coat and tie, also sports a turban. His companion, with beautifully coifed hair and hoop earrings, is dressed in a formal, flowing shawl and skirt. Taking a closer look, we notice the dour man carefully cutting his food in the left corner of the frame bears a striking resemblance to James Beard, the culinary connoisseur who represented American food sophistication in the 1960s. We also read the restaurant's name printed on the menu tucked under the arm of the maître d': "Ye Olde Yankee Noodle Plantation Tea Roome," a play on the popular heritage-themed restaurants of the time. These restaurants tapped into nostalgic versions of the nation's founding history as decorative inspiration, from quaint New England–style colonial inns to grand southern slave plantations. The cartoon at once captures and is itself part of the materiality of American restaurants and the social practices of eating.

Yet, how do we know, looking at the cartoon, if the couple waiting to be seated is "authentically" African or impersonating Africans? What "discourses and structures of our society have predisposed us" to one interpretation or the other? The brilliance of the cartoon is that we cannot know—the cartoon's own medium reveals the layers of visual indeterminacy and exposes how, in the early 1960s, ideologies of race were recast as privilege, classifying Africans as white in the eyes of the US government and the white-dominated restaurant industry. The cartoon, though, is also a testament to the ironic success of ethno-national impersonation during a time when one rarely benefitted from "un-American" acts.

A 1961 Herblock Cartoon, © The Herb Block Foundation. Image courtesy of the Prints & Photographs Division, Library of Congress, reproduction #LC-DIG-ppmsc-03475.

CHAPTER 14

Freedom's Farms
Activism and Sustenance in Rural Mississippi

ANGELA JILL COOLEY

Growing up in early twentieth-century Sunflower County, Mississippi, as the twentieth child born to a poor, black farmer and his wife, Fannie Lou Hamer did not have much to eat. "So many times for dinner we would have greens with no seasonin'," she recalled for a *Nation* magazine article in 1964. "My mother would mix flour with a little grease and try to make gravy out of it. Sometimes she'd cook a little meal and we'd have bread."[1] Hamer's memories involve fairly typical fare for the poor farming families of the Mississippi Delta who labored long hours to put food on other peoples' tables. Decades later, after participating in the voting rights campaigns of the civil rights movement, Hamer understood that the sustenance needs of her community remained unmet.

In 1969, in an effort to provide for the daily subsistence needs of her neighbors, Hamer founded the agricultural cooperative Freedom Farm. She acquired the property from C. B. Pratt, a black landowner close to losing the land to tax liabilities. Freedom Farm provided free hogs and vegetables to poor farmers who had been displaced by agricultural allotments and mechanization. The cooperative intended to assist anyone in need, and it boasted an entirely African American leadership. In this way, Hamer's initiative represented an effort by rural black Mississippians to take control over their food systems. This was a significant development for a population that had little voice in the national policy debates over poverty and sustenance that dominated the latter half of the decade.[2]

Following in her parents' footsteps, Hamer had worked most of her adult life as a sharecropper. She came to prominence in 1964 as a member of the Mississippi Freedom Democratic Party, which traveled to the Democratic Convention in Atlantic City to attempt to unseat the state's all-white delegation. She worked for years as a voting rights activist for the Student Nonviolent Coordinating Committee (SNCC).[3] Her transition to focusing on the sustenance needs of her community represented a next step in her commitment to advance civil rights and was a typical one for this period of the movement, when many activists turned their attention to the problems of rural and urban poverty.

Freedom Farm sat in the Mississippi Delta, a fertile flood plain in the northwestern corner of the state that produced nearly half the state's crop values in the late 1960s. Much of the area's wealth, concentrated primarily in the hands of a small white minority, stemmed from federally subsidized crops. Two years before Hamer founded Freedom Farm, the US Department of Agriculture paid Sunflower County's farmers more than $10 million in price supports—going mostly to wealthy white landowners. One of these landowners, US senator James O. Eastland, received more than $160,000 in federal subsidies. Meanwhile, many of the black farmers who had worked Sunflower County's land for generations for barely subsistence wages no longer had any income.[4]

The incongruity between how the federal government allocated funds in farming communities in Mississippi in the 1960s and where the need was greatest is one of many paradoxes that surround the politics of poverty and hunger. Although the Mississippi Delta represented one of the most fertile agricultural areas in the world, accessing sufficient sustenance remained a significant challenge throughout the twentieth century. Politics played a role in subsistence especially after the New Deal introduced federal programs into poverty-stricken areas. The problem of sustenance was intertwined with issues of race and socioeconomic class because white landowners controlled both the land and the federal commodity programs upon which black farm families depended for food. Powerful white planters consistently manipulated food supplies to suit their desire for a vulnerable and pliable black laboring class.

In the 1960s African American farmers found allies in the civil rights activists who came to the Delta to advocate for black suffrage and, to a lesser extent, in the government officials who planned and executed antipoverty programs in the region. From 1962 to 1974, the problem of hunger represented a significant element in civil rights activism and in the development of federal poverty policy. As they executed voting rights campaigns in Mississippi, activists engaged in the political battles over food by soliciting donations to sustain poor communities and using distribution campaigns to educate hungry people on their constitutional rights. For federal lawmakers, food represented an important piece of more comprehensive programs targeted toward fighting poverty. They drafted legislation that had the potential to feed low-income communities, but local white administrators implemented these programs in ways that helped to maintain the racial status quo.

The late 1960s represented a period of change in civil rights activism as activists like Hamer turned their full-time attention to the matter of sustenance. The problem of hunger in the Delta, like the use of police dogs in Birmingham, was the result of purposeful acts of the white power structure to control and subjugate the region's black population. Yet, despite actions of a few dedicated activists and the genuine interest of some federal legislators who fought to bring attention to the problem of poverty in the Delta, hunger failed to generate the same type of national public outrage sufficient to produce real results.

Food Justice in the Mississippi Delta

This essay contributes to the emerging scholarly literature of food justice that considers how factors such as race, class, gender, ethnicity, and geography circumscribe access to food. Today, consuming food is widely recognized as a political act. Many best-selling volumes criticize the modern industrial food system with its heavy government subsidies for unhealthy foods and advocate for a return to the food practices of earlier generations. Yet, much of this work fails to adequately address the challenges marginalized communities face in accessing food. Food justice scholars and activists alleviate common oversights by addressing the ability of communities to access food in ways that provide for the health and autonomy of the people. Food justice offers a new vocabulary for discourse surrounding how food gets to our tables and the problems facing marginalized populations in accessing healthy sustenance. In food justice parlance, food security refers to a condition in which all individuals have regular access to sufficient food to satisfy their nutritional and energy needs. Food sovereignty refers to a population's ability to determine the best ways to fulfill their sustenance requirements.[5]

The political struggles over food access for black southern farmers during the civil rights era, however, remind us that only the vocabulary is new. The problems surrounding the lack of food sovereignty have been with us for generations—even for that population, the American farmer, commonly idealized as the person most closely connected to food and its source. Historically, poor black southern farm communities suffered food insecurity as a result of economic, racial, and geographical difference. Tenants, sharecroppers, and day laborers often had little say in how land was cultivated, and landowners preferred acreage to be planted in cash crops instead of food. Moreover, African Americans were disproportionally represented as sharecroppers because racial discrimination impaired the ability of black farmers to own and maintain their land. In rural areas after the New Deal, sharecroppers and farm laborers often relied on government assistance because of the seasonal nature of the work and the increasing mechanization of southern farming.[6] During the civil rights era, food justice issues helped to shape the interactions among African American farmers, white planters, government administrators, and civil rights activists.

Food Access in Rural Mississippi

As Hamer's childhood memories reveal, black Mississippi farmers suffered difficulty accessing healthy foods throughout the twentieth century. Dietary studies by the Mississippi extension services confirm that land tenure and race circumscribed food access in rural Mississippi. During World War II, most white farm families produced the majority of their food, but only landowners produced nearly sufficient quantities and varieties of food to maintain health and vigor. The diets

A Plantation Store near Clarksville, Mississippi. Here black sharecropper families may have purchased the majority of their food supplies. Photo by Dorothea Lange, 1936. Library of Congress, Prints and Photographs Division, reproduction #LC-USF34-009594-C.

of white tenant families fell well below recommended nutritional standards. Tenants generally did not have access to sufficient acreage to satisfy their dietary needs and to meet the demands of their cash crops. Although white tenants spent more of their limited cash resources on food than owners spent, they still failed to maintain a healthy diet based on contemporary standards.[7]

Black farmers, however, fared significantly worse in meeting these standards. According to one early twentieth-century study, black farmers in the Mississippi Delta produced less than half their food on the farm. This meant that, unlike white farmers at all tenure levels, African Americans purchased most of their food. They went into debt, most likely to their white landlord, to sustain their families. They paid more for food than they might have otherwise because they were limited in where they could purchase it and because their landowners charged interest on the loans. Dorothy Dickins, the state home economist responsible for conducting nutrition studies, acknowledged that some white landlords limited the ability of black tenants to cultivate gardens, but she also attributed the difference to a white supremacist understanding of African Americans as less intelligent than whites.[8]

Historical circumstances that Dickins did not recognize, however, likely account for this race-based difference in food access. Collectively, black farmers had less wealth—meaning they had fewer resources with which to produce food. For instance, nearly all white farmers—landowners and tenants—owned cows. But fewer than half of black farmers owned a cow. As a result, most black farmers could not produce milk.[9] Moreover, Hamer's life reveals that whites often sought retribution toward black farmers who experienced success. When her family moved to Sunflower County, they rented land—a step up from sharecropping. They purchased mules and equipment, fixed up their home, and bought a car. Then, a white neighbor, Hamer recalled, poisoned their mules and cow—stock necessary to the farm's success. After that, the family's fortunes fell, and they resorted to sharecropping. "That white man did it just because we were gettin' somewhere," Hamer later said. "White people never like to see Negroes get a little success."[10]

The differentiation in wealth between black and white farmers—either as the result of historical discrimination or racial spite—meant that black farm families had fewer resources with which to cultivate a healthy diet. But Dickins fails to attribute these discrepancies to arbitrary racial bias. White landowners often gave white tenants more control over the land. They established commissaries for black tenants rather than trusting them to cultivate food.[11] For all these reasons, in the general course of business, black farmers had less food sovereignty—or control over their sustenance—than whites had.

Starting in the New Deal, federal commodities supplemented black farm diets. As part of President Franklin D. Roosevelt's agricultural program, the federal government distributed surplus products, such as flour, cornmeal, and cheese, to needy families. New Deal policy provided such subsidies, not with the primary purpose to feed people, but rather to provide an outlet for surplus crops. Nevertheless, the programs did provide necessary sustenance to poor farm families when

Black Farm Workers Gathered in Plantation Stores to Collect Wages and Buy Supplies. Marcella Plantation, Mississippi. Photo by Marion Post Wolcott, 1939. Library of Congress, Prints and Photographs Division, reproduction #LC-USF34-052200-D.

they had access to the program. Like most federal agricultural programs, the white planter class controlled commodity benefits, deciding who received the food and when. Planters distributed commodities to farm laborers in the winter, meaning that the federal government maintained their workers in the off season. They stopped distributions during planting and harvesting to force laborers to accept paltry wages for their long hours of hard work.[12] In essence, white planters used federal food programs in the Mississippi Delta to sustain a compliant laboring class and not to generate a healthy, productive population.

Food Access and Civil Rights

During the civil rights era, white landowners and public officials took advantage of black food insecurity and white control over the region's sustenance to disrupt voting campaigns. Manipulation of food access took several forms. In many instances, landowners threatened black sharecroppers' access to the land if they participated in activism. In August 1962, Hamer traveled by bus to the county seat at Indianola to register to vote. Hamer's interest in voting stemmed from a mass meeting held in a church by SNCC activists. The Mississippi school system failed to educate African Americans on their rights as citizens, and until that point, no one had informed Hamer that she had the right to vote. Although the registrar refused to put her on the voter rolls, when she returned to the farm that she and her husband had worked for eighteen years, the planter dismissed her.[13]

White officials interfered with civil rights activism by using their control over the federal surplus commodities program. In Greenwood, Mississippi, the Leflore County Board of Supervisors administered the federal food program. In 1962, SNCC established a voting rights campaign in Greenwood. That winter, the board of supervisors, under the influence of the white supremacist Citizen's Council, stopped the distribution of federal food surpluses. The county's action prompted attention by federal civil rights investigators who, in January 1963, questioned the board's attorney, Aubrey Bell. Bell called the allegation "a damn lie," although there was no question that the food distributions had been eliminated. Bell admitted the county's white leadership resented the "outside agitators"—meaning civil rights workers—who encouraged black voter registration.[14]

Of course, the population that Leflore County officials attempted to starve into submission by eliminating commodity distributions represented the same people that SNCC activists targeted for suffrage drives—poor black citizens who had been politically disfranchised. Consequently, the actions of county officials in Greenwood gave activists a new opportunity to reach these individuals. Civil rights activists reached out to Friends of SNCC in Chicago to solicit food donations for needy Mississippians. A food drive poster read "Give Food for Freedom in Mississippi" and provided addresses for twelve drop-off locations across the city. The poster explained the need in more detail: "As you read this, thousands of Mississippi citizens face starvation because some of them dared to register as voters. In retaliation, Mississippi officials have withdrawn support from the U.S. surplus food distribution program on which these families must rely for subsistence during the winter." Friends of SNCC requested donations of flour, cornmeal, rice, sugar, cereals, dried beans, cooking oils, and canned meats. The well-known comedian and activist Dick Gregory escorted these donations to Mississippi, where he gave speeches, led marches, and pledged to stay "until . . . freedom was obtained."[15]

Sending food aid to the people of Greenwood fit SNCC's ideology of living among the people and of respecting the capabilities and humanity of the individuals they served. But activists also made savvy political use of these donations. Food drives in Chicago gave activists the opportunity to describe the dangerous and deceitful methods by which white authorities in Mississippi stripped black citizens of their constitutional rights and maintained white supremacy. In Greenwood, civil rights activists packed the donated food into boxes and distributed them to families who normally relied on the government surplus program. Activists took advantage of this time with community members to discuss voter registration, and many recipients later turned up at the county courthouse to register.[16]

County officials accused civil rights activists of offering African Americans free food in exchange for registering to vote.[17] But white supremacists in Leflore County failed to recognize that by manipulating government assistance they had undermined key components of the white patriarchy that had, in part, kept potential black voters away from the courthouse. First, by cutting off access to an important source of food, especially during the off-season, the county board of supervisors demonstrated the power of elected officials and the significance of voting. If the black community needed a civics lesson in the power of elections over life and death decisions, white county officials provided it. Second, SNCC's food drive afforded a convenient gathering point for activists to discuss voting rights with the local population and to gain their trust and loyalty. Finally, by withholding federal resources from the citizens who relied on assistance, white county officials lost any paternalistic claim of loyalty they may have had over the local black community.

The War on Poverty in Mississippi

After the legislative successes of 1964 and 1965, which ended officially sanctioned racial segregation and disfranchisement, respectively, federal officials and civil rights activists turned to poverty as the next civil rights battle.[18] On January 8, 1964, President Lyndon B. Johnson announced this new government initiative in his State of the Union address by declaring "unconditional war on poverty in America."[19] Food programs constituted a significant part of Johnson's comprehensive attack on poverty. Under the Food Stamp Act of 1964, low-income households purchased coupons that could be used at approved grocery stores to buy food. The coupons' purchase price depended upon each family's ordinary grocery expenditures. The idea behind the program was that poor families would continue to spend the same amount of their household income on food, but their money would buy more. Like the surplus commodities program, however, feeding people was subsidiary to providing price supports for American agriculture. In Mississippi, participation in the new program depended upon the county, but federal law prohibited a county from participating in both the commodity surplus and food stamp programs.[20]

Hamer and many of her activist colleagues in Sunflower County opposed the food stamp program because so many county residents either did not qualify for the program, could not afford to purchase the coupons, or both. Eligibility requirements differed from those set forth to receive surplus commodities, and many poor families no longer qualified for assistance. The federal government implemented a loan program to help those families who could not afford to purchase food stamps. But for Hamer, such loans represented one more way for poor black farm families to incur debt they could not repay. She circulated a petition advocating a free food stamp program.[21]

In addition to fundamental problems with the law, county officials implemented the food stamp program in a manner that demeaned those in need of assistance. Although many poor whites lived in the area, according to federal records from the late 1960s, they did not participate in food programs—most likely because of the perpetuation of segregation culture and a racialized interpretation of poverty programs by Mississippi's white population. The all-white staff at welfare offices serviced their all-black clientele in ways that helped to maintain white supremacy. Recipients had to make several trips to the welfare office before they were certified to participate in the program. In a rural county, this meant walking long distances into town. Once

POLITICS

clients were in the waiting room, white government officials treated them in ways that, as one observer described, "did not accord with human dignity." A sign posted in the waiting room read "No Talking," and, even though twenty or more recipients may wait for an entire day, officials threatened to remove anyone who violated the prohibition. In another case, welfare officials threatened to call the police to arrest anyone whose name did not appear on their list.[22]

Sunflower County Progress, a social service agency funded by federal monies, ran the Emergency Food and Medical program (EF&M) in the county that helped poor people purchase food stamps. Again, the administration of the program stripped recipients of their autonomy as well as their dignity. The social service agency gave the funds directly to the welfare office, which then issued the coupons. Low-income families qualified for assistance for six months, at which point the EF&M program assumed they would be in an improved financial position. The EF&M program could provide direct grants to needy families, but the staff rarely did so because they mistrusted recipients to make food choices that white administrators considered appropriate. In one case, for example, EF&M staff reported that they paid for the groceries selected by a beneficiary family, and the family purchased roast beef. The staff considered roast beef to be too expensive compared to the bologna or neckbones, on which they thought beneficiaries should subsist. As a result, program officials started selecting and purchasing foods for needy families.[23] The sole concern seemed to be price, and perhaps the quality of food considered to be fit for a poor black family. The EF&M staff made no mention of the preference, nutrition, or autonomy of the community members they served. For all these reasons, food programs largely failed to provide decent sustenance in the Mississippi Delta.

The absurdity of federal food programs that did not furnish basic subsistence for poor communities is explained by the fact that food stamps, like other government food assistance, were intended to promote price supports for wealthy farmers. The *Delta Democrat-Times* in Greenville, Mississippi, suggested as much when it questioned whether food stamps helped supermarket owners more than needy families because it provided an influx of federal monies into their cash registers.[24] In reality, it also aided a powerful lobby behind the big farmers who cultivated the food sold in supermarkets. In 1969, journalist Nick Kotz reviewed the history of federal food assistance and found that 1960s subsistence programs overwhelmingly failed because they were underfunded, bureaucratic, and not targeted toward solving the problem of hunger.[25]

Food Sovereignty in the Delta

As an alternative to disappointing federal programs, civil rights activists turned their attention to the problem of sustenance in ways that attempted to give local people some control over their food systems. This type of activism took place across the country in different forms. In Atlanta, the Southern Christian Leadership Conference (SCLC) conducted the Poor People's Campaign to advocate for guaranteed incomes sufficient for poor people to take care of their needs. In California, the Black Panthers initiated free breakfast programs for school children. Chicago-based activist Dick Gregory, who had delivered food to Greenwood in the early 1960s, advocated for more healthful eating. The Nation of Islam founded agricultural cooperatives to enable black Americans to maintain a religious-based diet.[26]

The Nation of Islam initiative was only one of many rural cooperatives designed to provide poor farmers with greater autonomy over their livelihoods and subsistence. In 1968, the National Sharecroppers Fund estimated that there were as many as seventy-five cooperatives in the rural South controlled by a democratic membership representing around seventeen thousand persons. The following year, this organization accompanied a team of black leaders, including SNCC veteran Charles Sherrod, to Israel to study communal farming methods as inspiration for a Georgia cooperative.[27] Although many of these programs anticipated transracial cooperation, a common objective was to provide food sovereignty—or control over their food systems— to poor black communities.

In Sunflower County, Hamer began Freedom Farm for this reason. She recognized that food insecurity threatened not only the health and well-being of Mississippi farmers but also their ability to claim their rights as citizens. In addition to founding an agricultural cooperative, Hamer actively engaged in the politics of poverty in the 1960s. In 1968, she participated in a public television documentary titled *Hunger— American Style* that attempted to bring attention to food insecurity in Mississippi.[28] Among other things, the show featured civil rights activist and pediatrician Dr. Aaron Shirley, who explained the nutritional problems Delta farm families faced. "Even though we see people who are not underweight, because they get enough calories," Dr. Shirley said. "They get a lot of starchy foods, but they don't get green vegetables, they don't get fruits, and they don't get some of the minerals and vitamins that they need." In other words, Sunflower County residents often had access to sufficient food to keep them from starving but not to the variety of foods necessary to maintain health and energy.[29]

Other reports offered a dimmer picture of health in the Delta. In 1967, US senator Robert F. Kennedy found desperate hunger when he visited Mississippi sharecropper shacks as part of his investigation into poverty. Medical testimony presented at Senate committee hearings depicted children with no access to milk, fruit, green vegetables, or meat. They survived on "scraps" offered by well-meaning neighbors. According to these reports, "Malnutrition is not quite what we found. ... They are suffering from hunger and disease and directly or indirectly they are dying from them—which is exactly what starvation means."[30] Kennedy and his Senate investigation found the children who were too poor to see a pediatrician, so they never made their way into Dr. Shirley's office.

Hamer and her colleagues in Freedom Farm, mostly civil rights veterans, understood that, given the history of Mississippi, where powerful whites intentionally kept black farm families hungry, solutions to poverty needed to empower the people with knowledge and resources. This approach paralleled the policy of SNCC, with which Hamer had worked for several years, to involve locals in civil rights programs. Starting in 1969, Hamer centered her activism on creating Freedom Farm to provide local farmers with a control over their food systems that they had never had before.

Freedom Farm provided black farmers with foods connected to traditional rural diets. Pig Bank, its most well known program, started with the donation of fifty hogs by the National Council of Negro Women. Freedom Farm loaned the pigs to needy families. A recipient family nurtured a pregnant sow until she gave birth. Then, they returned the sow and two offspring to the bank. The family kept the rest of the litter for their own sustenance. At least 865 families benefitted from Pig Bank. Freedom Farm also provided fresh vegetables to hungry families. They planted forty acres of vegetables and allowed families to pick what they needed for their subsistence. Freedom Farm workers grew a variety of vegetables, including cucumbers, butter beans, okra, snap beans, and squash, to serve the nutritional needs of beneficiaries. They also helped families purchase food stamps; provided clothing, medical assistance, and transportation; and continued to advocate for fair treatment of African Americans in the local community.[31]

Freedom Farm and similar initiatives represented more than simply sustenance. Promoting food sovereignty among African Americans in a region where white supremacy had been maintained, in part, by keeping people hungry, constituted a revolutionary act. Autonomy in food systems represented black independence, and there is evidence that in some areas of the South the white power structure tried to inhibit these developments. In December 1967, for example, fifty black farmers met in a church to plan a vegetable cooperative in Wilkes County, Georgia. In an action that evokes memories of the earlier suffrage campaigns, unknown arsonists set fire to the church in the middle of the night. In other areas, county sheriffs were known to break up meetings where African Americans were discussing marketing cooperatives.[32]

Freedom Farm did not suffer such terrorist threats, and Hamer's primary concerns mostly centered on raising money to sustain the venture. Like earlier civil rights activism, their work depended upon financial contributions from groups and individuals across the nation. In May 1969, entertainer and activist Harry Belafonte distributed a fundraising letter requesting that individuals and organizations support Freedom Farm. Belafonte described Freedom Farm as a "self-help" initiative by which "a community of free, independent people can be built." In response, supporters from across the nation sent small and large checks to support the new initiative.[33]

As Belafonte's advocacy suggests, most of Freedom Farm's funding came from individuals and organizations with a demonstrated commitment to social justice. Madison Measure for Measure, a Wisconsin organization dedicated to help with the Southern Freedom Movement, made several large contributions. In October 1970, this organization raised funds to help Freedom Farm purchase additional land.[34] Despite such generosity, Freedom Farm's financial situation remained tenuous and depended largely on Hamer's celebrity in the world of social justice. During her lifetime, Hamer succeeded in providing food support to hundreds of Sunflower County families, but Freedom Farm did not survive long past her 1977 death.

For Hamer, food sovereignty was intimately connected to civil rights for many reasons. The inability to control access to basic sustenance made black farm families vulnerable to the overbearing labor practices of white planters. They had to take work at any wages and had to remain in untenable labor relationships. Their ability to advocate for better circumstances, through demonstrations or the traditional political process, remained secondary to maintaining basic subsistence. Moreover, children who grew up in perpetual poverty had less access to education and medical care—conditions exacerbated by extreme hunger. Hamer's attempt to alleviate food insecurity by providing access to meat and fresh vegetables for Sunflower County's laboring poor represented an extension of her previous efforts to provide political opportunity to the disfranchised.

In conclusion, the history of sustenance struggles among Mississippi's poor black rural population reveals how food served to uphold white supremacy throughout the twentieth century. Power over land use as well as government food programs rested with the white planter class. The planters generally used this influence to maintain the African American population as an amenable work force—not to improve the health and vigor of their communities. When civil rights campaigns came to Mississippi advocating black suffrage, white officials and activists both made political use of food resources. White Mississippians found that they could continue using their control over the land and government commodities to inhibit activism by threatening to cut off much-needed aid. Activists, on the other hand, with a genuine desire to feed the needy, nevertheless recognized that food drives could also be used to educate and advocate.

The more expansive government programs of the 1960s-era "War on Poverty" failed to improve the subsistence of black Mississippians and instead served as another way by which white supremacists could maintain the status quo. By the end of the civil rights era, however, activists began to pursue sustenance measures as a primary objective of their activism—rather than simply a means to an end. In such efforts, like Freedom Farm in Sunflower County, local activists and farmers collaborated to pursue food sovereignty. Although Freedom Farm failed to achieve long-term success, its objectives and methods resemble more contemporary efforts to pursue food justice by providing local communities with autonomy over their food systems.

CHAPTER 15

After Forty Acres

Food Security, Urban Agriculture,
and Black Food Citizenship

VIVIAN N. HALLORAN

At the dawn of the twenty-first century in the United States, urban agriculture has become newly popular due to a combination of factors: concerns about the nation's obesity epidemic, fears about adverse health effects of processed foods and the presence of pesticides and genetically modified crops in the food chain, and efforts to improve homeland security after the terrorist attacks in 2001. Renewed emphasis has been paid to urban food systems since then, with government and law-enforcement leaders nationwide evaluating the potential threat of agroterrorism, or possible biological attacks against the nation's food supply.[1] Ironically, what began as a reactionary threat assessment and active effort to improve the safety and oversight over every level of the nation's food chain in the first decade of this new millennium has prompted some communities to reevaluate their own local food systems. At the local level, however, concerns about social justice and public health have supplanted civil defense drills and other measures to ensure the food supply against foreign attack. This shift in emphasis popularized the concept of "food security" as a condition or state of being, "when all people at all times have access to sufficient, safe, nutritious food to maintain a healthy and active life."[2]

First articulated at the World Food Summit sponsored in 1996 by the World Health Organization, "food security" and the essential tenets the term conveys continue to serve as a rallying cry and call for political mobilization and reform. In 2006, the US Department of

Agriculture developed terms to better reflect the relative levels of food insecurity or security an individual household experiences, replacing the umbrella term "hunger" with categories ranging from "high food security" to "very low food security."[3] Communities with low overall food security, or limited access to affordable fresh and healthy food, came to be called "food deserts."[4] Thus, urban farming, which was once popularized as the patriotic duty of citizens to augment the available food supply during World Wars I and II, has come into vogue in the wake of the terrorist attacks, now seen as an invaluable weapon in the combined battles against obesity and food insecurity, which can be understood as the social effects of urban blight and poverty.[5] These negative factors have a disproportionately large impact upon the lives of African Americans throughout the United States. This chapter examines how African American urban farmers have claimed the national spotlight to promote local food and agriculture as viable and necessary ways to combat food deserts.

Contemporary food activists and urban farmers, such as Ron Finley in Los Angeles and Will Allen in Milwaukee and Chicago, have garnered national attention for their efforts to popularize small-scale household food production through their deft manipulation of the public media landscape. Finley's TED talk, "A Guerrilla Gardener in South Central LA," and Allen's Midwestern urban farming memoir/manifesto, *The Good Food Revolution: Growing Healthy Food, People, and Communities*, both promote the combined economic and health benefits of locally grown food in urban centers.[6] Southerner Michael Twitty is the intellectual force behind the Twitter handle @koshersoul and author of *Afroculinaria.com*, a popular blog about Afro-diasporic foodways.[7] Through historical reenactments of African American farming and cooking techniques and the preservation of heirloom fruit and vegetable seeds dating back to the slavery era, Twitty demonstrates positive interactions between this community and the land's bounty and works to promote "food justice," which he defines as "creating community gardens, increasing support for local food systems, and increasing greener living and sustainability culture in Southern communities of color."[8] In her first book, *American Grown: The Story of the White House Kitchen Garden and Gardens Across America*, First Lady Michelle Obama has taken a different approach to achieve the same goal by reviving the concept of the "victory garden" pioneered by her predecessor, Eleanor Roosevelt, during the nation's involvement in World War II, in order to wage a national battle against her chosen opponent: childhood obesity.[9] Even media mogul Oprah Winfrey has joined this new back-to-the-land movement by turning some of her property in Maui into an organic farm.[10]

This chapter posits that these high-profile African American urban farmers' efforts to promote food security in their respective communities and across the nation should be interpreted as part of a larger civic project dating back to America's experience with food rationing and victory gardening during the two world wars. By simultaneously reclaiming their agrarian heritage and turning to urban agriculture to help ensure the safety and viability of the homeland's food supply, Will Allen, Michael Twitty, Michelle Obama, and Oprah Winfrey publicly perform their "food citizenship," a concept defined by Jennifer L. Winkins as

> the practice of engaging in food-related behaviors (defined narrowly and broadly) that support, rather than threaten, the development of a democratic, socially and economically just, and environmentally sustainable economic system.[11]

These celebrity urban farmers emphasize the connection between eating and agriculture by constantly asking their audiences to question what kind of food system they want to participate in. Embracing the combined legacies of slavery, sharecropping, and victory garden campaigns as crucial parts of their family heritage that have led directly to their public advocacy of food-related social justice causes, Allen, Twitty, Obama, and Winfrey open up new avenues for African Americans to reclaim their historical roots in this country and thus arrive at a sense of full citizenship and belonging.

Food Security Discourses and African American Urban Farmers

African American farmers, food activists, and community leaders from all walks of life have played a leading role in popularizing urban agriculture throughout the United States by teaching residents how to cultivate crops in so-called food deserts, neighborhoods with no easy access to fresh and affordable produce. Not only are these efforts meant to counteract urban blight and improve the health of individual communities by making the consumption of locally grown food feasible in low-income areas, but Finley and Allen have sought to invigorate the local economic climate by actively promoting urban agriculture as a viable business enterprise and job-training program in Los Angeles and Milwaukee/Chicago, respectively.[12] Michael Twitty foresees a future of "culinary security" for African Americans premised upon the reconceptualization of agriculture—gardening and farming—as part of the Afro-diasporic community's rich cultural heritage, a legacy to be reclaimed and cherished: "Culinary justice is when children of color have access to the land, traditional ecosystems, resources, clean water, and legal protections by which they can grow the heirlooms and raise the heritage breed of their ancestors, and do so in a way that they might come back to a greater connection with nature, and learn to live and eat better."[13] Twitty's utopian vision for culinary change and activism, borne out of his personal connection to the past, is being carried out in multiple fronts today.

Considered in isolation, each of these initiatives for urban renewal, nutritional activism, and social justice could be mistaken for timely efforts to join the latest food fad or trend; however, when read together, each project in its own way promotes the purposeful reconnection to the soil and the fruits of one's labor. Allen, Twitty, Obama, and Winfrey all see the potential of urban agriculture not only as an immediate method to improve food security in urban food deserts, but also as a means of both reclaiming and developing a fuller understanding of the black experience and African Americans' many contributions to national history, culture, and foodways.

Food Security and Victory Gardens New and Old

The events of 9/11 (September 11, 2001) and the country's subsequent decade-long engagement in wars in Iraq and Afghanistan prompted food activists and other proponents of urban agriculture to revive the notion of the "victory garden" as a way to connect the public's interest in locally grown and harvested food to the patriotism of the larger war effort, as had been done during both World War I and II. Food shortages and rationing were the primary causes behind the effort to promote victory gardens, first in the years 1917–19 and then after the bombing of Pearl Harbor in 1941. What started out as "war gardens" became rechristened as "victory gardens," not only to celebrate the defeat of enemy forces abroad, but also to serve as a reminder that peace must be waged through the cultivation of food to aid in reconstruction efforts in Europe.[14] Though millions of adults were disenfranchised—women due to their gender and African Americans due to Jim Crow discriminatory practices such as poll taxes—war propaganda promoted food citizenship directly tied to patriotic duty during the World War I era.[15] Two decades later, Howard R. Tolley's *The Farmer Citizen at War* addressed the lingering effects of this double standard head on, by strongly advocating the elimination of poll taxes in the "underprivileged parts of the South" so that citizens may have "a chance to vote" like everyone else because "now in time of war, we see more than ever that this is their country, too. More than that, this war is their war, too."[16]

By the outset of World War II, the US government aggressively advocated urban agriculture as a means to increase the available food supply through home canning and the yields of small, kitchen gardens. In April 1941, President Roosevelt issued an official statement urging all Americans to grow a "victory garden"; and First Lady Eleanor Roosevelt modeled this form of food citizenship by growing vegetables on the grounds of the White House.[17] Though the recent wars in Iraq and Afghanistan did not directly affect the national food supply, the current first lady, Michelle Obama, has followed Mrs. Roosevelt's example by setting up her own "kitchen" garden, an undertaking she chronicles in *American Grown*.[18] Whereas Eleanor Roosevelt's victory garden was a direct response to her husband's call to action, Mrs. Obama's kitchen garden may be best understood as the centerpiece to her Let's Move! Campaign, the first lady's signature initiative to fight childhood obesity through the promotion of physical activity and healthy eating.[19] In her book, Obama recalls that her mother's family grew vegetables in their own victory garden plot in Chicago, a city that led the nation in the cultivation of such urban gardens during World War II.[20] Thus, Obama provides a genealogy for her own fascination with urban agriculture, tracing it back professionally, as first lady, and personally, as the grandchild of victory gardeners.

Obama's backward glance to the end of World War II illustrates how social and political trends running on seemingly parallel tracks can lead to fundamentally divergent outcomes. The postwar years were an era of real progress for the African American community with a string of hard-fought political victories including the integration of the armed forces in 1948, the end of "separate but equal" schooling with the Supreme Court decision in *Brown v. the Board of Education* in 1954, and a large-scale social transformation that served as a precursor of the dismantling of Jim Crow laws and other institutional discriminatory mechanisms during the civil rights movement and beyond. Nonetheless, the economic disparity in communities across the nation meant that many communities were suffering from food insecurity. Even when wages and economic opportunities were growing, the advent of widely available, affordable, processed, and convenience foods eventually began to have a negative impact on the health and waistlines of the country as a whole, with a magnified impact on low-income communities in urban centers. In promoting the spread of urban gardens like hers "across America," Michelle Obama relies on the symbolic power of her position as first lady to encourage other citizens to simultaneously embrace healthy, local eating and combat the spread of food deserts across the United States. She also personalizes her message by turning to her Chicago roots and family history. Mrs. Obama mentions that though both of her parents grew up eating fresh-grown vegetables either from the victory garden or from the vegetable truck that used to cater to urban neighborhoods, she and her brother grew up eating fruits and vegetables bought from the supermarket, shipped there from far away. The account in *American Grown* of her visit to the Iron Street Urban Farm, a Southside Chicago outpost of Will Allen's Growing Power agriculture nonprofit suggests that in her personal experience of this city, things have come full circle: where once there was nothing but urban blight, Mr. Allen and his crew of volunteers have returned the city to its former tradition of urban gardening and local food production.[21]

While *American Grown* supplements Michelle Obama's personal family history with fresh food with historical accounts of previous presidential forays into farming, such as an image of Thomas Jefferson's hand-drawn plans for a White House garden, photos of Eleanor Roosevelt's victory garden, and a vignette discussing Lady Bird Johnson's penchant for growing wildflowers, its only reference to the especially freighted historical relationship African Americans have had with agriculture after the abolition of slavery—specifically, with sharecropping—comes in the section where Milwaukee agro-entrepreneur Will Allen shares his family story. Although the book features a diverse group of chefs, community gardeners, celebrities, and volunteers, Allen is the only person to refer to sharecropping as part of his family history.

Sharecropping, the Great Migration, and Culturally Appropriate Foods

Will Allen is the first high-profile African American urban farmer to publicly link his contemporary food-based social justice activism to his family's heritage of sharecropping. He does so proudly and without reservation, although he acknowledges that the children of those who left the South during the Great Migration often felt burdened by their families' agricultural background: "They saw no good in being associated with sharecropping" and considered it a stigma.[22] Not so Allen. In almost every interview he grants, including one with Elizabeth Royte from the *New York Times*, Allen attributes his current success as the CEO of the nonprofit organization Growing Power to his family's participation in the peonage system: "My father was a sharecropper in South Carolina. . . . He was the eldest boy of 13 children and he never learned to read."[23] Despite leaving the South during the Great Migration and moving to Maryland, Allen's mother and father never stopped farming whatever bit of land they could rent or own, and they made their children do farm chores before they could play sports or engage in any other leisure activity. Although these obligations initially made him eager to pursue the urban lifestyle that basketball offered—first through college scholarships and later as a professional in the American Basketball Association and the European leagues—Allen changed his mind after living in Belgium and seeing how much the organic agricultural practices of his youth played a part in everyday life in Europe. So, the very distance he sought from the circumstances of his upbringing made it easy for Allen to embrace his family's agricultural heritage—whether as backyard farmers or workers in the oppressive peonage system. Today, he uses his green thumb and entrepreneurial innovations to run a successful urban farm that also employs local youth, teaching them valuable time-tested skills.[24] Most importantly, even as he leads the fight to change discriminatory and outmoded administrative models that pit local and federal government agencies against urban farmers seeking environmental justice, Allen acknowledges the debt he owes to his forbearers and to their hard work and dedication. These combined missions—to effect change in the present and to honor the past—are what make him a modern food citizen.

Allen's civic mission is in evidence of his rejection of one-size-fits-all master narratives and insistence on the particularity of his own experience. Rather than providing blueprints to be followed directly, Allen's memoir-cum-manifesto, *The Good Food Revolution*, hopes to inspire readers to tackle their own community's food security and justice issues in culturally appropriate ways. Allen displays his civic enterprise most clearly when he discusses his multiple and oftentimes frustrating dealings with local, state, and federal government bureaucracies, such as the protracted process he endured before being allowed to run a stand in the local farmer's market. Despite these setbacks, some of which were clearly related to his race, Allen's faith in his ability to make the system fair is not shaken:

> I experienced similar feelings of unease a few years later when I first sought to bring my produce to Fondy Farmers market in Milwaukee. Located in a North Milwaukee neighborhood that was almost exclusively African American, the market was administered by the city government. It operated under a large steel awning that kept the stalls dry even on days of rain. I remember walking through the market for the first time and feeling that I could do well there. Though the community was black, all of the farmers who had stalls in the market were white.
>
> I saw older customers walking through the aisles and perusing the tables and I knew that they were members of the Great Migration. They were searching for the flavors of their youth, and

they could not find them there. The farmers weren't selling the produce that black people liked and that I was growing now in large quantities: collards, curly-leaf and slick leaf mustards, and turnip greens.[25]

This passage highlights Allen's philosophy in action: rather than dwell on personal slights or temporary setbacks, his dedication to serve the members of his community by providing the southern regional specialties they had enjoyed before embarking upon their Great Migration journeys remained strong. Allen's food activism is a grassroots mission borne out of the legacy of the parents who moved North to escape sharecropping but never stopped working the land. He acknowledges that his mother "taught [him] that food was a celebration. It brought people together who might differ otherwise because of race, religion, or politics."[26] As his mother's son, Will Allen has made it his life's mission to bring people together as grassroots participants in a "good food revolution" leading to improved food security in a large urban center, the reconnection of African Americans with what he calls "culturally appropriate foods," and increased healthy food options in a former food desert.

Though Allen claims he only really began appreciating the skills and knowledge he had inherited from his parents' experience as sharecroppers once he started growing food for himself following his professional basketball career, Allen imbues their agrarian labors with a sense of history and continuity that resonates as a way to contextualize food citizenship in the United States. Allen's urban food advocacy does important work reminding us how fraught African Americans' historical connection to agricultural production, past and present, can be. In order to fully appreciate the radicalism of Will Allen's reclamation of his family's sharecropping past, we need to understand the historical moment that gives rise to his statements.

This movement toward the reclamation of an agrarian connection with roots in the South has been underway for quite some time. Long before anyone heard of Paula Deen, there was Edna Lewis, the doyenne of southern cooking. With the publication of her memoir with recipes, *The Taste of Country Cooking* (1976), Lewis welcomed what she saw as two positive trends in popular culture that continue to this day: the sometimes-overlapping journeys of people returning to agriculture as a profession and of people reclaiming the South as their home.

> I am happy to see how many young people are going back to the land and to the South. They are interested in natural farming and they seem to want to know how we did things in the past, to learn firsthand from those who worked hard, loved the land, and relished the fruits of their labor. I hope this book will be helpful to them.[27]

Lewis interprets these social changes as harbingers of a renewed appreciation of the intrinsic dignity of physical labor and stewardship for the land, as well as the appeal of reclaiming their southern roots. Rather than continue such forward-looking meditations, however Lewis looks primarily to the past throughout *The Taste of Country Cooking*, lovingly recalling her rural childhood in Virginia, where "the spirit of pride in community and cooperation in the work of farming is what made Freetown a very wonderful place to grow up in."[28] Although the book contains helpful descriptions of how the rhythms and activities associated with farm life varied according to the seasons, which constitute the organizing principle according to which all the featured dinner menus and individual recipes appear, Lewis speaks with the authority of the cook, rather than claiming the subject position of the farmer, as does Allen. Her culinary expertise grew out of her farm life, but Lewis's life work was behind a stove and oven, not out in the fields.

Despite her personal great migration North and the many decades that passed between her girlhood in Freetown and the writing of her memoirs, Edna Lewis never relinquished her membership in the "imagined community" of Freetown, Virginia. The somewhat rosy gloss on what must have been a life of hard work and sacrifice is not unusual among texts in this genre.

Media mogul Oprah Winfrey's recent reminiscences about her own rural upbringing in Mississippi, published in *O* magazine as part of the feature story unveiling "Oprah's New Farm," strike a similar nostalgic note, perhaps due to the fact that the story—like Edna Lewis's memoir with recipes and even Allen's *The Good Food Revolution*—celebrates the benefits of eating locally grown, healthy food. Declaring that "being on Maui and creating a farm feel like coming home," Oprah goes on to portray her interactions with the grandmother who raised her as being mediated through agricultural labor:

> One of my strongest memories is being on the back porch helping my grandmother churn butter. We churned the butter, we milked the cows, we killed the hogs, we cured the meat in the smokehouse. Above all, we tended our little garden. That's where most of what we ate came from. And now I've returned to that way of living: We eat what's from the garden.

Oprah's current gloss on her Mississippi life has not always been this positive, highlighting the self-reliance and character-building competence that her grandmother found through farming her "little garden." In a televised interview with Harvard University African American studies professor and public intellectual extraordinaire Henry Louis Gates Jr., the entertainer once again alluded to butter churning as one of her assigned tasks in the household, but acknowledged she was not the most diligent helper to her grandmother.

> I remember standing on the back porch and looking through the screen door and my grandmother was boiling clothes in a big, black pot and she had the clothespins in an apron sash, and I was churning butter, or I was supposed to be churning anyway, so I was churning, and every time she turned around I'd churn, and when she was not looking I would stop churning, and she said, 'Oprah Gail, I want you to pay attention to me now, I want you to watch me—yeah Grandmama—because one day you're going to have to learn to do this for yourself,' she said to me. And I watched, and looked like I was paying attention, but I distinctly recall a feeling that 'no I'm not, no I'm not.' That this will not be my life.[29]

Oprah's silent rejection of her grandmother's vision of the limited future awaiting her conveys the shame she felt as a six-year-old. Somehow butter churning forms a connection between this image of herself as a member of the grassroots—someone helping the family— and the ambitious youngster yearning for broader horizons. The mundane task involves a transformation from milk into butter, much as Oprah took control of her circumstances, achieved professional success, and returned to farming on her own terms.

Even though the historian admits that "Oprah's ancestors . . . proved to be the exceptions" because they owned their own small farm, Gates insists on setting Oprah's early life in Mississippi against the backdrop of sharecropping, the "seemingly hopeless" economic system that trapped tenant farmers in cycles of debt and borrowing: "Oprah grew up surrounded by sharecroppers, people bound to the soil by a system that was intended to replace slavery with its mirror image, a system of peonage to which most blacks were chained economically."[30] By insisting upon reading Oprah's geographical, if not familial, connection to sharecropping, Gates's efforts to validate sharecroppers' labor have the unintended effect of effacing the successes of independent black farmers like Oprah's relatives and the families of Edna Lewis's Freetown.

Farming as Part of the Afro-diasporic Heritage

Michael Twitty, a southerner, has been pursuing a similar genetic/ genealogical project to Gates's for some time now through his blog, *The Cooking Gene.com*.[31] Twitty's commitment to celebrating how African Americans' culinary and agricultural contributions have shaped American life from colonial times through the Reconstruction period is made evident by his physical labor—planting, harvesting, seed saving, and cooking—as well as by his intellectual pursuits. In an interview for *Living on Earth*, the online environmental magazine hosted by Public Radio International, journalist Ike Sriskandarajah asked Twitty to share his views on African Americans' relationship to the land today:

> TWITTY: We were an agrarian people for millennia, even through the period of slavery—and we went from being 90 percent agrarian to 90 percent urban in less than a 100 years. Think about that.
>
> SRISKANDARAJAH: Freedom wasn't free; emancipation cost the slaves their link to the land. African Americans couldn't own or lease land; their only option was punitive sharecropping.
>
> TWITTY: All that oppression hurt us in the long run because it divorced us from the land; it divorced us from nature, and through food we can reconnect with that and begin to repair those links.[32]

What Twitty calls for, then, is a return to both the land and one's heritage, seen through the lens of a relationship to the land. His message goes beyond the specific action of growing food in one's own home space; what he advocates is a renewed appreciation of the very skills of working the land that urban dwellers have lost or chosen to forget. Like Allen's, Obama's, and Winfrey's, Twitty's working definition of "food citizenship" is expansive and includes all types of healthy food choices.

As Twitty argues in "A People's History of Carolina Rice," the promise of homesteads gave freedmen hope that they could earn a living with the agricultural skills they had relied upon during their bondage.[33] Some black southern farmers put these same acres to patriotic service by joining in the collective effort to strengthen our national food supply through their agricultural skills during World War II. Though many urban African Americans were called upon to do their part in support of the war effort by serving up chicken dinners for the troops, as Psyche Williams-Forson so powerfully chronicles, their rural counterparts, like Oprah's grandmothers' family, demonstrated their patriotism by growing victory gardens and necessary crops during World Wars I and II.[34] The short propaganda documentary *Henry Browne, Farmer*, made by the US Department of Agriculture in 1942, tells the story of one such patriotic African American farmer in Georgia, "Henry Browne, aged thirty-eight, father of three children, farming forty acres."[35] Mrs. Browne tends a victory garden that will feed the family through the winter, leaving the supermarket's canned foods for "people in cities who just can't grow their own food." For his part, Mr. Browne plants peanuts in fifteen of his acres in hopes of contributing some of the much-needed "fats and oils to make up for what the Japs got," as the "government man" tells him.[36] The narrator, Canada Lee, concludes the voiceover by proclaiming that "we" are proud of Henry Browne "for being an American that we can count on at a time when every American has an important job to do." Nowhere in the film or in its narration is Mr. Browne's race mentioned, whereas his Americanness and patriotism are emphasized several times.

Conclusion

In celebrating the inherent dignity of growing one's own food, contemporary agro-luminaries validate the historical self-sufficiency of slaves cultivating the small plots allotted to them, sharecroppers who fed their families from small garden plots while also working fields owned by others, and patriots busily contributing to the war effort by tending their victory gardens. While achieving full "food citizenship" is a goal of these African American agro-luminaries, Alison Hope Alkon reminds us that "individuals participate in the green economy not as equal citizens, but as consumers with unequal access to wealth and products, and as producers with unequal access to capital and markets."[37] Thus, though the message of food security and food citizenship is being broadcast to the masses through the publications of these books, the problem of culinary justice remains. Urban agriculture, whether on a commercial or a personal scale, is but one way to level the playing field and bring healthier food to more people. A love of fresh food rooted in heritage is these writers' legacy to the next generation.

Afterword

In the spring of 2014, provocative artist Kara Walker installed a seventy-five-foot-long sculpture of a sphinx in the soon-to-be-demolished Domino sugar refinery in Brooklyn. The sculpture depicted the crouching figure of an African American woman wearing a mammy-style head kerchief with her vulva exposed. The entire figure was coated with refined sugar crystals, giving it a white, sparkling veneer. It was sponsored by the nonprofit group Creative Time. Walker entitled the work *A Subtlety or the Marvelous Sugar Baby: An Homage to the unpaid and overworked Artisans who have refined our Sweet tastes from the cane fields to the Kitchens of the New World on the Occasion of the demolition of the Domino Sugar Refining Plant.*

As most of Walker's work has been wont to do, *A Subtlety* stirred commentary, both positive and negative, about African American women, sexuality, and exploitation. Walker's title deliberately and pointedly brought global and local systems of food into the discussion, recalling the millions of enslaved workers who died in the cane fields of the Caribbean and the African American women, both slave and free, who cooked for white families for centuries. Yet, as critic Carol Diehl points out, the controversy went beyond mere representation. The installation brought positive attention to Domino Sugar, a company that was a subsidiary of Flo-Sun, a multinational corporation that engaged in all manner of questionable business practices, including slave-like conditions for their child workers.[1]

When the subject is African Americans and food, to use William Faulkner's often-quoted phrase, "the past isn't dead; it isn't even past." As Kara Walker asks her viewer to think about the transgressions that the world's craving for sweetness brought about in the past, critics like Diehl remind us that cruelty persists into the present. And so the essays in this book, encapsulating much of the most recent scholarship in African American foodways, also prompt us to look both behind and forward. The topic has been complicated and difficult since the seventeenth century and it remains so today.

As Jennifer Wallach reminds us in her introduction, food studies have come into their own only in the past fifteen years or so. The daily stuff of life was for many years considered too ordinary to be taken seriously by academics, but that is generally no longer the case. Complex and loaded with physical, cultural, and social meaning, food is now seen as a worthy lens to engage the many dilemmas of being human. Each of these essays takes its subject seriously, with no winks or ironic nods, realizing that food presents scholars with yet another tool to grapple with huge topics such as power and race.

Although food studies can spin out in variations as wide as the imagination allows, they can also be categorized under a few broad rubrics. I would like to think about those rubrics, what they say about the essays in this book, and suggest a few avenues for future studies of African Americans and food.

First there is the food itself: the cassava, the corn, the sugar, the beans, the cayenne, the Big Gulp soda. The substances themselves have stories, but they are made most meaningful by looking at how people relate to them. In this volume, Kelly Wisecup, Robert A. Gilmer, and Christine Marks examine ways that African American people brought together—whether willingly or by force—the foodways of their native continent with those of Native Americans and Europeans to create a new and vibrant American cuisine. The Columbian Exchange and the shock waves that followed it truly altered the ways that people lived across the globe, and this trend of globalization continues unabated, for good and for ill. The possible topics for thinking about foodstuffs and African Americans are endless. As several authors in this collection hint, the recent trend toward locavorism has special meaning for African Americans. Other scholars might consider the ongoing meanings of globalization, which are in tension and discussion with the increased emphasis on local foods. Along with localization, regional foods appear to maintain strong presences. A continued consideration of the meaning of region and regional cooking is certainly warranted, both historically and in the present, beyond the South. Do and did African Americans in the San Francisco Bay area eat like those in the northern neck of Virginia? What do the differences and commonalities mean? Foodways have evolved over the centuries, and they continue to change. Scholars and popular media like to quarrel about what constitutes "genuine" cuisines, but the truth is that African American food has never been defined solely only by collard greens and chitlings. Future scholars can continue the analysis of that evolution.

Another direction for study is the labor that people put into producing and cooking food. It's a long way from hoeing sugarcane to that Big Gulp soda (assuming that it has any sugar in it), but it's all a part of a continuum that begins either in a field or a chemical plant, with actions by people, and ends up in eaters' bodies. Christopher Farrish shows that colonial slaves took significant risks to bring food to their families, while Angela Jill Cooley and Vivian N. Halloran demonstrate the importance of people having a hand in the production of their own food, in the past and in the present. Scholars should persist in asking how African Americans have worked with food: growing it, processing it, cooking it, serving it, and eating it. They should also continue to ask how shortages have affected African Americans, as food insecurity has been an important factor from Jamestown to the present, and how an overabundance of poor, calorie-laden food contributes to the ongoing health difficulties of many people. Further studies of the eating habits of the poor will shed light on the historical and current-day health problems of certain parts of the population. As the Americans in power (usually white) have used food as a means of oppression, African Americans have used it to resist such hegemony. Food supplies also can include both making meals directly for one's family or cooking as a means of making money, either as a domestic worker or to sell for a profit to make money. Among African Americans, mere survival has equaled resistance to the dominant power structure. And people use food to express their creativity, as cooks and as businesspeople. Thoughtful explorations of food entrepreneurs of all kinds will surely yield rich results in thinking about risk taking, feeding others, and feeding one's family. African American chefs bring together a cuisine, and they deserve study both as workers and as cultural arbiters. As Anthony J. Stanonis demonstrates, African

American attitudes toward and uses of food have not been monolithic, and further investigations of food in this context can complicate and show the rich variations in African American culture

As numerous authors have pointed out, food carries social and cultural meaning, and it plays central roles in many cultural productions, whether novels, films, or television. As long as Americans are still working out their issues with race through cultural media, this is likely to persist. African Americans and others represent food in alternative lights: the books that Marcia Chatelain explores and Freda De Knight's work, explicated by Katharina Vester, surely diverge from the work of white authors with dramatically different points of view. The cultural products that Kimberly D. Nettles-Barcelón and Jessica Kenyatta Walker consider are but recent examples of the outrages committed by white cultural arbiters, using African American subjects. US society at large seems to have a bottomless supply of examples to parse.

The search for historical sources will surely continue to yield, however grudgingly, new clues to the past. These essays amply demonstrate the importance of cookbooks as sources, often the only printed glimpses of foods of the past. As academics continue to take a spatial turn, mapping will surely become more common and more useful in thinking about how people and food are physically located in the world. Material culture will also yield greater insights with an increasing number of artifacts and new ways to think about them.

New questions will rise as old ones persist. When the essays in this book consider gender, it is almost always female. Men and masculinity need to be a part of the conversation. Now that an African American has occupied the highest office in the United States, as Lindsey Swindall points out, discussions need to continue over the discrepancies among African Americans. What do the foods of the 1 percent and those people in the poorest areas of the rural South have to say to one another?

Michelle Obama and Oprah Winfrey, among the most powerful and wealthy African Americans in the nation, are good exemplars through which to project future studies: Winfrey with her Maui farm and Obama with her various food-related reforms through the White House. Obama and Winfrey bring together three strands of analysis: the healthy food that is being grown at the White House and Maui and encouraged throughout the United States; the people who come together to grow the food and disseminate it and information about it; and, particularly in the case of Obama, the symbolism of a powerful African American woman influencing public policy and receiving harsh criticism for doing so.

Racists will continue to try to put Winfrey and Obama back into the context of Mammy, but the allusions will not hold. Although anyone studying African American food must keep in mind the enslaved people who grew and cooked food, the story has moved beyond that one, and the Kara Walkers of the world must acknowledge the shift. At the same time, the past is prologue, and it will never be irrelevant to the present. Past and present become yet another dyad for study. In the meantime, the field of African American food studies will continue to expand, growing ever more complicated, sophisticated, and thoughtful. And in so doing, it will continue to teach us about ourselves and one another.

REBECCA SHARPLESS
Texas Christian University

NOTES

Introduction

1. Myrlie Evers, with Williams Peters, *For Us, the Living* (New York: Doubleday, 1967).

2. The books that signaled the ascendency of food studies include the following: Warren Belasco, *Appetite for Change: How the Counterculture Took on the Food Industry* (Ithaca, NY: Cornell University Press, 2006); Amy Bentley, *Eating for Victory: Food Rationing and the Politics of Domesticity* (Chicago: University of Illinois Press, 1998); Judith Carney, *Black Rice: The African Origins of Rice Cultivation in the Americas* (Cambridge, MA: Harvard University Press, 2001); Hasia R. Diner, *Hungering for America: Italian, Irish, and Jewish Foodways in the Age of Migration* (Cambridge, MA: Harvard University Press, 2001); Donna R. Gabaccia, *We Are What We Eat: Ethnic Food and the Making of Americans* (Cambridge, MA: Harvard University Press, 1998); Sherrie A. Inness, ed., *Kitchen Culture in America: Popular Representatives of Food, Gender, and Race* (Philadelphia: University of Pennsylvania Press, 2001); Harvey Levenstein, *Paradox of Plenty: A Social History of Eating in Modern America* (New York: Oxford University Press, 1993); Lucy M. Long, ed., *Culinary Tourism* (Lexington: University of Kentucky Press, 2004): James McWilliams, *A Revolution in Eating: How the Quest for Food Shaped America* (New York: Columbia University Press, 2005); and Jeffrey Pilcher, *¡Que vivan los tamales! Food and the Making of Mexican Identity* (Albuquerque: University of New Mexico Press, 1998).

3. Jennifer K. Ruark, "A Place at the Table: More Scholars Focus on Historical, Social, and Cultural Meanings of Food, but Some Critics Say It's Scholarship-Lite," *Chronicle of Higher Education,* July 9, 1999, A17.

4. Psyche Williams-Forson, *Building Houses out of Chicken Legs: Black Women, Food, and Power* (Chapel Hill: University of North Carolina Press, 2006). Williams-Forson graciously reflected on the paucity of secondary sources she had to work with by acknowledging, "When I first began researching, there was very little literature available on the meanings associated with African American food consumption" (3).

5. Doris Witt, *Black Hunger: Food and the Politics of U.S. Identity* (Oxford: Oxford University Press, 1999), 4.

6. Williams-Forson, *Building Houses out of Chicken Legs,* 1–2.

7. Ann L. Bower, ed., *African American Foodways: Explorations of History and Culture* (Urbana: University of Illinois, 2007).

8. The titles of three recent books about African American foodways testify to the predominance of southern cooking in most studies about black cuisine. See Frederick Douglass Opie, *Hog and Hominy: Soul Food from Africa to America* (New York: Columbia University Press, 2008); Jessica B. Harris, *High on the Hog: A*

Culinary Journey from Africa to America (New York: Bloomsbury, 2011); Adrian Miller, *Soul Food: The Surprising Story of an American Cuisine, One Plate at a Time* (Chapel Hill: University of North Carolina Press, 2013).

9. W.E.B. Du Bois, "Food," *Crisis*, August 1918, 165.

CHAPTER 1. Foodways and Resistance: Cassava, Poison, and Natural Histories in the Early Americas

1. On foods imported and cultivated for Africans' diets, see John H. Parry, "Plantation and Provision Ground: An Historical Sketch of the Introduction of Food Crops into Jamaica," *Revista de Historia de America* 39 (June 1955): 1–20.

2. David Collins, *Practical Rules for the Management and Medical Treatment of Negro Slaves, in the Sugar Colonies. By a Professional Planter* (London, 1811), 22.

3. Ibid., 100.

4. Vivian Nun Halloran, "Recipes as Memory Work: Slave Food," *Culture, Theory and Critique* 53, no. 2 (2012): 148.

5. See Judith Carney, *Black Rice: The African Origins of Rice Cultivation in the Americas* (Cambridge: Harvard University Press, 2002). For an early manifestation of debates about the degree to which Africans retained or had to remake their Old World knowledge, see E. Franklin Frazier, *The Free Negro Family: A Study of Family Origins before the Civil War* (Nashville: Fisk University Press, 1932); and Melville Herskovits, *Acculturation: The Study of Culture Contact* (Gloucester, MA: J. J. Augustin, 1938). For more recent studies of acculturation and retention, see, for example, Sidney Mintz and Richard Price, *The Birth of African-American Culture: An Anthropological Perspective* (Boston: Beacon Press, 1976); and Edward Brathwaite, *The Development of Creole Society in Jamaica, 1770–1820* (Oxford: Clarendon Press, 1971).

6. David Eltis, Philip Morgan, and David Richardson, "Agency and Diaspora in Atlantic History: Reassessing the African Contribution to Rice Cultivation in the Americas," *American Historical Review* 112, no. 4 (1997): 1357.

7. Ibid., 1357.

8. Richard Ligon, *A True and Exact History of the Island of Barbados*, ed. Karen Ordahl Kupperman (Indianapolis: Hackett Publishing Company, 2011), 81.

9. Christopher P. Iannini, *Fatal Revolutions: Natural History, West Indian Slavery, and the Routes of American Literature* (Chapel Hill: University of North Carolina Press, 2012), 3.

10. Henry Lowood, "The New World and the European Catalog of Nature," *America in European Consciousness, 1493–1750*, ed. Karen Ordahl Kupperman (Chapel Hill: University of North Carolina Press, 1995), 296.

11. See, for example, Daniela Bleichmar and Peter C. Mancall, eds., *Collecting across Cultures: Material Exchanges in the Early Modern Atlantic World* (Philadelphia: University of Pennsylvania Press, 2011).

12. Iannini, *Fatal Revolutions*, 9.

13. Ibid., 37.

14. Ibid., 47.

15. Karen Ordahl Kupperman, introduction to *A True and Exact History of Barbados*, by Richard Ligon (Indianapolis: Hackett, 2011), 6.

16. Ligon, *A True and Exact History*, 78.

17. Ibid., 77.

18. Ibid., 81.

19. Ibid., 93.

20. Ibid., 93.

21. Ibid., 93–94.

22. Ibid., 75.

23. Ibid., 75–76.

24. Ibid., 76.

25. J. D. La Fleur, *Fusion Foodways of Africa's Gold Coast in the Atlantic Era* (Leiden, The Netherlands: Brill, 2012), 155 n. 1.

26. See Achim von Oppen, "Cassava, 'The Lazy Man's Food'? Indigenous Agricultural Innovation and Dietary Change in Northwestern Zambia (ca. 1650–1970)," *Food and Foodways* 5, no. 1 (1991): 21; and James C. McCann, *Stirring the Pot: A History of African Cuisine* (Athens: Ohio University Press, 2009), 51.

27. See Stanley B. Alpern, "The European Introduction of Crops into West Africa in Precolonial Times," *History in Africa* 19 (1992): 13–14; and D. L. Jennings, "Cassava," in *Evolution of Crop Plants*, ed. N. W. Simmonds (London: Longman, 1976), 81–84.

28. John Frechione, "The Root and the Problem: Cassava Toxicity and Diffusion to Africa," in *The Globalization of Food*, ed. Leonard Plotnicov and Richard Scaglion (Prospect Heights, IL: Waveland Press, 2002), 44.

29. La Fleur, *Fusion Foodways*, 8.

30. See Alfred W. Crosby, *The Columbian Exchange: Biological and Cultural Consequences of 1492* (Westport, CT: Greenwood Press, 1972).

31. The natural historian Guillaume Thomas Raynal made this suggestion. See Barbara S. Renvoize, "The Area of Origin of *Manihot esculenta* as a Crop Plant—a Review of the Evidence," *Economic Botany* 26, no. 4 (1972): 352.

32. La Fleur, *Fusion Foodways*, 181.

33. See Kenneth F. Kiple, *The Caribbean Slave: A Biological History* (Cambridge: Cambridge University Press, 1984), 66.

34. McCann, *Stirring the Pot*, 165–66.

35. Ligon, *A True and Exact History*, 81.

36. Ibid., 75.

37. This word refers to a searce, or sieve.

38. Hans Sloane, vol. 1 of *A Voyage To the Islands . . . With The Natural History of the Herbs and Trees, Four-footed Beasts, Fishes, Birds, Insects, Reptiles, &c. of the last of those Islands* (London, 1707), xviii.

39. Hans Sloane, vol. 2 of *A Voyage To the Islands . . . With The Natural History of the Herbs and Trees, Four-footed Beasts, Fishes, Birds, Insects, Reptiles, &c. of the last of those Islands* (London, 1707), 363.

40. Henry Barham, *Hortus Americanus . . . Interspersed with many curious and useful Observations, respecting their Uses in Medicine, Diet, and Mechanics* (Kingston, Jamaica, 1794), 34.

41. Griffith Hughes, *The Natural History Of Barbados. In Ten Books* (London, 1750), 123–24.

42. See John Savage, "'Black Magic' and White Terror: Slave Poisoning and Colonial Society in Early 19th Century Martinique," *Journal of Social History* 40, no. 3 (2007): 636.

43. Ibid., 646.

44. Ligon, *A True and Exact History*, 75.

45. Ibid., 75.

46. Sloane, vol. 1 of *Voyage*, xviii.

47. Iannini, *Fatal Revolutions*, 37.

CHAPTER 2. Native American Contributions to African American Foodways: Slavery, Colonialism, and Cuisine

I owe a debt of gratitude to a number of individuals and organizations for making this essay possible. I would like to thank Mike Wise for encouraging me to submit a proposal for the volume, as well as Jennifer Wallach for providing valuable editorial assistance and patience throughout the writing process. Jean O'Brien provided helpful suggestions during the research stage of my work, particularly in regards to Native American foodways. I would also like to thank the Institute for Southern Studies at the University of South Carolina for providing support during the early stages of this project, as well as the staffs at the South Caroliniana Library and the library of Midlands Technical College for research assistance. Finally, I would like to thank my wife, Shanna Hoff-Gilmer, for copyediting numerous drafts and providing unending support.

1. Adrian Miller, *Soul Food: The Surprising Story of an American Cuisine, One Plate at a Time* (Chapel Hill: University of North Carolina Press, 2013), 44–45.

2. For examples, please see Miller, *Soul Food*, 19; Frederick Douglass Opie, *Hog and Hominy: Soul Food from Africa to America* (New York: Columbia University Press, 2008), 20–21; Anne Yentsch, "Excavating African American Food History," in *African American Foodways: Explorations of History and Culture*, ed. Anne L. Bower (Urbana: University of Illinois Press, 2009), 61–62, 65, 70; Jessica B. Harris, *High on the Hog: A Culinary Journey from Africa to America* (New York: Bloomsbury USA, 2011), 43–45.

3. John Egerton, introduction to *Cornbread Nation 1: The Best of Southern Food Writing*, ed. John Egerton (Chapel Hill: University of North Carolina Press, 2002), 2. While southern and African American foodways are not synonymous, there is a substantial degree of overlap between the two as African American cuisine played a profound role in shaping the diets of all southern peoples.

4. Andrew B. Munkacsi, Sam Stoxen, and Georgiana May, "Ustilago Maydis Populations Tracked Maize through Domestication and Cultivation in the Americas," *Proceedings: Biological Sciences* 275, no. 1638 (2008): 1037–38.

5. Miller, *Soul Food*, 187–90, 194, 198.

6. Judith Carney, "African Rice in the Columbian Exchange," *Journal of African History* 42, no. 3 (2001): 381.

7. William Frank Mitchell, *African American Food Culture* (Westport, CT: Greenwood Press, 2009), 7.

8. Millie Evans interview, WPA Slave Narrative Project, Arkansas Narratives, Vol. 2, pt. 2, 250–51; Allen Sims interview, WPA Slave Narrative Project, Alabama Narratives, Vol. 1, 342–43; Sarah H. Hill, *Weaving New Worlds: Southeastern Cherokee Women and Their Basketry*, (Chapel Hill: University of North Carolina Press, 1997), 8.

9. There is some division over the origin of the word "barbeque" (or even barbecue, BBQ, etc.). While most sources suggest that it was derived from the Taíno or Timucua languages, others have argued that it could be derived from French, or through French from other Native American sources. See Mark Morton, "Barbecue Mania," *Gastronomica: The Journal of Food and Culture* 2, no. 3 (Summer 2002): 11; Ginny Carney, "Native American Loanwords in English," *Wicazo Sa Review* 12, no. 1 (Spring 1997): 191, 201n14; G. Dixon Hollingsworth Jr., "The Story of Barbecue," *Georgia Historical Quarterly* 63, no. 3 (1979): 391–92; J. M. Carriére, "Indian and Creole Barboka, American Barbecue," *Language* 13, no. 2 (April–June 1937): 148–50.

10. William C. Wirt, "Soul Food as a Cultural Creation," in *African American Foodways*, ed. Bower, 48–49.

11. Opie, *Hog and Hominy*, 20–21.

12. Robert L. Hall, "Food Crops, Medicinal Plants, and the Atlantic Slave Trade," in *African American Foodways*, ed. Bower, 26–27.

13. Wirt, "Soul Food as a Cultural Creation," 48–49; Alfred W. Crosby Jr., *The Columbian Exchange: Biological and Cultural Consequences of 1492* (Westport, CT: Praeger Publishing, 2003), 170–72; and Shannon Lee Dawdy, "'A Wild Taste': Food and Colonialism in Eighteenth-Century Louisiana," *Ethnohistory* 57, no. 3 (Summer 2010): 407.

14. Rayna Greene, "Mother Corn and Dixie Pig: Native Food in the Native South," *Southern Cultures* 14, no. 4 (Winter 2008): 124.

15. Carney, "African Rice in the Columbian Exchange," 378.

16. Miller, *Soul Food*, 113.

17. Greene, "Mother Corn and Dixie Pig," 117–18.

18. Miller, *Soul Food*, 19.

19. Yentsch, "Excavating African American Food History," 65.

20. Harris, *High on the Hog*, 43–45.

21. Jean M. O'Brien, *Dispossession by Degrees: Indian Land and Identity in Natick, Massachusetts, 1650–1790* (Lincoln: University of Nebraska Press, 1997), 201–2.

22. Claudio Saunt, *A New Order of Things: Property, Power, and the Transformation of the Creek Indians, 1733–1816* (Cambridge: Cambridge University Press, 1999), 207–13.

23. Greene, "Mother Corn and Dixie Pig," 20. See also the excellent work of Malinda Maynor Lowery, *Lumbee Indian in the Jim Crow South: Race, Identity, and the Making of a Nation* (Chapel Hill: University of North Carolina Press, 2010).

24. Carney, "African Rice in the Columbian Exchange," 381.

25. Dawdy, "'A Wild Taste,'" 407.

26. Carney, "African Rice in the Columbian Exchange," 381–88.

27. Mitchell, *African American Food Culture*, 6–8.

28. As Michael Guasco points out, the majority of captives taken during the Pequot War were kept locally as slaves, though the terms of their captivity differed significantly from African slavery. Seventeen others were shipped to the West

Indies. See "'Doe Some Good Upon Their Countrymen': The Paradox of Indian Slavery in Early Anglo-America," *Journal of Social History* 41, no. 2 (Winter 2007): 398–400. Owen Stanwood, "Captives and Slaves: Indian Labor, Cultural Conversion, and the Plantation Revolution in Virginia," *Virginia Magazine of History and Biography* 114, no. 4 (2006): 442.

29. One famous victim of this trade is Tituba, who was one of the first accused during the Salem witch trials. Tituba was originally from Barbados and later brought to New England and was variously described as being of Native American and African origin (and quite possibly European as well) in records from the trials. Her multiracial and multiethnic identities (and the intractability of determining precisely what that identity was) reflect the degree to which the daily lives of various peoples, American Indian, Native Caribbean, and African, were forced together through the development of slavery across the Atlantic world during the seventeenth and eighteenth centuries. See Veta Smith Tucker, "Purloined Identity: The Racial Metamorphosis of Tituba of Salem Village," *Journal of Black Studies* 30, no. 4 (March 2000): 624–33.

30. Stanwood, "Captives and Slaves," 444–45.

31. Ibid., 445.

32. See Robin A. Beck Jr., "Catawba Coalescence and the Shattering of the Carolina Piedmont, 1540–1675," in *Mapping the Mississippian Shatter Zone: The Colonial Indian Slave Trade and Regional Instability in the American South*, ed. Robbie Ethridge and Sheri M. Shuck-Hall (Lincoln: University of Nebraska Press, 2009), 134–38.

33. The Province of Carolina split into northern and southern halves during the midst of this trade, but the bulk of it was centered in what became South Carolina.

34. Stanwood, "Captives and Slaves," 435–37.

35. Alan Gallay, *The Indian Slave Trade: The Rise of English Empire in the American South, 1670–1717* (New Haven: Yale University Press, 2002), 346.

36. Juliana Barr, "How Do You Get from Jamestown to Santa Fe? A Colonial Sun Belt," *Journal of Southern History* 73, no. 3 (August 2007): 564–65; Juliana Barr, *Peace Came in the Form of a Woman: Indians and Spaniards in the Texas Borderlands* (Chapel Hill: University of North Carolina Press, 2007), 247–48.

37. L. H. Roper, "The 1701 'Act for the Better Ordering of Slaves': Reconsidering the History of Slavery in Proprietary South Carolina," *William and Mary Quarterly* 64, no. 2 (April 2007): 399–400.

38. Gallay, *The Indian Slave Trade*, 347–48.

39. Ibid., 347; Tiya Miles, *Ties That Bind: The Story of an Afro-Cherokee Family in Slavery and Freedom* (Berkeley: University of California Press, 2005), 31–34.

40. Claudio Saunt, "The Paradox of Freedom: Tribal Sovereignty and Emancipation during the Reconstruction of Indian Territory," *Journal of Southern History* 70, no. 1 (February 2004): 64–65.

CHAPTER 3. Black Women's Food Writing and the Archive of Black Women's History

1. Research for this essay was collected at the David Walker Lupton African American Cookbook Collection in the W. S. Hoole Special Collections Library at the University of Alabama, Tuscaloosa. I am grateful to the Frances S. Summersell Center for the Study of the South for research support.

2. The motto "We specialize in the wholly impossible" comes from Nannie Helen Burroughs's National Training School for Women and Girls, an industrial school in Washington, D.C., for African Americans, which operated from 1909 through the 1940s. This motto is also the title of a reader on black women's history: Darlene Clark Hine, Wilma King, and Linda Reed, *We Specialize in the Wholly Impossible: A Reader in Black Women's History* (New York: New York University Press, 1995).

3. Rebecca Sharpless, *Cooking in Other Women's Kitchens: Domestic Workers in the South, 1865–1960* (Chapel Hill: University of North Carolina Press, 2013); Psyche Williams-Forson, *Building Houses out of Chicken Legs: Black Women, Food, and Power* (Chapel Hill: University of North Carolina Press, 2006); and Jessica B. Harris, *High on the Hog: A Culinary Journey from Africa to America* (New York: Bloomsbury, 2012).

4. The strongest archive for African American food publications is the David Walker Lupton African Cookbook Collection at the University of Alabama's W. S. Hoole Special Collections Library, Tuscaloosa. Doris Witt published an excellent appendix on African American cookbooks with a bibliographic essay in Doris Witt, *Black Hunger: Soul Food and America* (Minneapolis: University of Minnesota Press, 2004), 217–29.

5. Intersectionality, outside of the legal context that innovated the idea, is useful for avoiding simplistic reductions of privileging race or gender in the lives of black women and instructs the historian to see them as mutually operational. See Kimberle Crenshaw, "Demarginalizing the Intersection of Race and Sex: A Black Feminist Critique of Antidiscrimination Doctrine, Feminist Theory, and Antiracist Politics," *University of Chicago Legal Forum* (1989), 139–67. Evelyn Brooks Higginbotham used the idea of politics of respectability to understand the motivations and actions of black club women at the turn of the twentieth century, see Evelyn Brooks Higginbotham, *Righteous Discontent: The Women's Movement in the Black Baptist Church: 1880–1920* (Cambridge: Harvard University Press, 1993).

6. Legal scholar Patricia Hill Collins coined the term "controlling image" to discuss the way racism and sexism portrayed black women in popular and political culture. Patricia Hill Collins, "Mammies, Matriarchs, and Other Controlling Images," *Black Feminist Thought: Knowledge, Consciousness, and the Politics of Empowerment* (New York: Routledge, 2008), 69–96.

7. See, for example, Doris Witt, "Look Ma, the Real Aunt Jemima: Consuming Identities under Capitalism," in her *Black Hunger*, 21–53; and Maurice Manring, *Slave in a Box: The Strange Career of Aunt Jemima* (Charlottesville: University of Virginia Press, 1998).

8. The actresses who portrayed Aunt Jemima for the Quaker Oats Company included the first live-action Aunt Jemima, Nancy Green. Anna Robinson, Anna Short Harrington, and Edith Wilson, among many others, played the iconic mammy.

9. An example of this is Katherin Bell, *Mammy's Cookbook* (Katharin Bell, 1927). Bell wrote in the foreword to the recipe collection: "With the dying out of the black mammies of the South, much that was good and beautiful has gone out of life."

10. Natalie V. Scott, *Mandy's Favorite Louisiana Recipes* (Gretna: Pelican Publishing Company, 1980), n.p.

11. One of the clearest examples of a newspaper column written by a white editor pretending to be a black cook was the *Baltimore Sun's* "Aunt Priscilla" feature. Penned by a white writer named Eleanor Purcell, the newspaper articles and the cookbooks bearing Priscilla's name were infused with stereotypes about black loyalty as well as with dialect. For more, see Jennifer Jensen Wallach, *How America Eats: A Social History of U.S. Food and Culture* (New York: Rowman and Littlefield, 2013), 186–88.

12. "Omar Cake Mix Advertisement," *Mason City (NE) Globe-Gazette*, n.d.

13. For more on the politics of respectability, see Higginbotham, *Righteous Discontent.*

14. The 1934 version of the film *Imitation of Life* was based on a 1933 novel by Fannie Hurst. The film features a Mammy-like character named Delilah Johnson. Hurst was a lifelong dieter and frequent writer of tales that discussed women's fraught relationship with food. Scholars such as Julia Erhardt argue that Hurst used black women characters to consume in ways that would be considered inappropriate or unfeminine for white women. For more on Hurst and the two film versions of *Imitation of Life*, see Miriam Thaggert, "Divided Images: Black Female Spectatorship and John Stahl's *Imitation of Life*," *African American Review* 32, no. 3 (Autumn 1998), 481–91.

15. Slave narratives often included testaments from whites that such texts were indeed authored by emancipated or escaped slaves. These certifications often included passages about the slave's literacy, moral fitness, and truthfulness.

16. Sarah Helen Mahammitt, *The Mahammitt School of Cookery: Recipes and Domestic Service* (Omaha, NE: Mrs. T. P. Mahammitt, 1939), foreword.

17. *Ibid.*, 133.

18. Williams-Forson, *Building Houses out of Chicken Legs*, 80–81.

19. *Ibid.*, 144.

20. Ibid.

21. Ibid., 145.

22. Ibid., 145.

23. Rebecca Sharpless's study of Idella Parker, a black maid, and her employer, Marjorie Rawlings, illustrated the unequal relationship between black and white women in the kitchen. Parker published a memoir revealing that famed author Rawlins took credit for many of her recipes. Rebecca Sharpless, "The 'Soul Sisters' in the Kitchen," *New York Times*, July 29, 2013, A19; Sharpless, *Cooking in Other Women's Kitchens*, and Rebecca Sharpless, "Neither Friends nor Peers: Idella Parker, Marjorie Kinnan Rawlings, and the Limits of Gender Solidarity at Cross Creek," *Journal of Southern History* 78, no. 2 (May 2012), 327–60.

24. Black women's labor history has focused on the period after slavery and provides insights into the negotiation of new relationships of power between blacks and whites. See Tera Hunter, *To Joy My Freedom: Southern Black Women's Lives and Labors after the Civil War* (Cambridge: Harvard University Press, 1998).

25. Black women's economic mobility and the hair care industry are well documented in Tiffany Gill, *Beauty Shop Politics: African American Women's Activism in the Beauty Industry* (Urbana: University of Illinois Press, 2010); and Susannah Walker, *Style and Status: Selling Beauty to African American Women, 1920–1975* (Lexington: University of Kentucky Press, 2007).

26. Sharpless, *Cooking in Other Women's Kitchens*, 173–76.

27. Rebecca West, *Rebecca's Cookbook* (Washington, DC: Rebecca West, 1942), 1–2. Historians of black women after Emancipation have examined an array of issues surrounding black women and urbanization: see Kali Gross, *Colored Amazons: Crime, Violence, and Black Women in the City of Brotherly Love* (Durham: Duke University Press, 2006); Cynthia Blair, *I've Got to Make My Livin': Black Women's Sex Work in Turn-of-the-Century Chicago* (Chicago: University of Chicago Press, 2010); and Erin D. Chapman, *Prove It on Me: New Negroes, Sex, and Popular Culture in the 1920s* (Oxford: Oxford University Press, 2012).

28. "Bungleton Green" appeared in the *Chicago Defender* between 1920 and 1963, and four artists worked on the strip throughout its life. Sheena C. Howard and Ronald L. Jackson, *Black Comics: Politics and Representation* (New York: Bloomsbury, 2013), 13–15.

29. West, *Rebecca's Cookbook*, 1–2.

30. Ibid., 2.

31. Ibid., 3.

32. Ibid., 51.

33. Ibid.

34. Ibid., 21.

35. Gillian Clark, *Out of the Frying Pan: A Chef's Memoir of Hot Kitchens, Single Motherhood, and the Family Meal* (New York: St. Martin's Press, 2007).

36. Ibid., 3.

37. Ibid., 8.

38. Ibid., 97.

39. For a look at black women's labor as wet nurses, child nurses, and nannies, see Kimberly Wallace Sanders, *Mammy: A Century of Race, Gender, and Southern Memory* (Ann Arbor: University of Michigan Press, 2008); and Micki McElya, *Clinging to Mammy: The Faithful Slave in Twentieth-Century America* (Cambridge: Harvard University Press, 2007).

40. Clark, *Out of the Frying Pan*, 162.

41. Ibid., 199.

42. "Gillian Clark: The Chef People Love to Hate," *Washington Post*, February 1, 2011.

43. Clark, *Out of the Frying Pan*, 243.

CHAPTER 4. *A Date with a Dish:* Revisiting Freda De Knight's African American Cuisine

I would like to thank Lauren Duval, who assisted me with my research for this project, and Max Paul Friedman and Jennifer Wallach for their comments and editorial suggestions.

1. Freda De Knight, *A Date with a Dish* (New York: Hermitage Press, 1948).

2. A note on the spelling of De Knight's name: De Knight published her column in *Ebony* magazine under "DeKnight" and in contemporary accounts her name (and that of her husband, René) is usually spelled without a space. But in *A Date with a Dish* her name is given as "De Knight."

3. Gertrude Blair, foreword, in *A Date with a Dish*, by De Knight, ix.

4. Roi Ottley, "Negro Authors Find Topics in Many Fields," *Chicago Daily Tribune*, May 29, 1960, sw 3, accessed January 15, 2014, http://search.proquest.com/docview/182498203?accountid=8285.

5. Roi Ottley, "Party Menu Launches Woman on a Career as Culinary Editor," *Chicago Daily Tribune*, October 23, 1955, sw 17, accessed January 15, 2014, http://search.proquest.com/docview/179595084?accountid=8285. See also Gertrude Blair's foreword to *A Date with a Dish*, in which she, too, mentions De Knight's research and claims that she had "collected over a thousand wonderful recipes from Negro sources, during the last twenty years" (ix).

6. Frederick Douglass Opie's *Hog and Hominy: Soul Food from Africa to America* (New York: Columbia University Press, 2008) and Doris Witt's *Black Hunger: Soul Food and America* (Minneapolis: University of Minnesota Press, 2004) do not mention *A Date with a Dish*. The quote in this paragraph comes from Witt's later book chapter, "From Fiction to Foodways: Working at the Intersections of African American Literary and Cultural Studies," in *African American Foodways: Explorations of History and Culture*, ed. Anne L. Bower (Urbana: University of Illinois Press, 2007), 113. William Frank Mitchell lists *A Date with a Dish* in the bibliography of his *African American Food Culture* (Westport, CT: Greenwood Press, 2009), but it appears neither in the text nor in his complex timeline of events relevant to African American cooking. Jessica Harris devotes a bit over a page to Freda De Knight in her *High on the Hog: A Culinary Journey from Africa to America* (New York: Bloomsbury, 2011), 195–96.

7. See, for instance, Marisa Chappell, Jenny Hutchinson, and Brian Ward's remarks on Freda De Knight in "'Dress Modestly, Neatly . . . As if You Were Going to Church': Respectability, Class, and Gender in the Montgomery Bus Boycott and the Early Civil Rights Movement," in *Gender and the Civil Rights Movement*, ed. Peter John Ling and Sharon Monteith (New Brunswick, NJ: Rutgers University Press, 2004), 75.

8. Vertamae Smart Grovenor, *Vibration Cooking: The Travel Notes of a Geechee Girl* (New York: Doubleday, 1970); or *The Historical Cookbook of the American Negro*, ed. Sue Bailey Thurman (Washington, DC: Corporate/National Council of Negro Women, 1958).

9. Freda De Knight's "Tamale Pie for New Year," *Ebony*, January 1947, 42–43; "Lena Horne's Valentine Party," *Ebony*, February 1947, 17–18; and "Baked Fish," *Ebony*, April 1948, 33.

10. Freda De Knight's "Salad Bowl," *Ebony*, April 1947, 46; and "Red, White, and Blue Supper," *Ebony*, July 1948, 65.

11. For more information on *Ebony*, see Jason Chambers, "Equal in Every Way: African Americans, Consumption, and Materialism from Reconstruction to the Civil Rights Movement," *Advertising and Society Review* 7, no. 1 (2006), accessed January 1, 2014, http://muse.jhu.edu.proxyau.wrlc.org/journals/advertising_and_society_review/v007/7.1chambers.html.

12. "Goodbye Mammy, Hello Mom," *Ebony,* March 1947, 36.

13. "Lena Horne's Valentine Party," 17–18.

14. Freda De Knight, "Ebony Dates a Turkey," *Ebony,* November 1946, 36–37.

15. Freda De Knight, "New Orleans Gumbo for Thanksgiving," *Ebony,* November 1947, 25.

16. De Knight, *A Date with a Dish,* 23, 43, 55, 57, 63, 69, 77, 86.

17. Norma Jean and Carole Darden, *Spoonbread and Strawberry Wine, Recipes and Reminiscences of a Family* (New York: Fawcett Crest, 1978).

18. Rafia Zafar, "The Signifying Dish: Autobiography and History in Two Black Women's Cookbooks," *Feminist Studies* 25, no. 2 (1999): 449. See also Psyche Williams-Forson's reading of the mammy in her *Building Houses out of Chicken Legs: Black Women, Food and Power* (Chapel Hill: University of North Carolina Press, 2006), 188–89.

19. De Knight, *A Date with a Dish,* 265, 232, 168.

20. Adelle Davis, *Let's Cook It Right: Good Health Comes from Good Cooking* (New York: Harcourt, Brace & World, 1947), lists, for instance, recipes for "Tongue," "Pig's Feet," and "Head Cheese," 140, 142.

21. This is perhaps most famously represented in Ralph Ellison's *Invisible Man,* in which the protagonist is initially embarrassed by his desire for yams (New York: Random House, 2010 [1952]), 262–66.

22. See, for instance, Opie, *Hog and Hominy,* 17–30.

23. See, for instance, Opie, *Hog and Hominy,* 124.

24. In 1965 Eldridge Cleaver wrote: "The emphasis on Soul Food is counter-revolutionary black bourgeois ideology." He continued: "You hear a lot of jazz about Soul Food. Take chitterlings: the ghetto blacks eat them from necessity while the black bourgeoisie has turned it into a mocking slogan. Eating chitterlings is like going slumming to them. Now that they have the price of the steak, here they come prattling about Soul Food. The people in the ghetto want steaks. *Beef Steaks.* I wish I had the power to see to it that the bourgeoisie really *did* have to make it on Soul Food." Eldridge Cleaver, *Soul on Ice* (New York: Delta, 1991 [1968]), 49.

In a portrait of Edna Lewis in *Southern Living* the author writes that Lewis "shudders" when asked about soul food and says: "That's hard-times food in Harlem—not true Southern food." Denise Gee, "The Gospel of Great Southern Food," *Southern Living,* June 1996, 128.

And in her discussion of representations of soul food in the 1970s in *Ebony Jr!* Laretta Henderson argues that it was used to "define and postulate a middle-class, Christian, and politically moderate (at least more so than those of the Nation of Islam) black identity for the child reader." "*Ebony Jr!* and 'Soul Food': The Construction of Middle-Class African American Identity through the Use of Traditional Southern Foodways," *MELUS* 32, no. 4 (2007): 88.

On the question of resistance against soul food on the basis of health, see the chapter "Food Rebels" in Opie's *Hog and Hominy,* 155–73.

25. For biographical information on Russell, see Patricia E. Clark, "Cookbooks Help Tell the Story of African-American Women Coming into Their Own," *Post-Standard* (Syracuse, NY), February 26, 2012. Accessed February 27, 2014, http://blog.syracuse.com/opinion/2012/02/patricia_e_clark_cookbooks.html.

26. For a more detailed analysis of the dishes in *A Domestic Cook,* see Harris, *High on the Hog,* 164–65.

27. In the introduction a Mrs. W. T. Hayes names herself the author, but research by Toni Tipton Martin casts doubt on whether she was also the "colored woman" who is credited as the creator of the recipes. "Mrs. W. T. Hayes: Courageous Cook or Benefactor?" *The Jemima Code*, April 20, 2010. Accessed February 15, 2014, http://thejemimacode.com/2010/04/20/mrs-w-t-hayes-courageous-cook-or-benefactor/.

28. Emma Allen Hayes, *Kentucky Cook Book* (St. Louis: J. H. Tomkins Printing Company, 1912), 6, 7, 14, 18, 20, 24, 25, 29, 40.

29. Bob Jeffries writes in his *Soul Food Cookbook* (New York: Bobbs-Merrill, 1969) that moving the focus from cooking to eating was an important point in the conceptualization of soul food:

> The word soul, when applied to food, means only those foods that Negroes grew up eating in their own homes; food that was cooked with care and love—with soul—by and for themselves, their families, and friends. This, of course, included much of what is now termed traditional southern fare, dishes such as Deep-Fried Chicken, Spareribs, and Country Ham, but it was also much more. (ix)

With the "much more," Jeffries seems to mean that recipes that use easily available, fresh ingredients with little reference to European preparation styles can count as soul food.

30. Harris, *High on the Hog*, 119.

31. Ibid., 122.

32. Ibid., 125–30.

33. De Knight, *A Date with a Dish*, xiii.

34. "A Date with a Dish," Advertisement, *Ebony*, June 1948, 27.

35. De Knight, *A Date with a Dish*, 227.

36. Or if African Americans appeared in white cookbooks, it was generally in (often racist) asides or as colorful illustrations, as in Patsie McRee's excruciating *The Kitchen and the Cotton Patch* (Nashville: Cullom & Ghertner, 1948), which happened to be published in the same year as De Knight's *A Date with a Dish*. That coincidence illustrates how much De Knight challenged the conventional depiction of African Americans in the culinary realm.

37. "A Date with a Cook Book," *Ebony*, June 1948, 44.

38. Some texts explicitly appealed to their readership to explore other people's cuisines, such as Davis, *Let's Cook It Right*.

39. De Knight, *A Date with a Dish*, 90.

40. Ibid., 30–32.

41. Mary Meade, "East and West Indian Cookery Demonstrated," *Chicago Tribune*, January 14, 1950, http://search.proquest.com, accessed May 27, 2014.

42. De Knight, *A Date with a Dish*, 245.

43. See Bertha Gehrke, "What's Cooking in a Colleague's Test Kitchen," *Chicago Tribune*, December 13, 1957. Accessed January 14, 2014. http://search.proquest.com/docview/180244017?accountid=8285

44. De Knight, *A Date with a Dish*, 34.

45. Ibid., xiv.

46. Ibid., 17–18.

47. Irma S. Rombauer, *The Joy of Cooking: A Compilation of Reliable Recipes with an Occasional Culinary Chat* (Philadelphia: Blakiston Company, 1943 [1931]).
48. De Knight, *A Date with a Dish*, 1.
49. Dorothy Malone, *How Mama Could Cook!* (New York: A. A. Wyn, 1946).
50. De Knight, *A Date with a Dish*, 3.
51. Ibid., 9, 6.
52. Davis, *Let's Cook It Right*, ix–x.

CHAPTER 5. What's the Difference between Soul Food and Southern Cooking? The Classification of Cookbooks in American Libraries

1. Patrick Wilson, *Two Kinds of Power: An Essay on Bibliographic Control* (Berkeley: University of California Press, 1968). See also Hope A. Olson, *The Power to Name: Locating the Limits of Subject Representation in Libraries* (Dordrecht, Netherlands: Kluwer Academic Publishers, 2002); and Hope A. Olson, "The Power to Name: Representation in Library Catalogs," *Signs: Journal of Women in Culture and Society* 26 (2001): 639–68.

2. Library of Congress, *Library of Congress Subject Headings* (Washington, DC: US Government Printing Office, 1910–). This has been in publication under various titles from 1910 to the present.

3. The original title was *Subject Headings Used in the Dictionary Catalogues of the Library of Congress*. The title was changed to *Library of Congress Subject Headings* in 1975.

4. For more information about the history and structure of the *Library of Congress Subject Headings*, please see Lois Mai Chan, *Library of Congress Subject Headings: Principles and Application*, 4th ed. (Westport, CT: Libraries Unlimited, 2005).

5. Library of Congress, *Library of Congress Classification* (Washington, DC: US Government Printing Office).

6. Except for subclass KF (Law of the United States), which was first published in 1969.

7. For more information about the history and structure of the *Library of Congress Classification*, please see Lois Mai Chan, *A Guide to the Library of Congress Classification*, 5th ed. (Englewood, CO: Libraries Unlimited, 1999); and Francis Miksa, *The Development of Classification at the Library of Congress* (Champaign: University of Illinois at Urbana-Champaign, 1984).

8. Olson, *The Power to Name*, 6.

9. Hope A. Olson, "Mapping beyond Dewey's Boundaries: Constructing Classificatory Space for Marginalized Knowledge Domains," *Library Trends* 47 (1998): 233–54. See also Olson, "The Power to Name," 639–68.

10. There are many critiques of the *Library of Congress Subject Headings*. For example, see Joan Marshall, "LC Labeling: An Indictment," in *Revolting Librarians*, ed. Celeste West and Elizabeth Katz (San Francisco: Booklegger Press, 1972), 45–49; Sanford Berman, *The Joy of Cataloging: Essays, Letters, and Other Explosions* (Phoenix: Oryx Press, 1981); Marielena Fina, "The Role of Subject Headings in Access to Information: The Experience of One Spanish-Speaking Patron,"

Cataloging & Classification Quarterly 17 (1993): 267–74. Newer critiques include Emily Drabinski, "Queering the Catalog: Queer Theory and the Politics of Correction," *Library Quarterly* 83 (2013): 94–111.

11. Sanford Berman, *Prejudices and Antipathies: A Tract on the LC Subject Heads Concerning People* (Jefferson, NC: McFarland & Co., 1971). This is a classic critique of the *Library of Congress Subject Headings*.

12. Library of Congress, *Classification and Shelflisting Manual*, 2013 ed. (Washington, DC: US Government Printing Office, 2013).

13. Library of Congress, *Subject Headings Manual*, 2008 ed. (Washington, DC: US Government Printing Office, 2008).

14. "Cookery" was changed to "Cooking" "to modernize the subject headings for cooking and cookbooks, but it reflects usage in the United States. See Library of Congress Cataloging and Acquisitions, "Revision of Headings for Cooking and Cookbooks," Library of Congress, http://www.loc.gov/catdir/cpso/cooking.pdf, accessed January 12, 2014.

15. "Floribbean Cuisine," in *American Regional Cuisine*, ed. The Art Institutes (New York: John Wiley, 2002), 133–42.

16. The subject headings "Mexican American cooking" and "Indian cooking" also are treated as exceptions in the *Library of Congress Subject Headings*.

17. "African American Food," in *The Oxford Encyclopedia of Food and Drink in America*, 2nd ed., ed. Andrew F. Smith (Oxford: Oxford University Press, 2013).

18. Frederick Douglass Opie, *Hog and Hominy: Soul Food from Africa to America* (New York: Columbia University Press, 2008), xi.

19. Jessica B. Harris, *High on the Hog: A Culinary Journey from Africa to America* (New York: Bloomsbury, 2011), 1.

20. "Soul food cooking" should be a separate subject heading related to "Cooking, American—Southern style." Yet, "soul food" may be a difficult subject for the *Library of Congress Subject Headings* because other groups have begun to use the expression to describe their foodways. For example, see Laura Silver, *Knish: In Search of the Jewish Soul Food* (Waltham, MA: Brandeis University, 2014). In the *Library of Congress Subject Headings*, which group gets to claim "Soul food"?

21. There are over nine thousand titles in the Library of Congress collection classified at TX715. Library of Congress. *Library of Congress Online Catalog*, http://catalog.loc.gov/, accessed January 12, 2014.

22. Until 1990, the subject heading also could be classified at TX357, a "general-special" number for works on nutrition or the food supply.

23. Elizabeth S. D. Engelhardt, *A Mess of Greens: Southern Gender and Southern Food* (Athens: University of Georgia Press, 2011).

24. Psyche A. Williams-Forson, *Building Houses out of Chicken Legs: Black Women, Food, and Power* (Chapel Hill: University of North Carolina Press, 2006).

25. Anne L. Bower, ed., *African American Foodways: Explorations of History and Culture* (Chicago: University of Illinois Press, 2007).

CHAPTER 6. Creole Cuisine as Culinary Border Culture: Reading Recipes as Testimonies of Hybrid Identities and Cultures

I am grateful to the CUNY Faculty Fellowship Publication Program, sponsored by the Office of the Dean for Recruitment and Diversity, for the opportunity to work on this chapter during the spring of 2014. Thank you to Moustafa Bayoumi, Habiba Boumlik, Claudia Calirman, Ruth Garcia, Sarah Kate Gillespie, Jayashree Kamble, and Michael Lacy for your insightful feedback and collegiality.

1. Mary Douglas, "Deciphering a Meal," in *Food and Culture: A Reader*, ed. Carole Counihan and Penny Van Esterik (New York: Routledge, 1997), 36.

2. Unlike the two previous examples, Célestine Eustis's *Cooking in Old Créole Days* was not published in New Orleans but in New York. The author, however, draws on her Creole heritage and New Orleans background.

3. Kyla Wazana Tompkins, *Racial Indigestion: Eating Bodies in the Nineteenth Century* (New York: New York University Press, 2012), 16–17.

4. Judith Ann Carney and Richard Nicholas Rosomoff, *In the Shadow of Slavery: Africa's Botanical Legacy in the Atlantic World* (Berkeley: University of California Press, 2009), 4.

5. Paul Gilroy, *The Black Atlantic: Modernity and Double Consciousness* (Cambridge, MA: Harvard University Press, 1993), 2.

6. Gwendolyn Midlo Hall, *Africans in Colonial Louisiana: The Development of Afro-Creole Culture in the Eighteenth Century* (Baton Rouge: Louisiana State University Press, 1992), 157.

7. Jessica B. Harris, *Beyond Gumbo: Creole Fusion Food from the Atlantic Rim* (New York: Simon and Schuster, 2003), 2–3.

8. Ibid., 4–5.

9. Ania Loomba, *Colonialism/Postcolonialism*, 2nd ed. (1988; reprint, London: Routledge, 2005), 145.

10. Marie Louise Pratt, "Arts of the Contact Zone," *Profession* (1991): 34, http:// www.jstor.org/stable/25595469, accessed January 10, 2013.

11. Tompkins, *Racial Indigestion*, 17.

12. See Hall, *Africans in Colonial Louisiana*, 10.

13. Susan E. Dollar, "Ethnicity and Jim Crow: The Americanization of Louisiana's Creoles," in *Louisiana beyond Black and White: New Interpretations of Twentieth-Century Race and Race Relations*, ed. Michael S. Martin (Lafayette: University of Louisiana at Lafayette Press, 2011) 1–16, 1–2.

14. See also Hall, *Africans in Colonial Louisiana*, 34; and Ralph Bauer and José Antonio Mazzotti, "Introduction: Creole Subjects in the Colonial Americas," in *Creole Subjects in the Colonial Americas: Empires, Texts, Identities*, ed. Ralph Bauer and José Antonio Mazzotti (Chapel Hill: University of North Carolina Press, 2009), 3.

15. Daniel Usner, "Between Creoles and Yankees: The Discursive Representation of Colonial Louisiana in American History," in *Colonial Louisiana and the Atlantic World*, ed. Bradley G. Bond (Baton Rouge: Louisiana State University Press, 2005), 2.

16. Ibid., 13.

17. Bauer and Mazzotti, "Introduction," 33.

18. "Okra, or 'Gumbo,' from Africa," *Aggie Horticulture*, http://aggie horticulture.tamu.edu/archives/parsons/publications/vegetabletravelers/okra. html, accessed January 20, 2014. For parts of present-day Senegal, Gambia, Ghana, and Mali, see Marcelle Bienvenu, Carl A. Brasseaux, and Ryan A. Brasseaux, *Stir the Pot: The History of Cajun Cuisine* (New York: Hippocrene Books, 2005), 134. Hall suggests that the majority of slaves in Louisiana came from the same region. See Hall, *Africans in Colonial Louisiana*, 29. For the West African forest-savanna ecotone, see Carney and Rosomoff, *In the Shadow*, 14. For Central Africa, see Karen Hess, *The Carolina Rice Kitchen: The African Connection* (Columbia: University of South Carolina Press, 1992), 111.

19. See, for an example on the Middle Passage, Marvalene H. Hughes, "Soul, Black Women, and Food," in *Food and Culture: A Reader*, ed. Carole Counihan and Penny van Esterik (New York: Routledge, 1997), 272. For cheap slave food, see Harris, *Beyond Gumbo*, 12.

20. Harris, *Beyond Gumbo*, 12.

21. Ibid.

22. As early as 1836, Mary Randolph introduced several recipes containing "ochra" in *The Virginia Housewife*. Sarah Rutledge's *The Carolina Housewife* (1851) presented two recipes for okra soup. Fannie Merritt Farmer's *The Boston Cooking-School Cook Book* (1896) also includes two references to okra, in recipes for oyster and chicken gumbo. In 1889, the first Jewish American cookbook, *Aunt Babette's Cook Book: Foreign and Domestic Receipts for the Household: A Valuable Collection of Receipts and Hints for the Housewife, Many of Which Are Not to Be Found Elsewhere* (1889), included a recipe for okra gumbo.

23. Lafcadio Hearn, *La Cuisine Creole: A Collection of Culinary Recipes from Leading Chefs and Noted Creole Housewives, Who Have Made New Orleans Famous for Its Cuisine* (New Orleans: F. F. Hansell, 1885), 18.

24. Due to their abundant presence in the American South, turtles were considered a slave food before the Civil War. See "Turtle and Mock Turtle Soup," in *The Oxford Companion to American Food and Drink*, ed. Andrew F. Smith (Oxford: Oxford University Press, 2007), 551. Hearn, *La Cuisine Creole*, 32.

25. Marvalene H. Hughes reads the consumption of chitterlings by white people as a "food cultural plunge" and an act of acculturation. See Hughes, "Soul, Black Women, and Food," 276. Black feminist writer Mikki Kendall has recently observed the rise of "food gentrification," the appropriation of cheap vegetables or animal parts like offal by haute cuisine. See, for example, Anna Brones, "Food Gentrification: Whole Foods Market and the Rise of the Trendy Vegetable," last modified March 18, 2014, http://foodieunderground.com/ food-gentrification-whole-foods-market-trendy-vegetable/.

26. Hearn, *La Cuisine Creole*, 2.

27. Rice, like okra, was brought to the North American continent from Africa. For an extensive analysis of the interconnection between the histories of rice and slavery, see Hess, *The Carolina Rice Kitchen*. See also Judith A. Carney, *Black Rice: The African Origins of Rice Cultivation in the Americas* (Cambridge: Harvard University Press, 2001).

28. Hearn, *La Cuisine Creole*, 19.

29. Ibid., 106.

30. Hess, *The Carolina Rice Kitchen*, 64–66.

31. See Donna Gabaccia, *We Are What We Eat: Ethnic Food and the Making of Americans* (Cambridge: Harvard University Press, 1998), 14.

32. For a detailed account of Native American corn cultivation, see Betty Fussell, *The Story of Corn: The Myths and History, the Culture and Agriculture, the Art and Science of America's Quintessential Crop* (New York: Knopf, 1994).

33. For a recent study of *The Picayune's Creole Cook Book*, see Rien Fertel's "'Everybody Seemed Willing to Help': *The Picayune Creole Cook Book* as Battleground, 1900–2008," *The Larder: Food Studies Methods from the American South*, ed. John T. Edge et al. (Athens: University of Georgia Press, 2013), 10–31. While Fertel gives a comprehensive introduction to many editions of the cookbook and notes the "symbolic whitening of the kitchen" and the silencing effected by the "mammification" performed by the text, he presents little material from the actual recipes.

34. *The Picayune's Creole Cook Book*, 4th ed. (New Orleans: The Times Picayune Publishing Company, 1910), 32, http://babel.hathitrust.org/cgi/pt?id=nyp.33433085767030;view=1up;seq=38, accessed June 10, 2014.

35. Ibid., 32–33.

36. Ironically, sassafras is today classified as a human carcinogen by the FDA.

37. *The Picayune's Creole Cook Book*, 10.

38. Ibid.

39. Ibid.

40. Ibid., 168.

41. Ibid., 169.

42. Ibid., 381.

43. Célestine Eustis, *Cooking in Old Créole Days: La Cuisine Créole a l'Usage des Petits Ménages* (New York: R. H. Russell, 1904), 13, http://digital.lib.msu.edu/projects/cookbooks/books/creolelausage/cclu.pdf, accessed August 3, 2013.

44. In *Hog and Hominy*, Frederick Douglas Opie suggests that Hopping John likely evolved from West African cuisine and was a variant of rice and bean combinations that slaves subsisted on during the Middle Passage. See Frederick Douglass Opie, *Hog and Hominy: Soul Food from Africa to America* (New York: Columbia University Press, 2008), 29. Karen Hess argues that "congri" stands for "Cajanus cajan," a pea grown in Africa for millennia. See Hess, *The Carolina Rice Kitchen*, 105.

45. Eustis, *Cooking in Old Créole Days*, 78.

46. In her French introduction, she describes gumbo as an Indian dish. Eustis, *Cooking in Old Créole Days*, xvi.

47. Eustis, *Cooking in Old Créole Days*, 78–79.

48. Ibid., 79.

49. Ibid., 69.

50. Tompkins, *Racial Indigestion*, 8.

51. Psyche A. Williams-Forson, *Building Houses out of Chicken Legs: Black Women, Food, and Power* (Chapel Hill: University of North Carolina Press, 2006), 2.

52. Andrew Warnes, "'Talking Recipes': *What Mrs Fisher Knows* and the African-American Food Tradition," in *The Recipe Reader: Narratives, Contexts, Traditions*, ed. Janet Floyd and Laurel Forster (Burlington, VT: Ashgate, 2003), 67.

CHAPTER 7. Feast of the Mau Mau: Christianity, Conjure, and the Origins of Soul Food

1. Louis Jordan, "Beans and Cornbread," *Let the Good Times Roll* (1949; rereleased, 1994, Eclipse Record Group).

2. Yvonne Chireau, *Black Magic: Religion and the African American Conjuring Tradition* (Berkeley: University of California Press, 2003), 143; Carolyn Long, *Spiritual Merchants: Religion, Magic, and Commerce* (Knoxville: University of Tennessee Press, 2001), 99–157, quote from 129. Also see Jeffrey Anderson, *Conjure in African American Society* (Baton Rouge: Louisiana State University Press, 2005), 112–59; Katrina Hazzard-Donald, *Mojo Workin': The Old African American Hoodoo System* (Urbana: University of Illinois Press, 2013), 116–85; Stephanie Mitchem, *African American Folk Healing* (New York: New York University Press, 2007), 119–62.

3. Judith Carney and Richard Rosomoff, *In the Shadow of Slavery: Africa's Botanical Legacy in the Atlantic World* (Berkeley: University of California Press, 2009); Jessica Harris, *High on the Hog: A Culinary Journey from Africa to America* (New York: Bloomsbury, 2011), 44–59, 199–219; Frederick Opie, *Hog and Hominy: Soul Food from Africa to America* (New York: Columbia University Press, 2008), 20–22, 155–73; Tracy Poe, "The Origins of Soul Food in Black Urban Identity: Chicago, 1915–1947," *American Studies International* (February 1999), 4–27; Doris Witt, *Black Hunger: Soul Food and America* (Minneapolis: University of Minnesota Press, 1999, 2004), 79–125.

4. "Who I Love and Why," New Lisbon (OH) *Anti-Slavery Bugle*, March 3, 1855; "From Wilberforce to Texas," *Freeman*, February 16, 1895.

5. "Our Cleveland District Conference," *Cleveland (OH) Gazette*, May 17, 1919; "Church News," *Advocate*, June 1, 1923; June Day, "Beautifying the Home," *Cleveland Gazette*, May 20, 1945.

6. Sallie Hill, "Alabama Food Ways," address to the Alabama Historical Association April 22, 1960, W. S. Hoole Special Collections Library, University of Alabama, Tuscaloosa.

7. Opie, *Hog and Hominy*, 82; "Jet, Ok. Ter.," Oklahoma City *Guide*, July 20, 1899.

8. Robert Graetz, *A White Preacher's Memoir: The Montgomery Bus Boycott* (Montgomery, AL: Black Belt Press, 1998), 28–29.

9. Opie, *Hog and Hominy*, 96; Psyche Williams-Forson, *Building Houses out of Chicken Legs: Black Woman, Food, and Power* (Chapel Hill: University of North Carolina Press, 2006), 135–62.

10. Isaac Hayes, *Cooking with Heart and Soul* (New York: G. P. Putnam, 2000), 2; W. Ralph Eubanks, *Ever Is a Long Time: A Journey into Mississippi's Dark Past* (New York: Basic, 2003), 31, 37; D'Army Bailey, *The Education of a Black Radical: A Southern Civil Rights Activist's Journey, 1959–1964* (Baton Rouge: Louisiana State University, 2009), 11. On the black Christian home, see John Giggie, "Refining Religion: Consumerism and African American Religion in the Delta, 1875–1917," in *Dixie Emporium: Tourism, Foodways, and Consumerism in the American South*, ed. Anthony J. Stanonis (Athens: University of Georgia Press, 2008), 94–119.

11. Peter Jan Honigsberg, *Crossing Border Street: A Civil Rights Memoir* (Berkeley: University of California Press, 2000), 59; Harris, *High on the Hog*, 206.

12. Witt, *Black Hunger*, 96.

13. Laretta Henderson, "'Ebony Jr!' and 'Soul Food': The Construction of Middle-Class African American Identity through the Use of Traditional Southern Foodways," *MELUS* (Winter 2007): 87.

14. Mahalia Jackson, *Mahalia Jackson Cooks Soul* (Nashville, TN: Aurora, 1970), xii (emphasis in original), David Walker Lupton African American Cookbook Collection, W. S. Hoole Special Collections Library, University of Alabama, Tuscaloosa, hereafter cited as AACC.

15. Doris Witt, "From Fiction to Foodways: Working at the Intersections of African American Literary and Culinary Studies," in *African American Foodways: Explorations of History and Culture*, ed. Anne Bower (Urbana: University of Illinois Press, 2007), 104.

16. For insight on conjure and slaves' beliefs about medicine, see Sharla Fett, *Working Cures: Healing, Health, and Power on Southern Slave Plantations* (Chapel Hill: University of North Carolina Press, 2007).

17. Hortense Powdermaker, *After Freedom: A Cultural Study in the Deep South* (1939; reprint, Madison: University of Wisconsin Press 1993), 295–96; John Dollard, *Caste and Class in a Southern Town*, 3rd ed. (1937; reprint, Garden City, NY: Doubleday, 1957), 85.

18. William Craig Brownlee, *Letters in the Roman Catholic Controversy* (New York: self-published, 1834), 98.

19. John Albert Phillips, *Roman Catholicism Analyzed: A Dispassionate Examination of Romish Claims* (New York: Fleming R. Revell, 1915), 86.

20. Olin Marvin Owen, *Rum, Rags, and Religion: Or in Darkest America and the Way Out* (Syracuse, NY: A. W. Hall, 1892), 53.

21. *Chambers's Encyclopaedia: A Dictionary of Universal Knowledge* (Philadelphia: J. B. Lippincott, 1888), vol. 2, new ed., 710.

22. Horace Smith Fulkerson, *The Negro: As He Was, As He Is, As He Will Be* (Vicksburg, MS: Commercial Herald, 1887), 9; Robert Wilson Schufeldt, *The Negro: A Menace to American Civilization* (Boston: Richard G. Badger, 1907), 179. Schufeldt was curator of the Army Medical Museum and honorary curator at the Smithsonian Institution. For similar discussion of cannibalism and African Americans, see Robert Wilson Schufeldt, *America's Greatest Problem: The Negro* (Philadelphia: F. A. Davis Company, 1915).

23. Paul Brandon Barringer, *The American Negro: His Past and Future* (Raleigh, NC: Edwards and Broughton, 1900), 15–16. Barringer was a doctor at the University of Virginia.

24. "Political Cranks," *Washington (DC) Bee*, August 18, 1883; "Voudooism," *Wisconsin Labor Advocate*, August 27, 1886; "Southern Gleanings," *Huntsville (AL) Gazette*, September 29, 1888.

25. Rudolph Dunbar, "Robeson, Welch Take Top Roles in 'Song of Freedom,'" *Capital Plaindealer*, October 11, 1936.

26. Franklin Frank, "Things Theatrical," *Capital Plaindealer*, April 4, 1937.

27. *Soul Food: 50 Black American Recipes* (Seattle: Washington Natural Gas Company, 1969), 1, AACC.

28. Mary Jackson and Lelia Wishart, *Integrated Cookbook: Or the Soul of Good Cooking* (Chicago: Johnson Publishing Company, 1971), 1, AACC; Sidney Bechet, *Treat It Gentle: An Autobiography* (1960; reprint, Cambridge, MA: Da Capo, 2002), 10.

29. Chireau, *Black Magic*, 141–49.

30. Ibid., 145–46, songs quoted; Memphis Minnie, "Hoodoo Lady," *Hoodoo Lady* (1936; rereleased 1991, Columbia Records).

31. Pauline Coggs, "Black Power," *Milwaukee Star*, October 28, 1967.

32. Powdermaker, *After Freedom*, 289; Harry Middleton Hyatt, *Hoodoo-Conjuration-Witchcraft-Rootwork*, vol. 3 (Cambridge, MA: Western Publishing, 1973), 2297.

33. Ibid., 3:1974–75.

34. Ibid., 3:2332.

35. Ibid., 3:2084.

36. Harry Middleton Hyatt, *Hoodoo-Conjuration-Witchcraft-Rootwork*, vol. 2 (Cambridge, MA: Western Publishing, 1970), 1023.

37. Harry Middleton Hyatt, *Hoodoo-Conjuration-Witchcraft-Rootwork*, vol. 1 (Cambridge, MA: Western Publishing, 1970), 416, 424, 431, 445, 462, 466, 709, 710.

38. Harry Middleton Hyatt, *Hoodoo-Conjuration-Witchcraft-Rootwork*, vol. 5 (Cambridge, MA: Western Publishing, ca. 1972), 3821.

39. Ibid., 2:1353.

40. Ibid., 2:1402.

41. Ibid., 1:90, 95, 96.

42. Zora Neale Hurston, *Mules and Men* (1935; reprint, New York: HarperCollins, 1990), 185.

43. Hyatt, *Hoodoo-Conjuration-Witchcraft-Rootwork*, 5:4503; Alice Walker, *In Love and Trouble: Stories of Black Women* (New York: Harcourt Brace Jovanovich, 1973), 93.

44. For examples, see *Heavenly Dining: Compiled by the Living Testament C.O.G.I.C. in Crossett, AR* (Collierville, TN: Fundcraft, 1999), AACC; Claudia Green, *Little Bit of Soul: Preserving Our Black Heritage* (Kearney, NE: Morris Press, 1994), AACC. Morris Press, for instance, advertises, "Cookbooks by Morris Press has developed a simple step-by-step program that helps you from start to finish, from collecting recipes to selling your books" (back cover).

45. Tiffany Graham, "Small Town Festivals in the Lower Mississippi Delta Region: Organization, Motivation, and Religion" (PhD diss.: University of California–Los Angeles, 2009), 253.

46. Freda De Knight, *A Date with a Dish: A Cook Book of American Negro Recipes* (New York: Hermitage Press, 1948), 1, AACC.

47. Lynn Hudson, *The Making of 'Mammy Pleasant': A Black Entrepreneur in Nineteenth-Century San Francisco* (Urbana: University of Illinois Press, 2003), 80.

48. Helen Holdredge, *Mammy Pleasant's Cookbook* (San Francisco: 101 Productions, 1970), 23; Hudson, *The Making of 'Mammy Pleasant,'* 5–7, AACC.

49. Richard Dorson, *American Folklore* (Chicago: University of Chicago Press, 1959), 198; Dorothy Kuffman, *West Oakland Soul Food Cook Book* (Oakland, CA: Peter Maurin Neighborhood House, circa 1969), 46–47, AACC.

50. Screamin' Jay Hawkins, "Feast of the Mau Mau," *Spellbound! 1955–1974* (1969, rereleased 1999, Bear Family).

CHAPTER 8. The Sassy Black Cook and the Return of the Magical Negress: Popular Representations of Black Women's Food Work

1. *The Help*, 2011, from DreamWorks Pictures and Reliance Entertainment, directed and written by Tate Taylor and adapted from Kathryn Stockett's 2009 novel of the same name. "Black Female Voices: A Public Dialogue between bell hooks and Melissa Harris-Perry," The New School, November 8, 2013, http://colorlines.com/archives/2013/11/watch_bell_hooks_and_melissa_harris_perry_talk_about_black_feminism.html, accessed February 15, 2014 (transcription done by the author).

2. I had to reiterate the need to follow basic rules of engagement: raise your hands; be respectful of each other; minimize sudden outbursts, etc.

3. This student was engaged and intrigued by the course material. She enthusiastically contributed her thoughts often and forcefully in class. I came to associate her with a certain amount of unconscious privilege and entitlement, which had to be delicately maneuvered in a class where I was the sole black person actually present but while we were critically reading black women's representations closely.

4. My reading of this is informed by bell hooks, in her "Eating the Other: Desire and Resistance," in *Black Looks: Race and Representation* (Boston, MA: South End Press, 1992); Kyla Wazana Tompkins, *Racial Indigestion: Eating Bodies in the Nineteenth Century* (New York: New York University Press, 2012), particularly 43–52; and Lisa Heldke, *Exotic Appetites: Ruminations of a Food Adventurer* (New York: Routledge, 2003).

5. *Merriam-Webster's Collegiate Dictionary*, 10th ed. (Springfield, MA: Merriam-Webster, 1998): 1037–38.

6. Dictionary.com, accessed February 2, 2014.

7. Minnie is initially fired by Ms. Hilly because she breaks the house rules and uses the indoor bathroom when she can not go to the specially constructed outdoor toilet for the black help. A subplot in the film is rooted in Miss Hilly's concern about the cleanliness of allowing the help to use the same toilets that whites use. When Minnie is let go, Miss Hilly tells all of the women in her social group that she is dishonest and has been caught stealing. No other family will take her on. Minnie is frustrated with this situation and wants to get her revenge. She bakes a chocolate pie with feces (her own we are to presume) baked into it. Miss Hilly gladly accepts the pie and while she is eating it, exclaiming at its deliciousness at the same time as she is laying down the ground rules for taking Minnie back as her domestic. Minnie can no longer hold her tongue and tells Miss Hilly that she is not there groveling for her old job back and that, in fact, Miss Hilly can "eat my shit!" And she literally is.

8. See "Issues of Our Time—The Help," JENdA: A Journal of Culture and African Women Studies, ISSN: 1530-5686 (September 2011), www.africa knowledgeproject.org/index.php/jenda/issue/view/124, accessed February 2, 2014; Association of Black Women Historians, "An Open Statement to the Fans of *The Help*" August 12, 2011, http://www.abwh.org/index.php?option=com_content&view=article&id=2%3Aopen-statement-the-help, accessed March 6, 2015 ; Manohla Dargis, "'The Maids' Now Have Their Say," review of *The Help* in the *New York Times*, August 10, 2011, http://movies.nytimes.com/2011/08/10/movies/the-help-spans-two-worlds-white-and-black-review.html?ref=manohladargis&_r=0; Nelson

George, "Black-and-White Struggle with a Rosy Glow," August 10, 2011, http://
movies.nytimes.com/2011/08/10/movies/the-help-spans-two-worlds-white-and-
black-review.html; Melissa Harris-Perry, "On 'The Help': Appalled at the Gross
Historical Inaccuracies," Huffington Post Media, February 26, 2012, http://www.
huffingtonpost.com/2012/02/26/melissa-harris-perry-the-help_n_1302275.html;
UNC Press Blog, "Historians Respond to The Help," August 8, 2011, http://uncpress
blog.com/2011/08/24/historians-on-the-help-vanessa-may-and-rebecca-sharpless-
respond/; Blanca E. Vega, "Choosing between The Help or Faces at the Bottom of
the Well: On Reproducing Racially-Easy Work or Constructing Courageously,"
January 5, 2012, http://www.racialicious.com/2012/01/05/choosing-between-the-
help-or-faces-at-the-bottom-of-the-well-on-reproducing-racially-easy-work-or-
constructing-courageously/#more-19677.

9. Rebecca Sharpless, *Cooking in Other Women's Kitchens: Domestic Workers
in the South, 1865–1960* (Chapel Hill: University of North Carolina Press, 2010);
Patrica Turner, *Ceramic Uncles and Celluloid Mammies: Black Images and Their
Influence on Culture* (Charlottesville: University of Virginia Press, 1994); Psyche
Williams-Forson, *Building Houses out of Chicken Legs: Black Women, Food, and
Power* (Chapel Hill: University of North Carolina Press, 2006).

10. We see this same dynamic in the 1934 version of *Imitation of Life*.

11. All quotes are from the movie *The Help* and are transcribed by the author.
According the Crisco website (http://www.crisco.com/About_Crisco/History.aspx,
accessed March 3, 2014), this product was "introduced by Proctor & Gamble in 1911
to provide an economical alternative to animal fats and butter."

12. In her doctoral study of personal and private chefs, Alexandra Hendley
notes that "scholars have shown that it is not uncommon for employers to try to
turn domestic workers into confidantes. Because domestic workers do not share
the same social circles, employers are safe from having their secrets get out."
Alexandra Hendley, "Inequalities on the Menu: How Private and Personal Chefs
Negotiate Tensions about Status and Self" (PhD diss., University of California,
Santa Barbara, 2014).

13. The scene begins with a comical reference to the very real threats of sexual
and physical assault perpetuated on black women by their white male employers.
Minnie is walking along a wooded area leading to the home of Celia Foote. As she's
walking, slightly out of the frame we see a small red roadster with the top down,
following closely behind her. She keeps walking but is also looking over her
shoulder, and when he stops the car and gets out, Minnie starts running, dropping
the grocery bags and grabbing a tree branch for protection. All the while she is
running, Mr. Johnnie is telling her that he will not hurt her and that he is the
husband of Celia Foote. Minnie relaxes and they walk side by side to the house.

14. Those scholars and film critics engaged in the debate around *The Help*
were always certain to make clear that their criticism lay with the romanticized
representations and the lack of historical veracity and not with the actors portray-
ing those roles. And, in fact, many praised the stellar performances of Viola Davis
(as "Aibileen Clark"), Octavia Spencer (as "Minnie Jackson"), and the other black
actresses in the film, only lamenting the fact that black actors continue to have
access to limited roles.

15. In *Black Feminist Thought* Patricia Hill Collins outlines the "controlling

images" that have shaped black women's lived experiences in the United States. Those images—the Mammy, Matriarch, Aunt Jemima, and Jezebel—have served disciplining functions felt in a variety of spaces from popular culture to public policy. Patricia Hill Collins, "Mammies, Matriarchs, and Other Controlling Images," in her *Black Feminist Thought: Knowledge, Consciousness, and the Politics of Empowerment, 2nd ed.* (New York: Routledge, 2000). See also Kimberlé Crenshaw, "Mapping the Margins: Intersectionality, Identity Politics, and Violence against Women of Color," *Stanford Law Review* 43, no. 6 (July 1991): 1241-99; Melissa Harris-Perry, *Sister Citizen: Shame, Stereotypes, and Black Women in America* (New Haven: Yale University Press, 2011); K. Sue Jewell, "The Social Significance of Cultural Imagery," in her *From Mammy to Miss America and Beyond: Cultural Images and the Shaping of US Social Policy* (London: Routledge, 1993); Lakesia D. Johnson, *Iconic: Decoding the Images of the Revolutionary Black Woman* (Baylor, TX: Baylor University Press, 2012).

16. The Paula Deen controversy began with a lawsuit in which employees at her *Uncle Bubba's Oyster House* restaurant accused her and her co-owner brother of creating a hostile work environment in her use of racist "jokes." In her deposition for the case, she admits to using the "n-word" in the past and to wanting to organize a plantation-themed wedding with an all-black wait and serving staff outfitted in ways which might recall the slave era. See Julia Moskin, "Deen Begs Forgiveness, Loses Contract," *Sacramento Bee*, June 22, 2013. For the tweet, see https://twitter.com/carlahall/status/348229286072836096, accessed June 24, 2014.

17. The co-hosts at the table were Chef Michael Symon, Daphne Oz (billed as a health and wellness expert), and Clinton Kelly (billed as an entertainment expert). Chef Mario Batali, the other co-host on the show, did not participate in this conversation.

18. See https://www.youtube.com/watch?v=2hf3-4qVLJg, June 26, 2013. At the end of this scripted "conversation" the audience breaks into applause. But as the camera pans around the studio, I am struck by one woman in the audience, a heavy-set black woman seated just to the right of frame. She was clapping along with others in the predominately "white-looking" audience, but her facial expression belied her seeming agreement with Carla Hall's reflections. Her face communicated to me that the work of racial reconciliation that this conversation was designed to foster fell short of its intended goal.

19. Carla Hall graduated from Howard University with a major in accounting and then worked for Price-Waterhouse. She has been quoted in various articles and interviews as saying that she absolutely hated the work and quit to pursue modeling in Paris and Milan—to seek a temporary "resting" place. It was in Paris, hanging out and eating with other models (who she says "really eat") and talking about food that she realized she liked food. So, while in Paris she educated herself about food—by dining out, reading cookbooks, and so on. When she returned to the United States, she moved in with her sister in Washington, D.C., and started a small food-delivery business. She then decided to go to culinary school because, although she knew how to cook and knew the business of food, cooking school taught her the theory.

20. This aired November 12, 2008, through March 4, 2009.

21. The show's producers create a mini-documentary of a select number of *cheftestants'* experiences during the season; these are aired on the reunion show.

22. "Top Chef Season 5 Reunion Show," http://www.youtube.com/watch?v= vaOokYhW-uM, accessed March 1, 2014 (transcription by author). Chef Carla ultimately garnered the respect of the judges and was one of three chefs in the finale. And, though she didn't win, 65 percent of the viewers reportedly said that she should have been named "Top Chef." Chef Carla later appeared in "Top Chef All-Stars" (season 8: December 1, 2010, through April 6, 2011) and, though she did not win, she was voted "fan favorite."

23. When I presented a version of this section of the paper in an undergraduate course, The Black Female Experience, several students were not convinced that there was anything racialized in her performance. Some asked: "Maybe she's just being her natural self?" But, as professor Laurie Lambert and I discussed after her class, the question here is, Why *this* "natural self"? While there have been a few black women *cheftestants* on the *Top Chef* series, none have made it to the finale. I argue that this particular representation, so well played by Chef Carla Hall, struck a familiar and "comforting" cord with judges and audience members. In this way, I understand her food work on *Top Chef* and *The Chew* and in all of her media productions as performative—perhaps not reflective of who she is as a person, but rather an image or brand crafted to appeal to as broad an audience as possible.

24. Chef Carla is rarely referred to as Chef Carla on the show; though the two male chefs, Mario Batali and Michael Symon, are. The difference might be that they are restaurant chef-owners and, while she is classically trained and worked as a sous chef and executive chef in hotel kitchens, her primary food work was in catering. In Hendley's research, based on interviews with public and private chefs, we learn that in the world of professional cheffing boundaries, restaurant chefs are at the top of the hierarchy and are most likely to be called and understand themselves as chefs. Henley, "Inequalities on the Menu."

25. Although many of *The Chew* episodes are readily available for view on sites like YouTube, TV.com, and the network itself, episode 15, season 1 (which aired on October 14, 2011) is no longer available to view. This episode featured Paula Deen; and since her public fall from grace, her shows have been pulled from television and she lost her endorsements and business partnerships with WalMart, Kmart, and other retailers. I refer to this controversy at the opening of this section and will return to a discussion of it at the end.

26. Although Chef Carla jokes in one of the *Top Chef* outtakes that when she was in cooking school she went back to her grandmother and exclaimed to her that "she [her grandmother] had been serving them a broken sauce for all those years!"

27. "Celebrity Chef Carla Hall Cooks up Success as a Media Maven: *The Chew*'s top chef dishes on how she turned a passion for food into a business and brand," *Black Enterprise Magazine*, March 8, 2012, http://www.blackenterprise.com/ lifestyle/celebrity-chef-carla-hall-cooks-up-success-as-a-media-maven/. While this quote appears in a publication geared toward an African American audience, the message she gives is one that is repeated on her website, through her product endorsements, and in her cookbooks.

28. See http://carlahall.com/, accessed February 1, 2015.

29. Carla Hall's cookbooks include *Carla's Comfort Food: Favorite Dishes from around the World* (Atria Books, 2014), *Cooking with Love: Comfort Food that Hugs*

You (New York: Atria Books, 2012), and those with the cast of *The Chew: What's for Dinner? 100 Easy Recipes for Every Night of the Week* (Kingswell, 2013) and *The Chew: Food, Life, Fun* (Kingswell, 2012).

30. See https://www.kickstarter.com/projects/carlahall/carla-halls-southern-kitchen, accessed February 1, 2015. Her campaign was successfully funded on October 29, 2014.

31. See Kim Severson, "Friendship Cools for Queen of Deen Kitchens: Once a 'Soul Sister,' she reveals woes under food maven," *Sacramento Bee*, July 25, 2013; and Michael W. Twitty, "An Open Letter to PaulaDeen," *Huffington Post*, June 26, 2013, http://www.huffingtonpost.com/michael-w-twitty/an-open-letter-to-paula-deen_b_3502048.html.

32. See Sharpless, *Cooking in Other Women's Kitchens*.

33. "Where Are the Black Chefs?," *Black/Culture/Connection*, http://www.pbs.org/black-culture/explore/black-chefs/, accessed February 1, 2015.

34. Though one might argue that the use of the term "glass ceiling" implies gender discrimination.

35. Journalist and public historian Toni Tipton Martin is doing some of this work with her *The Jemima Code*, http://thejemimacode.com/, accessed February 1, 2015. She writes: "So in an era when everyone from Food Network stars, to executive chefs, food scholars, nutritionists, authors and entrepreneurs tells us what we should eat and how we should cook it, it seems only natural that the nation's most recognized cook should be stirring the pot, too. When we break the Jemima Code, America's most maligned kitchen servant, Aunt Jemima is transformed into an inspirational and powerful symbol of culinary wisdom and authority—a role model." See also the work of scholars like Williams-Forson, *Building Houses out of Chicken Legs*; and Saru Jayaraman, *Behind the Kitchen Door* (Ithaca, NY: ILR Press, 2014).

CHAPTER 9. Mighty Matriarchs Kill It with a Skillet: Critically Reading Popular Representations of Black Womanhood and Food

I would like to thank Psyche Williams-Forson for mentorship and guidance. Ideas for this paper were initially developed in the classrooms of Sheri L. Parks, Mary Sies, A. Lynn Bolles, and Michelle V. Rowley. Thank you to the always grounding Cristina J. Pérez and Paul Saiedi for helping me process through ideas. Thanks also to Doug Ishiee, Darius Bost, and Melissa S. Rogers for your invaluable critiques and input.

1. Douglas Kellner, "Cultural Studies, Multiculturalism, and Media Culture," in *Gender, Race, and Class in Media: A Critical Reader*, ed. Gail Dines and Jean M. Humez (Thousand Oaks: Sage, 2011), 10.

2. Herman Gray, *Watching Race: Television and the Struggle for "Blackness"* (Minneapolis: University of Minnesota Press, 1995), xiii.

3. Sarah Murray, "Food and Television," in *Routledge International Handbook of Food Studies*, ed. Ken Albala (New York: Routledge, 2013) 191.

4. Heterosexuality here is assumed based on the presence of a husband in the majority of episodes. However, family is rarely presented as nuclear. Members of the mamas' families could include cousins, siblings, parents, friends, and children.

5. *My Momma Throws Down: Squash Casserole and Green Salad,* directed by Eytan Keller, 2012, Atlanta, GA, TV One, digital file.

6. All contestants are referred to as "Mama" during the show by comedian and host Ralph Harris. Harris also locates himself as a son of a mother, naming himself "one of Carol's boys" in the first episode. This act, while venerating the work and time that goes into mothering, also serves to limit the viewer's ability to conceive of her as anything but a mother.

7. Psyche Williams-Forson, "More than Just the 'Big Piece of Chicken': The Power of Race, Class, and Food in American Consciousness," in *Food and Culture: A Reader,* ed. Carole Counihan and Penny Van Esterik (New York: Routledge, 2008), 342–53.

8. Niche mini-networks are a current industry standard; they value flexible, frequent, and cheaply made content in contrast to the structured sitcom. This means shows can be developed and produced quickly and with greater frequency, making MMTD's cancellation an indication of its limited viewing audience and the ruthless "survival of the fittest" standard, where turnover rates for new television shows are high.

9. Jonathan Rodgers, quoted in Felicia R. Lee, "A Network for Blacks with Sense of Mission," *New York Times,* December 11, 2007.

10. Catherine Pinkeney, quoted in Lee, "A Network for Blacks With Sense of Mission," 1.

11. David Lionel Smith, "What Is Black Culture?," in *The House That Race Built,* ed. Wahneema Lubiano (New York: Vintage Books, 1998), 180–81. Smith raises the question of what opera, normally perceived to be "white" music, becomes when a Black person sings and creates it. This makes it clear that "no one can define blackness, but we Americans embrace it as a matter of common sense." Smith draws from Antonio Gramsci's "Critical Notes on an Attempt at a Popular Presentation of Marxism by Bukharin," in his *The Modern Prince and Other Writings* (New York: International Publishers, 1967), arguing that the ideology of common sense "is not critically self-conscious, and its function is to facilitate conformity and adaptation to familiar circumstances," evidenced by the inability to define Blackness. Sentiment comes to stand in for how we draw racial boundaries around cultural products so that "we feel we know who and what is truly black." Smith, "What Is Black Culture?," 180–81.

12. Catherine Pinkeney, quoted in Lee, "A Network for Blacks with Sense of Mission," 1.

13. Mammy remains a lasting trope of Black womanhood and food, circulating widely in the American imagination. Donald Bogle traces the evolution of mammy from her 1914 emergence as a strong-willed, "big, fat, and cantankerous" Black woman to the more subdued version of Aunt Jemima, who could easily navigate white spaces. Donald Bogle, *Toms, Coons, Mulattoes, Mammies, and Bucks* (New York: Continuum Press, 1973), 1–10. Other studies of the mammy trope include Trudier Harris, *From Mammies to Militants: Domestics in Black American Literature* (Philadelphia: Temple University Press, 1982), xi–xvi; Marylin Kern-Foxworth and Alex Haley, *Aunt Jemima, Uncle Ben, and Rastu: Blacks in Advertising, Yesterday, Today, and Tomorrow* (New York: Praeger, 1994); and Maurice Marning, *Slave in a Box: The Strange Career of Aunt Jemima* (Charlottesville: University of Virgina Press, 1998).

14. Although I deal with representations of Black women and food that harkens back to mammy tropes, scholars like Miki McElya do the meticulous work of historically contextualizing the development of a yearning and longing for mammy in the antebellum South. Miki McElya, *Clinging to Mammy* (Boston: Harvard University Press, 2007).

15. Alice Deck reads advertisements of Aunt Jemima products from 1905 through 1953, arguing that the commoditization of Aunt Jemima through packaged goods like biscuit mix and flour influenced ideologies of race, gender, and domesticity. See Alice Deck, "'Now Then—Who Said Biscuits?': The Black Woman Cook as Fetish in American Advertising, 1905–1953," in *Kitchen Culture in America: Popular Representations of Food, Gender, and Race,* ed. Sherrie A. Inness (Philadelphia: University of Pennsylvania Press, 2001), 69–93.

16. Kimberly Wallace-Sanders underscores the need to push past formulations of mammy as a docile servant to understand her conflicting role as a maternal figure to both white and Black children. Kimberly Wallace-Sanders, *Mammy: A Century of Race, Gender, and Southern Memory* (Ann Arbor: University of Michigan Press, 2008), 1–3.

17. An online chat room conversation titled "Stepin Fetchit Is Real—American Black 'Entertainment' Is a Minstrel Show" on The Coli (a site geared toward men interested in sport, hip-hop, and entertainment) featured users praising the show as authentic, while others disagreed, noting that "we" don't speak or act like that. Another online forum, Lipstick Alley, featured women in a conversation about how the show went overboard with segments, including, most prominently, the signifying battle, which was deemed too obvious. The conversation mentioned outrage over the use of store-bought ingredients, and one user even went as far as to call the show a "fucking mess." "Stepin Fetch it is real," The Coli, http://www.thecoli.com/threads/stepin-fetchit-is-real-american-black-entertainment-is-a-minstrel-show.7963/page-3, accessed June 15, 2013;
Lipstick Alley, http://www.lipstickalley.com/showthread.php/393992-My-Momma-Throws-Down; accessed May 20, 2013.

18. *My Momma Throws Down: Squash Casserole and Green Salad,* directed by Eytan Keller, May 4, 2012, Atlanta, GA, TV One, digital file.

19. Ibid.

20. The trope of motherhood, along with compulsory heterosexuality in these family narratives, wholly re-inscribes normative family structures that, while important to reading the show, deserve more attention than can be given in the scope of this essay.

21. Scripts refer to common language and imagery used to describe what soul food is. Scripts are not written in stone and can be revised or ignored. Robin Bernstein writes, "The term script denotes not a rigid dictation of performed action but, rather, a necessary openness to resistance, interpretation, and improvisation." Robin Bernstein, "Dances with Things: Material Culture and the Performance of Race," *Social Text* 27 (2009): 67–94.

22. Soul food is an overwhelming ideology that structures conceptions of what Black people eat in the present. Narratives of overcoming poverty, enslavement, or destitution through magic cooking by a Black woman dominate the story of soul food, obfuscating differences based on class, region, and gender. Doris Witt surmises that there are "contradictions inherent in maintaining the fiction of soul as

'a sum of all that is typically or uniquely Black' in the face of black geographic and economic diversity." However these "contradictions" fail to hinder the endurance of the term and the images it conjures. Doris Witt, *Black Hunger: Food and the Politics of U.S. Identity* (Minneapolis: University of Minnesota Press, 1999), 97.

23. Scripting reemphasizes the fact the soul food is discursively formed by notable Black arts figure Amiri Baraka, who coined the term in his 1966 book *Home: Social Essays* (New York: Morrow, 1966). Because Baraka's definition of what Black people ate was in response to a magazine article claiming Black people had no distinct culture, he defends the West African roots of African American food; and, in listing macaroni and cheese, fried chicken, and collard greens among dishes that typify soul food, Baraka unwittingly scripts how the food is to be referenced in relation to authentically black cultural productions. Not being able to name a distinctly African American food would delegitimize calls toward black nationalism. For more on soul food see Frederick Opie's *Hog and Hominy: Soul Food from Africa to America* (New York: Columbia University Press, 2008); and Jessica Harris's *High on the Hog: A Culinary Journey from Africa to America* (New York: Bloomsbury Publishing, 2011).

24. Psyche Williams-Forson, *Building Houses out of Chicken Legs: Black Women, Food, and Power* (Chapel Hill: University of North Carolina Press, 2006), 171.

25. bell hooks, *Black Looks: Race and Representation* (Boston: South End Press, 1990), 4–5.

26. Stuart Hall, "What Is This 'Black' in Black Popular Culture?," in *The Black Studies Reader,* ed. Jacqueline Bobo, Cynthia Hudley, and Claudine Michel (New York: Routledge, 2004), 259.

27. As Mamas Thea and Marilyn furiously cook against the clock, host Ralph Harris engages the family members in a game called "Know Your Mama," where they have to guess their mother's favorite foods. Also, in an obvious nod to *Family Feud's* "win as a team" dynamic, one member of each family gets elected to perform in an awkwardly staged, signifying battle. Family members engage in a language game, exchanging light-hearted barbs that usually begin with "your mama's cooking is so bad." The judges then decide the winner of the battle, and the contestant that family member represents receives more cooking time.

28. Mihaly Csikszentmihalyi, "Why We Need Things," in *History from Things: Essays on Material Culture,* ed. Steven D. Lubar and W. D. Kingery (Washington, DC: Smithsonian Institution Press, 1993), 26.

29. Jessica B. Harris, *Iron Pots and Wooden Spoons: Africa's Gifts to New World Cooking* (New York: Simon & Schuster, 1999), xii.

30. Indeed, when a viewer named the mere title of the show "ratchet" and "ghetto" on an online forum, the viewer pointed to the discomfort, perhaps, of the closeness of mammy to mamma as something that lacks classed Black respectability.

31. The phrase comes from Herman S. Gray's explanation of the Jazz Left as an alternative site for Black media production that resists the idea that the representation is always already made. Herman S. Gray, *Cultural Moves: African Americans and the Politics of Representation* (Berkeley: University of California Press, 2005), 5.

32. Patricia Hill Collins, *Black Sexual Politics: African-Americans, Gender, and the New Racism* (New York: Routledge, 2005), 122–23.

33. *My Momma Throws Down: Crab Cakes and Green Tomatoes,* directed by

Eytan Keller, 2012, Atlanta, GA, TV One, digital file. To be clear, Mama Avarita is a lawyer by trade, but apparently when she uses caterers she is more than willing to share her recipes with them.

34. The act is not foreign to depictions of Black women and food. A knife-wielding, kerchief-donning, Black woman cook was depicted in the 1930 Dixie Chicken Fryer advertisement featured on the cover to Williams-Forson's *Building Houses out of Chicken Legs*.

35. Williams-Forson, *Building Houses out of Chicken Legs*, 208.

36. For more on the politics of obesity, health, nutrition, and the racing of alternative food movements, see Alice Julier, "The Political Economy of Obesity: The Fat Pay All," in *Food and Culture: A Reader 2*, ed. Carole Counihan and Penny Van Esterik (New York: Routledge, 1997), 121–40. See also Rachel Slocum, "Whiteness, Space, and Alternative Food Practice," *Geoforum* 38, no. 3 (2007): 520–33; Julie Guthman, "Bringing Good Food to Others: Investigating the Subjects of Alternative Food Practice," *Cultural Geographies* 15, no. 4 (2008): 431–47; and Charlotte Biltekoff, *Eating Right in America: The Cultural Politics of Food and Health* (Durham: Duke University Press, 2013).

37. Tracy N. Poe, "The Origins of Soul Food in Black Urban Identity: Chicago, 1915–1947," *American Studies International* 37, no. 1 (1999): 4–33. These tensions between class, food, and Black authenticity are far from new. Similar tensions arose in Chicago from 1915 to 1947; as Poe notes, the foodstuffs of Blacks traveling to Chicago from the South were deemed unseemly, unhealthy, and impure by already settled northern Black communities. In the age of Black respectability, Poe argues that new Black cooks coming to Chicago who "were prized in the South's finest homes and dining rooms" prepared foods that were "not considered refined by an urban clientele." Differences in racialized health ideologies manifested in the food shamming of lower-class Blacks, adding more incentive to assimilate to middle-class food norms.

38. Dell Upton, "Ethnicity, Authenticity, and Invented Traditions," *Historical Archaeology* 30 (1996): 1–7.

39. Williams-Forson, *Building Houses out of Chicken Legs*, 198.

40. John Jackson, *Real Black: Adventures in Racial Sincerity* (Chicago: University of Chicago, 2005), 17.

CHAPTER 10. Looking through Prism Optics: Toward an Understanding of Michelle Obama's Food Reform

I am grateful for the assistance of Charles Bittner, Nancy Baker, Katherine Pierce, Erin Cassidy, and all of the participants at the 2013 Texas food writer's salon. Thanks to Jeffrey Pilcher for his comments when a draft of this essay was presented at the American Studies Association conference in November 2013. Many heartfelt thanks to Jennifer Jensen Wallach for editing the volume and tirelessly offering feedback on multiple drafts of this essay. This chapter is stronger because of all of their comments.

1. Marian Burros, "Pastry Chef to Obamas Hanging Up His Whisk," *New York Times*, March 18, 2014.

2. For example, Darlene Superville, "White House Losing Pastry Chef Bill

Yosses in June," Thebigstory.ap.org, March 18, 2014; Emily Heil, "White House Pastry Chef Bill Yosses Leaving," *Washington Post*, March 18, 2014.

3. Mike Tuttle, "White House Pastry Chef Leaves: Blame FLOTUS?" webpronews.com, March 21, 2014. See also Oliver Darcy, "Rumor Check: Was the White House Pastry Chef So Angry with Michelle Obama's Healthy Eating Push He Resigned?," theblaze.com, March 18, 2014.

4. "White House Pastry Chef Bill Yosses Announces 'Bittersweet' Departure," theweek.com, March 18, 2014.

5. Rush Limbaugh, quoted in "How a Pastry Chef's Resignation Became the First Lady's Fault," mediamatters.org, March 19, 2014.

6. Patrick Howley, "White House Pastry Chef Resigns: 'I Don't Want to Demonize Cream, Butter, Sugar and Eggs,'" dailycaller.com, March 18, 2014.

7. Psyche A. Williams-Forson, *Building Houses out of Chicken Legs: Black Women, Food, and Power* (Chapel Hill: University of North Carolina Press, 2006), 220.

8. Doris Witt, *Black Hunger: Food and the Politics of U.S. Identity* (New York: Oxford University Press, 1999), 4.

9. Rebecca Sharpless, *Cooking in Other Women's Kitchens: Domestic Workers in the South, 1865–1960* (Chapel Hill: University of North Carolina Press, 2010), xii.

10. J. Celeste Walley-Jean, "Debunking the Myth of the 'Angry Black Woman,'" *Black Women, Gender and Families* 3 (Fall 2009): 70.

11. David Pilgrim, "Sapphire Caricature," Jim Crow Museum of Racist Memorabilia at Ferris State University, http://www.ferris.edu/jimcrow/sapphire/, accessed February 2, 2015.

12. See, for example, Patricia Hill Collins, *Black Feminist Thought: Knowledge, Consciousness, and the Politics of Empowerment* (New York: Routledge, 2000), 75–76; Deborah Gray White, *Ar'n't I A Woman? Female Slaves in the Plantation South* (New York: W. W. Norton and Co., 1985), 166–67. The 1965 Moynihan Report, "The Negro Family: The Case for National Action," can be found on the Department of Labor's website: http://www.dol.gov/dol/aboutdol/history/webid-meynihan.htm, accessed March 15, 2015.

13. Collins, *Black Feminist Thought*, 76.

14. *New Yorker*, July 21, 2008, cover.

15. Melissa V. Harris-Perry, *Sister Citizen: Shame, Stereotypes, and Black Women in America* (New Haven: Yale University Press, 2011), 276.

16. An excerpt from the speech is available on You Tube: https://www.youtube.com/watch?v=LYY73RO_egw, accessed February 2, 2015. Also see Robin Abcarian, "Campaign Spotlight Shifts to Obama's Wife," *Los Angeles Times*, February 20, 2008; Matt Stearns, "Will Michelle Obama's Comment Matter Much in the Long Term?," *McClatchy Newspapers* (Washington, DC), February 20, 2008.

17. Michael Cooper, "Candidates' Wives Get Feet Wet on Muddy Campaign Trail," *Virginian Pilot* (Hampton Roads, VA), February 20, 2008; Greg Pierce, "Nation inside Politics," *Washington Post*, February 20, 2008; "Michelle Obama Hasn't Been Proud of America in at Least 26 Years?," hotair.com, February 18, 2008.

18. Ruben Navarrette Jr., "Obama Just Can't Win for Being African or American," *Salt Lake Tribune*, March 2, 2008.

19. "Michelle Obama's Remark Draws Fire from Conservatives," *Los Angeles*

Times, February 19, 2008; "Comment by Obama's Wife Riles Right," *Houston Chronicle*, February 20, 2008.

20. Michelle LaVaughn Robinson, "Princeton Educated Blacks and the Black Community" (Senior thesis, Princeton University, 1985).

21. "Putting Michelle Obama's Thesis under the Microscope," *Hannity's America*, TV program, March 2, 2008; Ilana Mercer, "Militant Mama Obama," WorldNetDaily.com, February 22, 2008.

22. Jodi Kantor, "The First Marriage," *New York Times*, November 1, 2009.

23. Jeffrey Ressner, "Michelle Obama Thesis Was on Racial Divide," Politico. com, February 22, 2008; Esther Breger, "Princeton Releases Michelle Obama's Senior Thesis," CBSnews.com, February 26, 2008.

24. Reid Cherlin, "How the East Wing Shrank Michelle Obama," *New Republic*, March 24, 2014.

25. Ibid.

26. Michelle Obama, *American Grown: The Story of the White House Kitchen Garden and Gardens across America* (New York: Crown Publishers, 2012).

27. *Late Night* with Jimmy Fallon, February 22, 2013. Clip available at https://www.youtube.com/watch?v=Hq-URl9F17Y, accessed February 2, 2015.

28. Sarah Kaufman, "Michelle Obama's Mom Dancing Genius," Washingtonpost.com, February 24, 2013.

29. Cherlin, "How the East Wing Shrank Michelle Obama."

30. Bill Yosses, quoted in Burros, "Pastry Chef to Obamas Hanging up His Whisk."

31. "Obama Food," Sodahead.com, September 3, 2011.

32. "Michelle Obama's Food Police Policies Raise Prices of School Lunches," www.gingpac.org, May 9, 2012.

33. "Junk Food Taxes and Regulations Are on the Way," Freedomoutpost.com, November 29, 2012.

34. "Watergate 2013," Winkprogress.com/teapartycat, December 9, 2013.

35. Jason Mattera, quoted in Leslie Rosenberg, "40 Right Wing Attacks and Conspiracy Theories Flung at Michelle Obama," Alternet.org, September 5, 2012.

36. Sharpless, *Cooking in Other Women's Kitchens*, xiii. Also see White, *Ar'n't I A Woman?*, 46–61.

37. M. M. Manring, *Slave in a Box: The Strange Career of Aunt Jemima* (Charlottesville: University Press of Virginia, 1998), 8.

38. Sharpless, *Cooking in Other Women's Kitchens*, xv.

39. *New York Times*, May 31, 2009, and April 17, 2013.

40. *New York Times*, May 31, 2009.

41. Anna Julia Cooper, *A Voice from the South* (University of North Carolina Documenting the American South, electronic edition, 2000), 31.

42. Manring, *Slave in a Box*, 8–9.

43. Angela Haupt, "Michelle Obama Speaks Out against Childhood Obesity," Usnews.com, March 11, 2013.

44. "Michelle Obama Describes Duty as Mother in Chief," USAToday.com, August 4, 2008; Krissah Thompson, "Cookie Contest Stirs Debate about Michelle Obama's Mom-in-Chief Role," *Washington Post*, July 6, 2012.

45. Courtland Milloy, editorial, *Washington Post*, February 26, 2013.

46. Linda Hirshman, *Washington Post*, January 18, 2013.

47. Michelle Cottle, "Leaning Out: How Michelle Obama Became a Feminist Nightmare," Politico.com, November 21, 2013.

48. Keli Goff, "Preach Michelle: Five Things We Want to Hear from the First Lady," TheRoot.com, November 5, 2013.

49. Kristin Rowe-Finkbeiner, "The Real Feminist Nightmare: It's Definitely Not Michelle Obama," Politico.com, November 25, 2013. See also Melissa Harris-Perry, "Don't Call the First Lady a Feminist Nightmare," msnbc.com, November 23, 2013; Jonathan P. Hicks, "Michelle Obama Called Feminist Nightmare? Hold On," BET.com, November 25, 2013; Brittney Cooper, "Lay Off Michelle Obama," Salon.com, November 29, 2013.

50. Courtland Milloy disapproved of Obama's hand jive with Jimmy Fallon: *Washington Post*, February 26, 2013.

CHAPTER 11. Theft, Food Labor, and Culinary Insurrection in the Virginia Plantation Yard

I would like to thank Jennifer Wallach for putting this wonderful collection of essays and scholars together. I must thank the generous and knowledgeable staff of the various archives that have supported my research, including the John D. Rockefeller Jr. Library at Colonial Williamsburg, the Virginia Historical Society, the Smalls Special Collections at the University of Virginia, and the Huntington Library. Thanks also to the keen eyes that have looked over this draft, including Bert Emerson, Bill Gleason, Katie Van Heest, and, of course, Nisha Kunte.

1. Mary Randolph, *The Virginia Housewife* (Washington, DC: Davis and Force, 1825), 14.

2. Kyla Wazana Tompkins, *Racial Indigestion: Eating Bodies in the Nineteenth Century* (New York: New York University Press, 2012), 2.

3. Judith A. Carney, *Black Rice: The African Origins of Rice Cultivation in the Americas* (Cambridge, MA: Harvard University Press, 2002), 1.

4. Ibid.

5. Ibid., 162.

6. Ibid., 2.

7. My framing of the yard does not include animals themselves, a category of life that mingles with conceptions of the human, notions of abjection, and the intimacy of life and death. For a more detailed account of the boundaries between the human and animal in the antebellum South, see Walter Johnson, *River of Dark Dreams: Slavery and Empire in the Cotton Kingdom* (Cambridge, MA: Harvard University Press, 2013), 176–208.

8. Ashli White, "The Character of a Landscape: Domestic Architecture and Community in Late Eighteenth-Century Berkeley Parish, Virginia," *Winterthur Portfolio* 34, nos. 2/3 (1999): 114.

9. Mechal Sobel, *The World They Made Together: Black and White Values in Eighteenth-Century Virginia* (Princeton, NJ: Princeton University Press, 1987), 45, 100; Rhys Isaac, *The Transformation of Virginia: 1740–1790* (Chapel Hill, NC: Omohundro Institute of Early American History and Culture, 1999), 32–42, 302–10;

Richard Bushman, *The Refinement of America, Persons, Houses, Cities* (New York: Knopf, 1992), passim; Dell Upton, *Early Vernacular Architecture in Southeastern Virginia* (PhD diss., Brown University, 1979), 142, 265. Dell Upton sees an increase in home size peaking around 1680; home sizes then decrease until the 1720s, a decrease he attributes to the ejection of servants from the master's home. In James Deetz, *In Small Things Forgotten: An Archaeology of Early American Life* (New York: Anchor, 1996), 150–51.

10. Elizabeth Fox-Genovese, *Within the Plantation Household: Black and White Women of the Old South* (Chapel Hill: University of North Carolina Press, 1988), 100–145.

11. Gordon McArthur, "Living Patterns in Antebellum Rural America as Depicted by Nineteenth-Century Women Writers," *Winterthur Portfolio* 19, nos. 2/3 (1984): 187.

12. R. Lewis Wright, "Key Baskets," *Journal of Early Southern Decorative Arts* 8, no. 1 (1982): 49–61. See also Catherine Clinton, *The Plantation Mistress: Woman's World in the Old South* (New York: Pantheon, 1984), 16–29; Fox-Genovese, *Within the Plantation Household*, 160–62; Henry Sharp, "Her Keys and Her Cares: The Holladay Women's Place and Space at Antebellum Prospect Hill" (MA thesis, University of Virginia, 1995), passim.

13. Wright, "Key Baskets," 49.

14. Huldah Lewis Holladay to James Minor Holladay, January 12, 1845, quoted in Sharp, "Her Keys and Her Cares," 10.

15. Frederick Law Olmsted, *A Journey in the Seaboard Slave States; with Remarks on their Economy* (New York: Dix and Edwards, 1856), 108.

16. Peter Kolchin, *American Slavery: 1619–1877* (New York: Hill & Wang, 1993), 113. A ration of cornmeal and bacon alone did not provide enough nutrients. And while theft supplemented a bondsperson's diet, it was not sufficient either. Subsequently, crops grown in kitchen gardens supplemented the diet of the enslaved. Planters frequently encouraged this "private" cultivation, as it aided in feeding the enslaved but did not negatively affect the planter's profit. Michael Twitty, "Gardens," in *World of a Slave: Encyclopedia of the Material Life of Slaves in the United States*, ed. Kym Rice and Martha Katz-Hyman (Santa Barbara, CA: Greenwood), 245–50.

17. For a discussion of diet and nutrients, see Kenneth Kiple and Virginia King, *Another Dimension to the Black Diaspora: Diet, Disease, and Racism* (New York: Cambridge University Press, 1981), 79–95, 117–33.

18. Robert Fogel and Stanley Engerman, *Time on the Cross: The Economics of American Negro Slavery* (New York: Norton, 1974), 59–106, 191–257.

19. See, most notably, Herbert Gutman, *Slavery and the Numbers Game: A Critique of* Time on the Cross (Urbana-Champaign: University of Illinois Press, 2003).

20. Johnson, *River of Dark Dreams*, 176–208, 463n7. Johnson's argument counters the notion that slavery was somehow "precapitalist." For an argument for the precapitalist and "paternalist" caste system of slavery, see Eugene D. Genovese, *Roll, Jordan, Roll: The World the Slaves Made* (New York: Vintage, 1976), passim.

21. Charles Perdue and Thomas Barden, eds., *Weevils in the Wheat: Interviews with Virginia Ex-Slaves* (Charlottesville: University of Virginia Press, 1991), 80, 81, 100, 226–27.

22. Diane Crader, "Slave Diet at Monticello," *American Antiquity* 55, no. 4 (1990): 690–717; Leland Ferguson, *Uncommon Ground: Archeology and Early African America, 1650–1800* (Washington, DC: Smithsonian, 2004): 93–108; Patricia Samford, "The Archeology of African-American Slavery and Material Culture," *William and Mary Quarterly* 53, no. 1 (1996): 13.

23. William Brooks, quoted in Perdue and Barden, *Weevils in the Wheat*, 57.

24. Beverly Jones, quoted in Perdue and Barden, *Weevils in the Wheat*, 181.

25. Philip Schwarz, *Slave Laws in Virginia* (Athens: University of Georgia Press, 1996), 67, 68, tables 3.2 and 3.3.

26. Alex Lichtenstein, "'That Disposition to Theft, with Which They Have Been Branded': Moral Economy, Slave Management, and the Law," *Journal of Social History* 21, no. 3 (1988), 418, 414, 415. See also E. P. Thompson, "The Moral Economy of the English Crowd in the Twenty-First Century," *South Atlantic Quarterly* 112, no. 3 (2013): 559–67; James Scott, *Domination and the Art of Resistance: Hidden Transcripts* (New Haven, CT: Yale University Press, 1999), 187–201.

27. Olmsted, *Journey in the Seaboard Slave States*, 117.

28. Frederick Douglass, quoted in William L. Van Deburg, *Hoodlums: Black Villains and Social Bandits in American Life* (Chicago: University of Chicago Press, 2004), 51.

29. On poisoning and conjuring in the antebellum South, see Sharla Fett, *Working Cures: Health, Healing, and Power on Southern Slave Plantations* (Chapel Hill: University of North Carolina Press, 2002), 84–92, 159–68.

30. John Michael Vlach, *Back of the Big House: The Architecture of Plantation Slavery* (Chapel Hill: University of North Carolina Press, 1993), 43–61. The extreme case is found in a 1760–1775 kitchen at Tuckahoe in Goochland County, Virginia. Ed Chappell, "Accommodating Slavery in Bermuda," in *Cabin, Quarter, Plantation: Architecture and Landscapes of North American Slavery*, ed. Clifton Ellis and Rebecca Ginsburg (New Haven, CT: Yale University Press, 2010), 97n55.

31. Donald Linebaugh, "All the Annoyance and Inconveniences of the Country: Environmental Factors in the Development of Outbuildings in the Colonial Chesapeake," *Winterthur Portfolio* 29, no.1 (1994): 1. For a comparative study of kitchens in the Tidewater and Bermuda, see Chappell, "Accommodating Slavery," 141–55.

32. Fox-Genovese, *Within the Plantation Household*, 164. See also Thavolia Glymph, *Out of the House of Bondage: The Transformation of the Plantation Household* (New York: Cambridge University Press, 2008); Stephanie Camp, *Closer to Freedom: Enslaved Women and Everyday Resistance in the Plantation South* (Chapel Hill: University of North Carolina Press, 2004).

33. Fox-Genovese, *Within the Plantation Household*, 160.

34. Caroline Gilman, *The Lady's Annual Register, and Housewife's Memorandum-Book of 1838* (Boston: T. H. Carter, 1837), 28

35. On the daily schedule of a cook in eighteenth-century Virginia, see Pat Gibbs, "Daily Schedule of a Cook in a Gentry Household," Colonial Williamsburg, accessed March 12, 2014, http://research.history.org/Historical_Research/Research_Themes/ThemeFamily/Cook.cfm.

36. Fox-Genovese, *Within the Plantation Household*, 159.

37. Olmsted, *Journey in the Seaboard Slave States*, 80.

38. Psyche Williams-Forson, *Building Houses out of Chicken Legs: Black*

Women, Food, and Power (Chapel Hill: University of North Carolina Press, 2006), 166–69. Williams-Forson builds her approach from philosopher Tommy Lott's concept of cultural malpractice. See Tommy Lott, *The Invention of Race: Black Culture and the Politics of Representation* (Malden, MA: Blackwell, 1999), 84–110.

39. Mary Randolph's 1824 *The Virginia Housewife* is considered by many as the first southern cookbook and by some as "the most influential American cookbook of the nineteenth century." It was also a text that created in its wake a genre of literature and a trope of white southern womanhood. Regional parvenus quickly emerged, including *The Kentucky Housewife* (Letice Brynt, 1839) and *The Carolina Housewife* (Sarah Rutledge, 1847), and stories of culinary prowess stretch from Randolph to Paula Dean. Quote in Hess, ed., *The Virginia Housewife by Mary Randolph*, facsimile ed. (Columbia: University of South Carolina Press, 1988), ix. See also Margaret Husted, "Mary Randolph's *The Virginia Housewife*: America's First Regional Cookbook," *Virginia Cavalcade* 30, no. 2 (1980): 6, 7.

40. Stephanie Camp, "The Pleasures of Resistance: Enslaved Women and Body Politics in the Plantation South, 1830–1860," *Journal of Southern History* 68, no. 3 (2002): 535–36.

41. For more on Native American foodways in pre-Columbian North America, see Rayna Green, "Mother Corn and the Dixie Pig: Native Food in the Native South," in *The Larder: Food Studies Methods from American Studies*, ed. John T. Edge, Elizabeth Engelhardt, and Ted Ownby (Athens: University of Georgia Press, 2013), 155–65.

42. Hess, *The Virginia Housewife by Mary Randolph*, xxix (benne and yams), 95–96 (okra and tomatoes), 135–36 (field pies).

CHAPTER 12. Dethroning the Deceitful Pork Chop: Food Reform at the Tuskegee Institute

I would like to thank the Culinary Historians of New York for funding that allowed me to travel to conduct research. I am grateful to Dana Chandler and the staff and volunteers at the Tuskegee University Archives for their outstanding research assistance. I received valuable feedback from the members of the 2013 Texas Food Writers' Salon, organized by Elizabeth Engelhardt, and from faculty and students affiliated with the Summersell Center for the Study of the South at the University of Alabama on an earlier version of these essay. I am also grateful to Jeffrey Pilcher and Anthony Stanonis for helpful comments, which I will continually draw upon as I expand this project.

1. "The Students Had Today," April 25, 1901, reel 438, Booker T. Washington Papers, Manuscript Division, Library of Congress, Washington, DC (hereafter cited as BTWP, LC).

2. For more insights into the politics of racial uplift, see August Meier, *Negro Thought in America: 1880–1915* (Ann Arbor: University of Michigan Press, 1988); Evelyn Brooks Higginbotham, *Righteous Discontent: The Women's Movement in the Black Baptist Church, 1880–1920* (Cambridge: Harvard University Press, 1992); Kevin Gaines, *Uplifting the Race: Black Leadership, Politics, and Culture in the Twentieth Century* (Chapel Hill: University of North Carolina Press, 1993).

3. Higginbotham used the phrase "politics of respectability" to describe the

work of middle-class church women who "equated public behavior with individual self-respect and with the advancement of African-Americans as a group." See Higginbotham, *Righteous Discontent*, 14.

4. Booker T. Washington, "An Address before the Alabama State Teachers' Association," June 8, 1892, in *The Booker T. Washington Papers*, vol. 3, ed. Louis R. Harlan (Urbana: University of Illinois Press, 1974), 234–35.

5. See, for example, "Fannie Merritt Farmer to Booker T. Washington," June 2, 1896, in *The Booker T. Washington Papers*, vol. 4, ed. Louis R. Harland (Chicago: University of Illinois Press, 1975), 176; "Booker T. Washington to John Harvey Kellogg," April 3, 1912, in *The Booker T. Washington Papers*, vol. 11, ed. Louis R. Harlan and Raymond W. Smock (Urbana: University of Illinois Press, 1981), 510; "Booker T. Washington to Edward Atkinson," November 7, 1897, in *The Booker T. Washington Papers*, vol. 4, 337–38; and "Wilber Olin Atwater to Booker T. Washington," April 17, 1895, in *The Booker T. Washington Papers*, vol. 3, 546. In "Booker T. Washington to Jabaz Lamar Monroe Curry," September 21, 1894, Washington refers to a letter he wrote to Ellen Richards (*The Booker T. Washington Papers*, vol. 3, 460–70).

6. "From Jabez Lamar Monroe Curry," April 17, 1894, in *The Booker T. Washington Papers*, vol. 3, 403–4.

7. *The Booker T. Washington Papers*, vol. 5, ed. Louis R. Harlan and Raymond W. Smock (Urbana: University of Illinois Press, 1976), 454; Robert J. Norrell, *Up from History: The Life of Booker T. Washington* (Chapel Hill: University of North Carolina Press, 2009), 102–3.

8. *The Booker T. Washington Papers*, vol. 3, 467.

9. "To Alice J. Kaine," September 5, 1894, in *The Booker T. Washington Papers*, vol. 3, 466–67; "To Elizabeth J. Scott," December 28, 1894, in *The Booker T. Washington Papers*, vol. 3, 494.

10. "From Alice J. Kaine," September 12, 1894, in *The Booker T. Washington Papers*, vol. 3, 467.

11. In comments on this essay, Anthony Stanonis pointed out that the presence of a white domestic scientist on campus also offered an interesting, if not deliberate, inversion of stereotypes claiming black women were natural cooks.

12. Charlotte Biltekoff, *Eating Right in America: The Cultural Politics of Food and Health* (Durham: Duke University Press, 2013), 24. See also Harvey Levenstein, "The New England Kitchen and the Failure to Reform Working-Class Eating Habits," in *Revolution at the Table: The Transformation of the American Diet* (Berkeley: University of California Press, 2003), 44–59; and Laura Shapiro, *Perfection Salad: Women and Cooking at the Turn of the Century* (Berkeley: University of California Press, 2009), 139–54.

13. Shapiro, *Perfection Salad*, 145.

14. Anna J. Atkinson, "Atlanta University: Student Dietaries," *New England Kitchen Magazine*, July 1896, 162.

15. Jennifer Jensen Wallach, *How America Eats: A Social History of U.S. Food and Culture* (Lanham: Rowman & Littlefield, 2013), 12–14; Clarissa Dickson Wright, *A History of English Food* (London: Random House UK, 2011); Colin Spencer, *British Food: An Extraordinary Thousand Years of History* (New York: Columbia University Press, 2002).

16. George M. Beard, "Axioms from Dr. George M. Beard's 'Sexual Neurasthenia,'" in *Pacific Medical and Surgical Journal*, ed. William S. Whitwell (San Francisco: W. S. Duncombe Publishers, 1885), 204.

17. W.E.B. Du Bois, "Food," *Crisis*, August 1918, 165.

18. Booker T. Washington, "A Sunday Evening Talk," October 6, 1907, in *The Booker T. Washington Papers*, vol. 9, ed. Louis R. Harlan and Raymond W. Smock (Urbana: University of Illinois Press, 1980), 368.

19. Booker T. Washington, "A Sunday Evening Talk," December 10, 1911, in *The Booker T. Washington Papers*, vol. 11, 409.

20. "To Warren Logan," November 23, 1899, *The Booker T. Washington Papers*, vol. 5, 270.

21. P. G. Parks to Booker T. Washington, September 18, 1906, reel 452, BTWP, LC; E. T. Atwell to P. C. Parks, April 17, 1906, reel 452, BTWP, LC.

22. W. O. Atwater and Chas. D. Woods, *Dietary Studies with Reference to the Food of the Negro in Alabama, 1895 and 1896* (Washington, DC: Government Printing Office, 1897), 20. Researchers at Tuskegee collaborated with the USDA in collecting the data for this study.

23. Roger Horowitz, *Putting Meat on the American Table* (Baltimore: Johns Hopkins, 2006), 13.

24. Atwater and Woods, *Dietary Studies with Reference to the Food*, 20.

25. Ibid., 16.

26. Ibid., 20.

27. There are literally hundreds of Tuskegee menus preserved in the Washington papers housed at the Library of Congress. For example, one sample menu was published in Booker T. Washington, *Working with the Hands* (New York: Doubleday, 1904), 50.

28. Booker T. Washington, *Up from Slavery: With Related Documents*, ed. W. Fitzhugh Brundage (Boston: Bedford St. Martin's, 2002), 66.

29. Washington, *Working with the Hands*, 183, 187; Cynthia Neverdon-Morton, *Afro-American Women of the South and the Advancement of the Race, 1895–1925* (Knoxville: University of Tennessee Press, 1989), 35.

30. Mrs. Booker T. Washington, "What Girls Are Taught," in *Tuskegee and Its People*, ed. Booker T. Washington (New York: D. Appleton and Company, 1905), 74.

31. Washington, *Working with the Hands*, 98.

32. Booker T. Washington, Cotton States and International Exposition address, 1895. The full text is available here: http://historymatters.gmu.edu/d/39/, accessed February 2, 2015.

33. Washington, *Up from Slavery*, 114–15.

34. Ibid., 115

35. Carla Willard, "Timing Impossible Subjects: The Marketing Style of Booker T. Washington," *American Quarterly* 53, no. 4 (December 2001): 647.

36. Warren Logan, "Resources and Material Equipment," in *Tuskegee and Its People*, ed. Washington, 38.

37. Ellen Weiss, *Robert R. Taylor and Tuskegee* (Montgomery, AL: New South Books, 2012), 177; Deborah Davis, *Guest of Honor: Booker T. Washington, Theodore Roosevelt, and the White House Dinner that Shocked a Nation* (New York: Atria Books, 2012), 100–101.

38. Booker T. Washington, "Negro Homes," *Colored American Magazine* (September 1902), reprinted in *Booker T. Washington Rediscovered*, ed. Michael Scott Bieze and Marybeth Gasman (Baltimore: Johns Hopkins University Press, 2012), 153.

39. Willard, "Timing Impossible Subjects," 647.

40. "An Item in the *Tuskegee Student*," October 29, 1910, in *The Booker T. Washington Papers*, vol. 10, ed. Louis R. Harlan and Raymond W. Smock (Urbana: University of Illinois Press, 1981), 428–29.

41. Paul Pierce, *Dinners and Luncheons: Novel Suggestions for Social Occasions* (Chicago: Brewer, Barse, & Company, 1907), 11, 25.

42. Mrs. F. L. Gillette and Hugo Ziemann, *The White House Cookbook* (1887). The recipe "Reed Birds on Toast" appears on page 279: "Remove the feathers and legs of a dozen reed birds, split them down the back, remove the entrails, and place them on a double broiler; brush a little melted butter over them and broil the inner side thoroughly first; then lightly broil the other side. Melt one quarter of a pound of butter, season it nicely with salt and pepper, dip the birds in it, and arrange them nicely on slices of toast."

43. Fannie Farmer, *Boston Cooking School Cook Book* (Boston: Little, Brown, & Co., 1906).

44. Booker T. Washington to Margaret Murray Washington, May 14, 1906, reel 499, BTWP, LC.

45. Booker T. Washington to Margaret Murray Washington, May 16, 1906, reel 499, BTWP, LC.

46. Although thus far my research has uncovered more evidence about Washington's beliefs about food and racial uplift, Margaret Murray Washington likely largely concurred with his ideas about food reform and was certainly charged with the task of helping implement his program. Mrs. Washington was the president of the local Tuskegee Women's Club, and the club hosted a number of talks and discussions related to proper food reform. Minutes from the meetings are documented in the "Margaret Murray Washington Notebook," which is housed in the archives of Tuskegee University, Tuskegee, AL.

47. Booker T. Washington, "An Invitation to a Possum Supper for Teachers," October 6, 1914, in *The Booker T. Washington Papers*, vol. 13, ed. Louis R. Harlan and Raymond W. Smock (Urbana: University of Illinois Press, 1984), 142.

48. "From James Carroll Napier," November 27, 1912; "To Jeannette Tod Ewing Bertram," November 15, 1913; "From Charles William Anderson to Emmett Jay Scott," November 21, 1913, all in *The Booker T. Washington Papers*, vol. 12, ed. Louis R. Harlan and Raymond W. Smock (Urbana: University of Illinois Press, 1982), 60, 334–35.

49. "To Jeannette Tod Ewing Bertram," November 15, 1913, 334.

50. Washington, *Working with the Hands*, 190.

51. "Booker T. Washington to Ernest Ten Eyck Attwell," July 15, 1912, in *The Booker T. Washington Papers*, vol. 11, 559.

52. Although Washington promoted beef as a healthful and symbolically significant meat and emphasized the right of his students to consume it, this does not mean that pork ever disappeared from Tuskegee tables or from Washington's private table. In *Working with the Hands*, he claims that he raised almost all of the

pork his family ate. He raised "common-bred pigs" as well as specialty Berkshires and Poland Chinas. He criticized other rural African Americans for not raising pork as scientifically as he did, indicating, once again, that the matter in which food was raised was as important as what was consumed. See Washington, *Working with the Hands*, 155–56.

53. Booker T. Washington, "A Sunday Evening Talk," March 27, 1910, in *The Booker T. Washington Papers*, vol. 12, 299.

54. Washington, *Working with the Hands*, 80; "A Tuskegee Student Bill of Fare, " in *The Booker T. Washington Papers*, vol. 6, ed. Louis R. Harlan and Raymond W. Smock (Urbana: University of Illinois Press, 1977), 428.

55. Booker T. Washington, "Teaching Domestic Economy at Tuskegee," *Good Housekeeping Magazine* (November 1910): 623–24. Washington also instructed his staff to serve in the dining halls as much food as possible that had been produced at Tuskegee. See E. T. Attwell to Booker T. Washington, May 2, 1905, reel 432, BTWP, LC.

56. J. H. Washington to Mr. E. T. Attwell, June 13, 1906, reel 432, BTWP, LC; J. H. Washington to Booker T. Washington, May 1, 1911, reel 496, BTWP, LC.

57. Booker T. Washington to Warren Logan, June 15, 1902, Booker T. Washington Collection, 001.004, folder 1902, Tuskegee University Archives, Tuskegee, AL.

58. "Canning," *Tuskegee Normal and Industrial Institute Catalogue, 1909–1910*, Tuskegee University Archives; J. H. Washington, "Our Canning Establishment," *Tuskegee Student*, July 20, 1900, Tuskegee University Archives.

59. *Tuskegee Student*, December 30, 1889, Tuskegee University Archives.

60. Washington, *Working with the Hands*, 32. In 1906, Tuskegee created the Jesup Agricultural Wagon, a mobile school that enabled faculty to travel and to instruct local farmers in the latest farming techniques.

61. Washington, *Working with the Hands*, 149–50.

CHAPTER 13. Domestic Restaurants, Foreign Tongues: Performing African and Eating American in the US Civil Rights Era

Many people provided valuable feedback at different stages of this project. Thanks especially to colleagues who participated in the Gender and Women's Studies faculty research series at Gustavus Adolphus College and to members of the American Studies Program at Carleton College. I also appreciate Amy Bentley's comments on an earlier version of this project presented at the 2012 American Studies Association Annual Meeting and John Thabiti Willis's insights that helped me take this material in new directions.

1. Howard Johnson's restaurants located in the US south were openly segregated prior to 1964. However, following a highly publicized episode of discrimination against K. A. Gbedemah, the finance minister of Ghana, at a Howard Johnson's restaurant in Delaware in 1957, company founder and president Howard D. Johnson falsely assured the State Department that "the organization's policy was to serve everyone without discrimination." Following the Fitzjohn scandal, the Russian media claimed that Fitzjohn selected a Howard Johnson's restaurant

because of the company president's assurance that no further incidents of discrimination would occur in his restaurants. Morrey Dunie, "Snubbed Ghana Visitor Gets Bid to Breakfast with President, Nixon," *Washington Post*, October 10, 1957; Press Release, "Statement by Acting Secretary of State, Chester Bowles," September 19, 1961, Pedro A. Sanjuan Papers, Box 1, John F. Kennedy Presidential Library, Boston, MA (hereafter cited as JFKL).

2. David Halberstam, "Restaurant Rebuffs African Diplomat," *New York Times*, April 10, 1961.

3. See Calvin B. Holder, "Racism toward Black African Diplomats during the Kennedy Administration," *Journal of Black Studies* 14, no. 1 (September 1983): 31–48; Renee Romano, "No Diplomatic Immunity: African Diplomats, the State Department, and Civil Rights, 1961–1964," *Journal of American History* 87, no. 2 (September 2000): 546–79; Faith Noelle Wassink, "Meeting in the Middle in Maryland: How International and Domestic Politics Collided along Route 40" (Master's thesis, University of Maryland, College Park , 2010); Nicholas Murray-Vachon, "The Junction: The Cold War, Civil Rights, and the African Diplomats of Maryland's Route 40," *Primary Source* 2, no. 2 (September 2012), http://www.indiana.edu/~psource/archive.html.

4. To differentiate between individuals who tried to pass as foreign and elude discovery and those who intended to expose the charade once completed, I turn to Brian McHale's three categories of hoaxes: "genuine" hoaxes, "trap-hoaxes," and "mock-hoaxes." "Genuine" hoaxes "are perpetrated with no intention of their ever being exposed." In contrast, "trap-hoaxes" are "designed with didactic . . . purposes" where the "deliberate inauthenticity always serves some ulterior extra-aesthetic purpose." "Mock-hoaxes" are also meant to be exposed; however, their intention is not punitive but aesthetic. I read individual efforts to pass as foreign to be a kind of genuine hoax, while the "spectacular performances" intended to *expose* the hypocrisy of domestic racism I read as "trap-hoaxes." See Brian McHale, "'A Poet May Not Exist': Mock-Hoaxes and the Construction of National Identity," in *The Faces of Anonymity: Anonymous and Pseudonymous Publication from the Sixteenth to the Twentieth Century*, ed. Robert J. Griffin (New York: Palgrave Macmillan, 2003), 233–52.

5. Tavia Nyong'o, *The Amalgamation Waltz: Race, Performance, and the Ruses of Memory* (Minneapolis: University of Minnesota Press, 2009), 7, 11, 15.

6. Martin A. Berger, *Sight Unseen: Whiteness and American Visual Culture* (Berkeley: University of California Press, 2005), 1. My analysis also builds on Kyla Wazana Tompkins's temporal use of "spectacular visibility" within nineteenth-century commodity culture and Daphne Brooks's framework of "spectacular performances of race" that "defamiliarize 'blackness' . . . in order to yield alternative racial and gender epistemologies" to suggest that we should first and foremost interpret these hoaxes not as performances of hyper-embodied Africanness or hyper-visible blackness but instead as spectacles of whiteness. See Kyla Wazana Tompkins, *Racial Indigestion: Eating Bodies in the Nineteenth Century* (New York: NYU Press, 2012), 149–50; Daphne Brooks, *Bodies in Dissent: Spectacular Performances of Race and Freedom, 1850–1910* (Durham: Duke University Press, 2006), 3–6.

7. Tompkins, *Racial Indigestion*, 11.

8. Ibid., 2.

9. "Address by Mr. Pedro Sanjuan to the Legislative Council of the General Assembly of Maryland," press release, September 13, 1961, Sanjuan Papers, Box 1, JFKL.

10. "Discriminatory Practices in New York City's Upper East Side Restaurants: A Pilot Survey," July 1960, Box 52, Folder 1155.2D, Ernest Dichter Papers (Accession 2407), Hagley Museum and Library, Wilmington, DE.

11. Mark S. Foster, "In the Face of 'Jim Crow': Prosperous Blacks and Vacations, Travel and Outdoor Leisure, 1890–1945," *Journal of Negro History* 84, no. 2 (Spring 1999): 141.

12. "Around the Country," *Cleveland Call and Post*, December 20, 1947.

13. "Negro Wears Turban, Feted in Alabama," *Washington Post*, November 17, 1947; Paul A. Kramer, "The Importance of Being Turbaned," *Antioch Review* 69, no. 2 (Spring 2011): 208–21.

14. "The Man in the Turban," *Meriden (CT) Record*, November 20, 1947.

15. Kenesaw M. Landis, *Segregation in Washington: A Report of the National Committee on Segregation in the Nation's Capital* (Chicago: National Committee on Segregation in the Nation's Capital, 1948), 14.

16. "Turbans Fail to Budge Bias," *Jet*, November 14, 1957, 8–9.

17. J. F. terHorst, "Maryland Restaurant Crusade Shows Some Signs of Success," *New London (CT) Day*, October 16, 1961.

18. Samuel F. Yette, "Remembering 'Mr. Carl' during Black Press Week," *Baltimore Afro-American*, March 20, 1971.

19. George Collins, "Everybody Eats but Americans," *Baltimore Afro-American*, September 2, 1961. Quotes in the following paragraphs are from this article.

20. "Just Thinking: Goban's Minister Dies; U.S. 40 Hoax Story Lives," *Baltimore Afro-American*, December 10, 1983.

21. Collins, "Everybody Eats but Americans."

22. Report, "Meeting with Representatives of State Governors," June 16, 1961, Sanjuan Papers, Box 1, JFKL.

23. Louis Hatchett, *Duncan Hines: The Man behind the Cake Mix* (Macon, GA: Mercer University Press, 2001), 33–47.

24. Duncan Hines, *Duncan Hines Adventures in Good Eating* (Ithaca, NY: Duncan Hines Institute, 1959), 136. Duncan Hines died in 1959, but his partner at the Duncan Hines Institute, Roy H. Park, assumed the editorial position and published new editions through 1962. See Roy H. Park, "Statement of Policy for the Years Ahead," *Pacific Coast Record*, July 1960, 7. Hines was the original author and publisher. As time went on, the publication needed to appear as if it were written solely by Hines for advertising purposes, even though he acknowledged that he had many trusted friends who contributed reviews. The institute wants the book to appear as single-authored.

25. Duncan Hines, *Duncan Hines Adventures in Good Eating*, 2nd ed. (Ithaca, NY: Duncan Hines Institute, 1961), 152–53.

26. Additional accounts of the *Negro Motorist Green Book* can be found in Kathleen Franz, "'The Open Road': Automobility and Racial Uplift in the Interwar Years," in *Technology and the African-American Experience*, ed. Bruce Sinclair (Cambridge, MA: MIT Press, 2004), 131–53; Cotton Seiler, *Republic of Drivers:*

A Cultural History of Automobility (Chicago: University of Chicago Press, 2008), 105–28.

27. Victor H. Green, *Negro Motorist Green Book* (New York: Victor H. Green and Co., 1940), 3.

28. "Meeting with Representatives of States Governments," report, April 27, 1961, Sanjuan Papers, Box 1, JFKL.

29. Most likely, "the Ford guide" is a reference to the *Ford Treasury of Favorite Recipes from Famous Restaurants Plus a Traveler's Guide to 820 Outstanding Eating Places*, which published multiple editions from 1950 to 1966.

30. "Meeting with Representatives of States Governments," April 27, 1961.

31. "Special Instructions on the Work of the Special Protocol Service Section," memorandum, August 4, 1961, Sanjuan Papers, Box 1, JFKL; J. Anthony Lukas, "Trouble on Route 40," *The Reporter*, October 26, 1961, 9, in the Sanjuan Papers, JFKL.

32. "Important! Signs and Other Advertising Material Bearing the Name of Duncan Hines," business pamphlet, Ivy House Records, College of William and Mary, Williamsburg, VA; "Eating for a Living," *Newsweek*, May 23, 1955, 75.

33. "Caroline Ramsay, Activist, 1962 GOP Candidate," obituary, June 13, 1992, *Baltimore Sun*, http://articles.baltimoresun.com/1992-06-13/news/1992165041_1_remak-ramsay-association-of-maryland-caroline-r; "Meeting with Representatives," June 16, 1961, Sanjuan Papers, JFKL (italics added for emphasis).

34. The elite status of diplomats fueled the attention surrounding their encounters with discrimination, attention based on social class that didn't sit well among all SPSS representatives. Some expressed concern that "only the present diplomats and the Prime Ministers" received publicity, while discrimination against foreign nationals without much money (such as students), who also had to eat out, "doesn't make the headlines." "Meeting with Representatives," June 16, 1961.

35. Stetson Kennedy, *Jim Crow Guide to the U.S.A.: The Laws, Customs and Etiquette Governing the Conduct of Nonwhites and Other Minorities as Second-Class Citizens* (London: Lawrence & Wishart, 1959), 47–57.

36. Berger, *Sight Unseen*, 8.

37. "Meeting with Representatives," June 16, 1961 (italics added for emphasis).

38. Ibid.

39. Ibid. (italics added for emphasis).

40. "Meeting with Representatives of States Governments," April 27, 1961.

41. Ibid.

42. "Hospitality to Africans Expected by Almond," *Washington Star*, April 21, 1961.

43. "Brothers of the Skin," *Ebony*, November 1961, 14.

44. "Foreign Diplomats Erased Bias in N.Y.," *Chicago Defender*, October 29, 1960.

CHAPTER 14. Freedom's Farms: Activism and Sustenance in Rural Mississippi

The author thanks Susan Levine, director of the University of Illinois at Chicago's Institute for the Humanities, and the Chicago Area Food Studies working group for inviting me to present an earlier draft of this essay. The meaningful discussion that followed my presentation provided valuable ideas for revising the essay for publication.

1. Jerry DeMuth, "Tired of Being Sick and Tired," *Nation* 198, no. 23 (June 1, 1964): 548–51.

2. Fannie Lou Hamer to Leslie Dunbar, November 16, 1971, Folder 24, Box 11, Fannie Lou Hamer Papers, Amistad Research Center, Tulane University, New Orleans, LA (hereinafter cited as the Hamer Papers); "Status Report," July 1973, Folder 24, Box 11, Hamer Papers; Kay Mills, *This Little Light of Mine: The Life of Fannie Lou Hamer* (New York: Plume, 1993), 255.

3. Mills, *This Little Light of Mine*, 105–33.

4. James Cobb, *The Most Southern Place on Earth: The Mississippi Delta and the Roots of Regional Identity* (New York: Oxford University Press, 1992), 4; "Hunger in the Mississippi Delta," Folder 17, Box 8, Hamer Papers; Public Broadcasting Laboratory, "Hunger—American Style," February 25, 1968, Folder 16, Box 3, Hamer Papers; Nick Kotz, *Let Them Eat Promises: The Politics of Hunger in America* (New York: Anchor Books, 1969), 3–4.

5. One successful critic of the industrial food system and advocate for more thoughtful eating patterns is Michael Pollan, author of *The Omnivore's Dilemma: A Natural History of Four Meals* (New York: Penguin Books, 2006) and *In Defense of Food: An Eater's Manifesto* (New York: Penguin Books, 2008). Food justice scholars (and Pollan critics) include Julie Guthman, *Weighing In: Obesity, Food Justice, and the Limits of Capitalism* (Berkeley: University of California Press, 2011); and Alison Hope Alkon and Justin Agyeman, eds., *Cultivating Food Justice: Race, Class, and Sustainability* (Cambridge: MIT Press, 2011). Definitions for food access and food sovereignty can be found at Alkon and Agyeman, *Cultivating Food Justice*, 3, 12. Sandy Brown and Christy Getz define food security in their essay "Farmworker Food Insecurity and the Production of Hunger in California" (in Alkon and Agyeman, *Cultivating Food Justice*, 121.

6. Pete Daniel, *Dispossession: Discrimination against African American Farmers in the Age of Civil Rights* (Chapel Hill: University of North Carolina Press, 2012). John J. Green, Eleanor M. Green, and Anna M. Kleiner, "From the Past to the Present: Agricultural Development and Black Farmers in the American South" (in Alkon and Agyeman, eds., *Cultivating Food Justice*, 47–64) also discusses the historical challenges of land and sustenance among black Mississippi farmers.

7. Dorothy Dickins, *Improving Levels of Living of Tenant Families* (State College: Mississippi Agricultural Experiment Station, 1942).

8. Dorothy Dickins, *A Nutritional Investigation of Negro Tenants in the Yazoo Mississippi Delta* (State College: Mississippi Agricultural Experiment Station, 1928), 17, 43, 45.

9. Ibid., 17.

10. DeMuth, "Tired of Being Sick and Tired," 549.

11. Dickins, *A Nutritional Investigation of Negro Tenants*, 25. Dickins compares this study of black farmers to similar research involving white subjects in Dorothy Dickins, *A Study of Food Habits of People in Two Contrasting Areas of Mississippi* (State College: Mississippi Agricultural Experiment Station, 1927).

12. Kotz, *Let Them Eat Promises*, 42–61.

13. Fannie Lou Hamer, interview by Neil McMillen, April 14, 1972, *Mississippi Oral History Project*, McCain Library and archives, University of Southern Mississippi, Jackson, http://www.usm.edu/msoralhistory/, accessed May 28, 2013.

14. "Greenwood Food Blockade (Winter)," *Veterans of the Civil Rights Movement*, updated August 2012, http://www.crmvet.org /tim/timhis62.htm# 1962food; Mississippi State Sovereignty Commission, "Leflore County," February 13, 1963, SCRID#2-45-1-62-1-1-1, Series 2515: Mississippi State Sovereignty Commission Records, 1994–2006, Mississippi Department of Archives and History, Jackson, http://mdah.state.ms.us/arrec /digital_archives/sovcom/, accessed February 2, 2015 (hereinafter cited as "Sovereignty Commission Online").

15. Chicago Area Friends of SNCC poster, Ben Burns Collection 133, Vivian G. Harsh Research Collection of Afro-American History and Literature, Chicago Public Library, Carter G. Woodson Regional Library, accessed May 27, 2013, http://mts.lib. uchicago.edu/artifacts/index.php?id=sncc; "Greenwood Food Blockade (Winter)," *Veterans of the Civil Rights Movement*, updated August 2012, http://www.crmvet.org/ tim/timhis62.htm#1962food; Mississippi State Sovereignty Commission, "Leflore County," February 13, 1963, SCRID#2-45-1-62-1-1-1, Sovereignty Commission Online; Mississippi State Sovereignty Commission, "Leflore County," April 4, 1963, SCRID #2-45-1-71-1-1-1, Sovereignty Commission Online.

16. Wazir (Willie B.) Peacock, interview by Bruce Hartford, July 2001, *Civil Rights Movement Veterans*, updated August 2012, http://www.crmvet.org/nars/ wazir1.htm.

17. Mississippi State Sovereignty Commission, "Leflore County," March 16, 1963, SCRID#2-45-1-65-3-1-1, Sovereignty Commission Online.

18. Passage of Civil Rights Act of 1964, Pub. L. No. 88-352, 78 Stat. 241 (1964); and Voting Rights Act of 1965, Pub. L. No. 89-110, 79 Stat. 437 (1965). This is generally viewed as the end of the traditional civil rights movement.

19. Lyndon B. Johnson, "Annual Message to the Congress on the State of the Union," January 8, 1964, in *The American Presidency Project*, ed. Gerhard Peters and John T. Woolley, accessed March 1, 1964, http://www.presidency.ucsb.edu/ ws/?pid=26787.

20. Food Stamps Act of 1964, Pub. L. No. 88-525, 78 Stat. 703 (1964).

21. Public Broadcasting Laboratory, "Hunger—American Style," February 25, 1968, Folder 16, Box 3, Hamer Papers; "What You Should Know about Food Stamps," Folder 41, Box 26, Hamer Papers.

22. "Composite On-Site Evaluation Report, Sunflower County Progress, Inc., Indianola, Mississippi," page 9, Folder MISS CG-3065, Box 11, RG 381, National Archives at Atlanta, Morrow, Georgia (hereinafter cited as Atlanta National Archives); Maggie Moody, "Target Area Individual Report," page 2, Folder MISS CG-3065, Box 11, RG 381, Atlanta National Archives; Eleanora Hines, "Individual Narrative Report on the Emergency Food and Medical Component of Sunflower County Progress, Inc.," page 2, Folder MISS CG-3065, Box 11, RG 381, Atlanta National Archives.

23. Hines, "Individual Narrative Report on the Emergency Food and Medical Component," pages 1–4.

24. "Reservation on Food Stamp Plan," *Delta Democrat-Times*, September 29, 1966, Folder 41, Box 26, Hamer Papers.

25. Kotz, *Let Them Eat Promises*, 216.

26. Michael K. Honey, *Going Down Jericho Road: The Memphis Strike, Martin Luther King's Last Campaign* (New York: W. W. Norton, 2007), 175–78; Edward P. Morgan, "Media Culture and the Public Memory of the Black Panther Party," in *In Search of the Black Panther Party: New Perspectives on a Revolutionary Movement*, ed. Jama Lazerowe and Yohuru Williams (Durham, NC: Duke University Press, 2006), 335–36; Doris Witt, *Black Hunger: Food and the Politics of U.S. Identity* (New York: Oxford University Press, 1999), 131–41; Priscilla McCutcheon, "Community Food Security 'For Us, By Us': The Nation of Islam and the Pan African Orthodox Christian Church," in *Cultivating Food Justice: Race, Class, and Sustainability*, ed. Alison Hope Alkon and Justin Agyeman (Cambridge: MIT Press, 2011), 177–96.

27. Fay Bennett, "The Condition of Farm Workers and Small Farmers in 1968," Folder 1, Box 10, Hamer Papers; Robert Swann, "Friends of the Institute," June 1969, Folder 1, Box 10, Hamer Papers.

28. Public Broadcasting Laboratory, *Hunger—American Style*, public television documentary, February 25, 1968, Folder 16, Box 3, Hamer Papers. This analysis is based on the script for a public television program filmed in Sunflower and Tallahatchie Counties in Mississippi, February 7–10, 1968. The actual recording should be stored with the PBS archives at the Library of Congress but is unavailable for viewing.

29. Public Broadcasting Laboratory, *Hunger—American Style*. Today, food justice activists might refer to such an area as a "food desert," although that term had not been coined in 1968. A food desert is typically defined as an area in which the population has limited access to sufficient nourishment and is determined based on a variety of factors, including distance to supermarkets, number and type of stores in the neighborhood, average family incomes in the area, and availability of transportation. USDA Economic Research Service, "Definition of a Food Desert," accessed March 1, 2014, http://www.ers.usda.gov/dataFiles/Food_Access_Research_Atlas/Download_the_Data/Archived_Version/archived_documentation.pdf.

30. US Senate, *Hunger and Malnutrition in America: Hearings before the Subcommittee on Employment, Manpower, and Poverty of the Committee on Labor and Public Welfare, United States Senate Ninetieth Congress, First Session* (Washington, DC: GPO, 1967), 46–47.

31. Freedom Farm Corporation, "Proposal for Funding," 1975, Folder 23, Box 11, Hamer Papers; Freedom Farm Corporation, "Status Report and Request for Funds," March 1973, Folder 3, Box 11, Hamer Papers.

32. Frank P. Graham to Friend, March 16, 1968, Folder 1, Box 10, Hamer Papers.

33. Harry Belafonte to Friend, May 1969, Folder 1, Box 10, Hamer Papers; Lester M. Salamon to Fannie Lou Hamer, July 14, 1969, Folder 1, Box 10, Hamer Papers; Marcia Rudeen to Harry Belafonte, ca. May 20, 1969, Folder 1, Box 10, Hamer Papers.

34. Fannie Lou Hamer to Jeff, October 21, 1970, Folder 2, Box 10, Hamer Papers; Fannie Lou Hamer to Madison Measure for Measure, November 13, 1970, Folder 2, Box 10, Hamer Papers; Fannie Lou Hamer to Mrs. Finney, July 26, 1971, Folder 3, Box 10, Hamer Papers.

CHAPTER 15. After Forty Acres: Food Security, Urban Agriculture, and Black Food Citizenship

1. Dean Olson, "Agroterrorism: Threats to America's Economy and Food Supply," *FBI Law Enforcement Bulletin*, February 2012, accessed January 16, 2014, http://leb.fbi.gov/2012/february/agroterrorism-threats-to-americas-economy-and-food-supply.

2. "Food Security," *World Health Organization*, accessed February 2, 2015, http://www.who.int/trade/glossary/story028/en/.

3. "Food Security in the U.S.," *United States Department of Agriculture Economic Research Service*, last modified September 4, 2013, http://www.ers.usda.gov/topics/food-nutrition-assistance/food-security-in-the-us/definitions-of-food-security.aspx.

4. The Centers for Disease Control defines "food deserts" as "areas that lack access to affordable fruits, vegetables, whole grains, low-fat milk, and other foods that make up the full range of a healthy diet." Centers for Disease Control, "A Look inside Food Deserts," http://www.cdc.gov/Features/fooddeserts/, accessed June 2, 2014.

5. During World War I, Charles Lathrop Pack formed the National War Garden Commission to encourage Americans to grow food in their own backyards and in vacant lots to help in America's war effort. At war's end, Lathrop advocated Americans turn their "war" gardens into "victory gardens" to free up national food reserves so that the United States could aid the European reconstruction effort by feeding the millions left homeless and hungry by the hostilities in his *Victory Gardens Feed the Hungry: The Needs of Peace Demand the Increased Production of Food in America's Victory Gardens* (Washington, DC: National War Garden Commission, 1919). Likewise, in 1942, Howard R. Tolley of the US Department of Agriculture urged his fellow Americans to fulfill their patriotic duty by growing food at home or helping out farmers who needed laborers to replace the men who were serving overseas during World War II in his *The Farmer Citizen at War* (New York: Macmillan, 1943).

6. Ron Finley, "A Guerrilla Gardener in South Central LA," *Ted.com*, last updated March 2013, www.ted.com/talks/ron_fubket_a_guerrilla_gardener. Though I acknowledge the importance of Finley's efforts in Los Angeles, and the real impact his campaign has had on zoning and urban planning, I will focus on discussing Will Allen's work in more detail throughout the rest of the chapter because his memoir/manifesto provides more data on the connection between urban farming and family history. Will Allen, *The Good Food Revolution: Growing Healthy Food, People, and Communities* (New York: Gotham Books, 2013).

7. Michael Twitty, *Afroculinaria.com*, accessed May 27, 2014, http://afroculinaria.com/about/.

8. Michael Twitty, *The Cooking Gene.com*, accessed May 27, 2014, http://thecookinggene.com/about/.

9. Michelle Obama, *American Grown: The Story of the White House Kitchen Garden and Gardens across America* (New York: Crown Publishers, 2012), Kindle ed.

10. Oprah Winfrey, "Dig It! How Oprah's Growing Healthier and You Can, Too," *O Oprah.com*, pp. 118–20, accessed May 14, 2013, http://www.oprah.com/home/Oprahs-Maui-Farm-Oprah-on-Growing-Her-Own-Food.

11. Jennifer L. Wilkins, "Eating Right Here: Moving from Consumer to Food Citizen," *Agriculture and Human Values* 22, no. 3 (2005): 271.

12. Collie Graddick has favored a more grassroots approach in Minnesota, where he urges local gardeners to rebrand themselves as farmers and establish cooperatives that can leverage more grants and federal support together than would be possible individually. Graddick explicitly acknowledges Allen's influence in his way of thinking about the adaptability of the farmer coop model for Minnesota. He also mentions the negative perceptions of farming that arose out of the exploitation of the sharecropping system as a source of contemporary alienation from the land felt by African Americans in an interview with Charles Hallman, "Urban Farming: It's Not Sharecropping Anymore," *Minnesota Spokesman-Recorder,* May 30, 2010, republished in *Twin Cities Daily Planet: Local News for Global Citizens,* accessed January 14, 2014, http://www.tcdailyplanet.net/news/2010/05/30/urban-farming-it%E2%80%99s-not-sharecropping-anymore. Since he has not published a volume of his own, nor given a TED or similar talk, I will not discuss him further here.

13. Michael Twitty, "A People's History of Carolina Rice," in *Guts, ed. David Chang* (San Francisco: McSweeney's Publishing, 2013), 52.

14. Pack, *Victory Gardens Feed the Hungry,* 3.

15. The tireless efforts of suffragists were rewarded with the passage of the Nineteenth Amendment in 1920. Although the Fourteenth Amendment extended citizenship to formerly enslaved people of color and the Fifteenth Amendment forbids discriminating against former slaves on the basis of race, many southern states instituted poll taxes and/or literacy tests to discourage them from exercising their full rights as citizens.

16. Tolley, *Farmer Citizen at War,* 195.

17. John Wooley and Gerhard Peters, "Franklin D. Roosevelt: Statement Encouraging Victory Gardens," *The American Presidency Project,* accessed January 14, 2014, http://www.presidency.ucsb.edu/ws/index.php?pid=16505.

18. Michelle Obama officially refers to the garden she and her staff dug in the White House grounds as a "kitchen garden" in the subtitle of her book, however, she spends a long time discussing World War II victory gardens, some of which are still in operation in her hometown of Chicago, as well as her best-known predecessor in this presidential gardening endeavor, Eleanor Roosevelt, and her famous White House victory garden.

19. Mrs. Obama's Let's Move! Campaign, http://www.letsmove.gov/, accessed February 2, 2015. Another of Michelle Obama's initiatives as first lady has been to champion military families during this time of war, reminding the nation of the sacrifices they undergo to ensure our national safety and preserve our way of life.

20. Obama, *American Grown,* 13.

21. Ibid., 146.

22. Allen, *The Good Food Revolution,* 49.

23. Elizabeth Royte, *NY Times Magazine,* and Will Allen, "Street Farmer." *New York Times Magazine,* July 1, 2009, http://mha-net.org/docs/temp/090705Street%20Farmer%20-%20NYTimes.pdf.

24. As he addresses audiences across the country during his public speeches, Allen warns those who seek to emulate his success that the nonprofit model of promoting urban agriculture as a job-creating engine and direct contribution to a

city's sustainability efforts is not easy to adapt and that the future success of urban gardening depends upon private industry making endeavors similar to his into profitable, self-sustaining enterprises. Allen's Milwaukee-based nonprofit organization is called *Growing Power, Inc.*

25. Allen, *The Good Food Revolution*, 97.

26. Ibid., 151.

27. Edna Lewis, *The Taste of Country Cooking* (New York: Alfred A. Knopf, 1980), xv.

28. Ibid., xiv.

29. Interview with Oprah Winfrey, *African American Lives*, directed by Henry Louis Gates Jr., PBS, 2006, DVD.

30. Henry Louis Gates Jr., *Finding Oprah's Roots, Finding Yours* (New York: Random House, 2007), 67. Gates uses details of Oprah's biography for his own interests, such as trying to motivate other African Americans to research their genealogy.

31. Michael Twitty's second blog, *The Cooking Gene.com,* chronicles a project aimed at helping people of all backgrounds trace their ancestral ties to specific foodways as they contribute to the living history of the United States. See http://thecookinggene.com/about/, accessed June 2, 2014. Twitty and Henry Louis Gates Jr. appeared together in the October 23, 2013, episode of the PBS series *The African Americans.*

32. Ike Sriskandarajah, "Food That Reaches Back through Slavery," *Living on Earth*, Public Radio International, June 18, 2010, http://www.loe.org/shows/segments.html?programID=10-P13-00025&segmentID=7.

33. Twitty, "A People's History of Carolina Rice," 56.

34. Psyche Williams-Forson, *Building Houses out of Chicken Legs: Black Women, Food, and Power* (Chapel Hill: University of North Carolina Press, 2006). She argues that "black men and women were fulfilling the mission of the U.S. Department of Agriculture" (72) in helping sustain the war effort through food work.

35. US Department of Agriculture, *Henry Browne, Farmer* (1942), https://archive.org/details/HenryBro1942, accessed June 6, 2014.

36. Ironically, by planting some peanuts instead of the usual cotton and corn, Mr. Browne will be improving his soil in the same way the pioneer African American agriculturalist George Washington Carver had been advocating in Tuskegee.

37. Alison Hope Alkon, *Black, White, and Green* (Athens: University of Georgia Press, 2012).

AFTERWORD

1. See http://artvent.blogspot.com/2014/06/dirty-sugar-kara-walkers-dubious.html, accessed March 15, 2015.

CONTRIBUTORS

MARCIA CHATELAIN is an assistant professor of history at Georgetown University. Her first book, *South Side Girls: Growing Up in the Great Migration* (Duke University Press, 2015), focused on the experiences of girls and young women, many of them domestics, in early twentieth-century Chicago. She is currently researching the relationship between fast food and race.

ANGELA JILL COOLEY is an assistant professor of history at Minnesota State University, Mankato, where she teaches about the US Constitution and civil rights. She previously held a post-doctoral fellowship at the University of Mississippi's Center for the Study of Southern Culture and has a PhD in history from the University of Alabama. She is the author of *To Live and Dine in Dixie: The Evolution of Urban Food Culture in the Jim Crow South* (University of Georgia Press, 2015).

CHRISTOPHER FARRISH is a PhD candidate in the Cultural Studies Department at Claremont Graduate University. He also teaches American studies at California State University, Fullerton. His research interests include race and gender in the nineteenth-century South, vernacular architecture, and food studies.

ROBERT A. GILMER earned a doctoral degree in history at the University of Minnesota in 2011, specializing in environmental and American Indian history. He recently completed a post-doctoral fellowship for the Institute for Southern Studies at the University of South Carolina and is currently teaching at Midlands Technical College and the University of South Carolina–Sumter. He has written articles for the *Journal of Mississippi History, Environmental Management,* and the *Radical History Review* and is currently working on a book manuscript examining Cherokee involvement in a series of controversies surrounding the construction of the Tellico Dam.

VIVIAN N. HALLORAN is an associate professor with joint appointments in the Department of American Studies and the Department of English at Indiana University. She is the author of *Exhibiting Slavery: The Caribbean Postmodern Novel as Museum* (University of Virginia Press, 2009). Professor Halloran's most recent article is "Recipes as Memory Work: Slave Food" in *Culture, Theory, and Critique*. She is currently at work on a monograph analyzing food memoirs written by immigrants to the United States.

GRETCHEN L. HOFFMAN is an associate professor of library and information studies at Texas Woman's University in Denton, Texas. Her research and teaching interests center on the organization of information, specifically, library cataloging. She focuses on issues surrounding the work of catalogers, the cataloging process, and the administration of cataloging departments, with the broader goal to understand how work is performed in libraries.

CHRISTINE MARKS is an assistant professor of English at LaGuardia Community College of the City University of New York. She received her doctorate from the Johannes Gutenberg University in Mainz, Germany, in 2011. Her research and teaching interests include literature and medicine, food studies, gender studies, relationality, and hybrid identities. She has published articles on hysteria, doctor-patient relationships, and narrative identity in American author Siri Hustvedt's works as well as an article on the use of metaphors in illness narratives. Her monograph, *"I Am Because You Are": Relationality in the Works of Siri Hustvedt*, was published by Winter, the Heidelberg University Press, 2014.

KIMBERLY D. NETTLES-BARCELÓN is an associate professor of women and gender studies at the University of California, Davis. Prior to joining the faculty at UC Davis, Nettles-Barcelón received her PhD in sociology from the University of California, Los Angeles, held a postdoctoral fellowship at the University of North Carolina, Chapel Hill, and then was an assistant professor of sociology at the University of Memphis. Her book, *Guyana Diaries: Women's Lives across Difference* (Left Coast Press, 2008), is based on field research with the Red Thread Women's Development Organization in Guyana. In it she writes about black and Indian women's activism in Guyana, using a narrative strategy combining ethnography and autobiography. Most recently, Nettles-Barcelón has published essays in *Gastronomica* ("Saving Soul Food") and *Boom: A Journal of California* ("California Soul: Stories of Food and Place from Oakland's Brown Sugar Kitchen") on issues of food and race. She is also the social science book review editor for the journal *Food and Foodways*.

AUDREY RUSSEK earned a PhD in American studies from the University of Texas at Austin and is an Andersen Fellow in American Studies at Carleton College. Her current book manuscript is a cultural history of regulation and consumption in twentieth-century US restaurants.

REBECCA SHARPLESS is a professor of history at Texas Christian University and is the author or editor of numerous publications, including the award-winning *Cooking in Other Women's Kitchens: Domestic Workers in the South, 1865–1960* (University of North Carolina Press, 2010) and *Fertile Ground, Narrow Choices: Women on Texas Cotton Farms, 1900–1940* (University of North Carolina Press, 1999).

ANTHONY J. STANONIS is a lecturer of American history at Queen's University Belfast. He is the author of *Creating the Big Easy: New Orleans and the Emergence of Modern Tourism, 1918–1945* (University of Georgia Press, 2006) as well as *Faith in Bikinis: Politics and Leisure in the Coastal South since the Civil War* (University of Georgia Press, 2014). He also edited *Dixie Emporium: Tourism, Foodways, and Consumer Culture in the American South* (University of Georgia Press, 2008).

LINDSEY R. SWINDALL completed a doctorate in Afro-American studies at the University of Massachusetts, Amherst, and is currently a teaching assistant professor at Stevens Institute of Technology in Hoboken, New Jersey. She has written *The Politics of Paul Robeson's Othello* (University Press of Mississippi, 2011), *Paul Robeson: A Life of Activism and Art* (Rowman and Littlefield, 2013), and *The Path to the Greater, Freer, Truer World: Southern Civil Rights and Anticolonialism, 1937–1955* (University Press of Florida, 2014). She is also coeditor, with Jennifer Jensen Wallach, of *American Appetites: A Documentary Reader* (University of Arkansas Press, 2014).

KATHARINA VESTER is an assistant professor of history and the director of the American Studies Program at American University in Washington, D.C. She received her PhD from the Ruhr–Universitaet Bochum, Germany. Her scholarship and publications focus on questions of food and identity as well as beauty, health, and citizenship. Her book *A Taste of Power: Food and American Identities* is under contract with the University of California Press.

JESSICA KENYATTA WALKER is a doctoral candidate in American studies and a certificate holder in women's studies at the University of Maryland, College Park. Her research explores the relationship between representations of black women's cooking practices and the evolving cultural meaning of "soul food."

JENNIFER JENSEN WALLACH is an associate professor of history at the University of North Texas and specializes in African American history and US food history. She is the author of *Closer to the Truth than Any Fact: Memoir, Memory, and Jim Crow* (University of Georgia Press, 2008), *Richard Wright: From Black Boy to World Citizen* (2010), and *How America Eats: A Social History of U.S. Food and Culture* (Rowman & Littlefield, 2013). She is the coeditor of *Arsnick: The Student Nonviolent Coordinating Committee in Arkansas* (University of Arkansas Press, 2011) and of *American Appetites: A Documentary Reader* (University of Arkansas Press, 2014).

PSYCHE WILLIAMS-FORSON is an associate professor of American studies at the University of Maryland and the author of the award-winning *Building Houses out of Chicken Legs: Black Women, Food, and Power* (University of North Carolina Press, 2006). She is also the coeditor of *Taking Food Public: Redefining Foodways in a Changing World* (Routledge, 2012).

KELLY WISECUP is an assistant professor of English at the University of North Texas. Her book *Medical Encounters: Knowledge and Identity in Early American Literatures* was published in 2013 by the University of Massachusetts Press and her scholarly edition of Edward Winslow's 1624 *Good News from New England* was published in 2014 by the University of Massachusetts Press.

INDEX

Boston Cooking School Cook Book.
    See Farmer, Fannie
botanical specimens, 5
Bower, Anne, xii, xxi–xxii, 74
Brooks, Gwendolyn, 47
Brooks, William, 157
Brown, Henry, 227
Brownlee, William Craig, 98
Brown v. Board of Education, 220
*Building Houses out of Chicken Legs:
    Black Women, Food, and Power.*
    See Williams-Forson, Psyche

Calas, 88
California, 70, 105, 210
Camp, Stephanie, 161–62
Caribbean, 3–16, 18, 19, 21, 24, 25, 26,
    29, 40, 48, 56, 57
Carmichael, Stokely, 17
Carnegie, Andrew, 176
Carney, Judith, 24, 152–53
Carolina, 23, 25, 26, 27, 152, 227, 240n.
    See also North Carolina; South
    Carolina
cashew nuts, 24
cassava, 5–16, 24, 230; flour, 13;
    poisonous qualities of, 9–10, 14,
    15, 16
caviar, 35
cayenne pepper, 94, 102, 230
celery, 35, 86
cheese, 164, 174, 178, 204, 262n
Cherokees, 20–21; See also Native
    Americans
Chestnut, Charles, 186
chestnuts, 19
Chicago, xii, 47, 52, 146, 186, 206, 207,
    210, 216, 218, 219, 220, 263n, 281n
Chew, The. See Hall, Carla
Chicago Defender, 38, 190
Chicago Tribune, 119
Chickasaws, 25. *See also* Native
    Americans
chicken, xxi, xxii, 49, 83, 85, 86, 89, 96,
    153, 227, 250n; fried, 35, 55, 112, 113,
    117, 129, 150, 246n, 262n, 263n; as

gospel bird, 96; library classifica-
    tion of, 73–74
Chinese food, 56, 66
chitterlings, xxii, 52, 85, 93, 245n, 250n
chocolate, 14
civil rights, 95, 181, 182
civil rights movement, 17, 34, 52, 97, 101,
    106, 199, 200, 201, 202; food access
    as civil rights issue, 205–8, 210,
    211, 213–14
Civil War, 27, 28, 80, 83, 250n
Clark, Gillian, 41–44, 45
Cleaver, Eldridge, 53, 139, 245n
clothing, 38–39
cocoyam, 11
Cold War, 181, 182
collard greens, xxiii, 20, 52, 63, 93,
    223, 231
Collins, David, 3
Collins, George, 187
Collins, Patricia Hill, 108, 131, 138,
    241n
colonial era, 4, 5, 6, 16, 18, 23, 25, 26,
    27, 56, 80, 226, 231
colonialism, 3, 26, 82, 83, 90
colonial style, 196
Columbian Exchange, 10, 17, 24
Columbus, Christopher, 10, 24
Comanches, *See also* Native Americans
cookbooks, xii, xii, 40, 45, 47–60, 89, 118
    126, 132, 174, 241n, 250n, 257n,
    258n; American, 75, 80, 84, 151, 162;
    authors of, 33, 82, 83, 88, 104, 242n;
    church published, 104; Creole, 80,
    81, 83, 84 87, 91; dialect and, 37;
    international, 85; library catalog-
    ing of, 61–75, 248n; power
    dynamics revealed in, 36, 79;
    prefaces and introductions to, 80;
    racism and, 82; representations of
    African Americans in, 32–33, 41,
    246n, 251n; respectability and, 34;
    as scholarly sources, 38, 232; soul
    food, 75, 97, 100, 103, 106
corn, 8, 11, 19–21, 22, 28, 42, 55, 86, 90,
    93, 112, 155, 160, 165, 169, 177, 179,
    204, 207, 230